Writers in Prison

Dedicated
to
Mikhail Bakhtin's cigarette papers

Writers
in
Prison

Ioan
Davies

Basil Blackwell

First published 1990

Basil Blackwell Ltd
108 Cowley Road, Oxford, OX4 1JF, UK

Basil Blackwell, Inc.
3 Cambridge Center
Cambridge, Massachusetts 02142, USA

British Library Cataloguing in Publication Data
A CIP catalogue record for this book is available from the British Library.

Library of Congress Cataloging in Publication Data
Davies, Ioan, 1936–
   Writers in prison/Ioan Davies.
       p.   cm.
   Includes bibliographical references.
   ISBN 0–631–16829–X
   ISBN 0–631–16831–1 (pbk.)
   1. Prisoners as authors.   2. Prisoners writings – History and criticism.   I. Title.
   PN494.D38 1990
   809'.8920692 – dc20   89–28538
                                                                          CIP

Typeset in 10½ on 12 pt Sabon
by Wessex Typesetters
(Division of The Eastern Press Ltd)
Frome, Somerset
Printed in Great Britain by T J Press Ltd., Padstow

Only that historian will have the gift of fanning the spark of hope in the past who is firmly convinced that *even the dead* will not be safe from the enemy if he wins. And this enemy has not ceased to be victorious . . .

There is no document of civilization which is not at the same time a document of barbarism. And just as such a document is not free of barbarism, barbarism taints also the manner in which it was transmitted from one owner to another. A historical materialist therefore dissociates himself from it as far as possible. He regards it as his task to brush history against the grain.

Walter Benjamin, *Illuminations* (trans. Harry Zohn)

Contents

Preface

This book is the product of many experiences and my attempts at making sense of them, although none of those experiences included spending any time in prison. Most of my life has been spent as an itinerant, a voyeur, as befits the son of Welsh missionaries to what was then the Belgian Congo. Every country to which I travelled might be a home but clearly I could never be at home, for was I not the product of a peripatetic culture whose mission had ended with the collapse of the old European empires? Christians, like Jews and Muslims, are more or less people of the Book, and those raised on a Book become bookish, avid readers of the literatures of the societies through which they are compelled to move. They become tourists of religious revivals, revolutions, carnivals, social movements, though never quite able to join in because they have read books before which seem to warn them against commitment and even personal ambition. But they go on reading, travelling, questioning.

Over time, certain forms of reading and the juxtaposition of events establish a pattern of questions which interpenetrate. Some of these stand out: the incarceration of missionaries in Zaïre (some of whom were relatives), meeting Hungarians who had escaped from mass prisons or mass executions after 1956, teaching at a university which had prisoners on parole sitting in the same class as policemen, an ex-wife marrying an inmate of a Canadian penitentiary, strong personal contact with Jews for whom the Holocaust was an everyday reality, friendship with writers and politicians who were subsequently murdered, executed, imprisoned or put under house arrest (Tom Mboya, Michel Raptis, Mehdi Ben Barka, Miklós Haraszti, György Krassó, Laszló Reyk, Maurice Bishop, Walter Rodney, Michael X, Václav Havel), meeting in Canada and Britain many people who were fugitives from other people's sense of justice and Canadian prisoners who started to write in prison. The books that I read began to suggest a formation around these events, making correspondences between different levels of incarceration and terror. Somewhere around 1984, a book began to be traced out in my notebooks which would connect some of the themes, though essentially emphasizing the production of text within the experience of prison and violent closure. In graduate and undergraduate classes at York University and at various conferences in Israel, France, India, Britain, the United States, New Zealand and Canada I explored my ideas with generous (and, sometimes, bemused) students and colleagues. A work-session with inmates at Collins Bay Penitentiary, Kingston, Ontario, Canada was particularly challenging.

What emerges out of these moments of deconstruction and reconstruction is therefore a literary autobiography – as an outsider. We can never be on the inside, nor know what it is like to be in solitary confinement or be faced with the firing squad, but in our gut we know our complicity in the entire process.

The book is therefore idiosyncratic in that it includes my own interpretation, interlaced with theoretical or philosophical concerns, but is also punctuated by quotations wherein the writers themselves speak out of the particular prisons to which they were confined. It is not universalistic (I have generally avoided most of Africa, Latin America and Asia, and also much of the growing literature on Australia) but I hope that it provides the beginnings of a study which will help us think about the elements of an alternative literacy which is at the heart of what we like to think of as Western civilization.

The book is divided into three parts. The first tries to establish a sense of the themes that pervade prison literature. The second, which I have called 'narratives', takes some issues in prison writing which involve the telling of a particular kind of story. In the final section I try to connect prison writing to our everyday concerns. In all of the chapters, however, I attempt to connect the actual products of prison writing with my own sense of how to read it. Thus there are longish quotations which can be used to question my own interpretations: quotations which are incisions into my own authorial stance.

Many people, organizations and traces of tangible ideas helped in the construction of this book. None of them should be seen to be complicit in the final production. The Social Sciences and Humanities Research Council of Canada provided a grant, which allowed time off to travel, employ a research assistant and collect material. York University, Toronto assisted in similar ways. The Canadian Broadcasting Corporation helped to fund a trip to Central Europe in conjunction with a radio programme. Alan O'Connor, as my teaching assistant in a course on prison literature, as research assistant and as colleague on the magazine *Borderlines* which we helped to set up together, was a wonderful co-conspirator. Nicky Drumbolis of 'Letters' bookstore in Toronto helped to find much out-of-print material (much more than I could refer to in this book). Jim Porter read most of the manuscript, and Andrew Ross, Derek Cohen, Phil Corrigan, Deborah Simmons, Diane Davies, Rhonda Hammer, John Keane, Barbara Harlow and Loretta Czernis parts of it. They all made valuable comments. Samuel Danzig, more than he knows, helped to make the text dance. Bob Gaucher, Hans Mohr, Ivan Varga and David Helwig were particularly helpful at an earlier stage in the project in suggesting ways of structuring my thoughts. Simon Prosser has been all that an author could wish for in a publisher. Gillian Bromley was an exacting and sensitive copy-editor and Andrew McNeillie a marvellous accomplice in the whole process. Claudio Colagourie and Graham Longford helped with the mechanics of preparation. But Diane, Eric, Justin, Todd and Benjamin Davies bore the brunt of the experience of seeing me locked in with these prisoners of script. For them, at least, I hope the long period of incarceration has been worth it.

Toronto
January 1990

Acknowledgements

I am grateful to acknowledge permission to reprint copyright material as follows. To *Social Text* for an excerpt from 'History and History's Problems' by Michael E. Brown, *Social Text*, no. 16: 158–9. To Penguin Books Ltd for excerpts from *The Consolation of Philosophy* by Ancius Boethius, translated by V. E. Watts, © V. E. Watts, 1969; and for excerpts from *Notes from the Underground* by Fedor Dostoievski, translated by Jessie Coulson, © Jessie Coulson, 1972. To Penguin Books Ltd and Pantheon Books for excerpts from *Whigs and Hunters: the Origin of the Black Act* by E. P. Thompson, © E. P. Thompson, 1975, 1977. To the estate of Sonia Brownell Orwell and to Secker and Warburg for excerpts from *Collected Essays and Journalism* 3, by George Orwell. To Grafton Books, a Division of William Collins and Company Ltd for excerpts from *The Jazz Scene* by E. J. Hobsbawm. To Michael Joseph Ltd and Simon and Schuster Inc for excerpts from *If not now, when?* by Primo Levi, translated by William Weaver, © Simon and Schuster Inc., 1985. To Jonathan Cape Ltd for excerpts from *Illuminations* by Walter Benjamin, translated by Harry Zohn. To the University of Minnesota Press for excerpts from *Problems of Dostoievski's Poetics* by Mikhail Bahktin, edited and translated by Carly Emerson, *Theory and History of Literature* 8. To Stoddart Publishing Company Ltd for excerpts from *Bingo* by Roger Caron, © Stoddart Publishing Company Ltd. To the *Canadian Journal of Political and Social Theory* for excerpts from 'The Dark Side of the Enlightenment' by David Cook, *TCJPST* 5, no. 3 (1981). To Oxford University Press for excerpts from *Selected Poems* by Osip Mandelstam, translated by Clarence Brown and W. S. Merwin, 1973; for excerpts from *Memoirs of a Revolutionary* by Victor Serge, translated by Peter Sedgwick, 1963; and for excerpts from *Rosa Luxemburg* by Peter Nettl, 1966. To Cornell University Press for excerpts from *Imagination in Confinement: Women's Writings in French Prisons*, © 1983 by Cornell University Press. Macmillan Publishing Company for 'In Memory of Eva Gore-Booth and Con Markievicz' from *The Poems of W. B. Yeats: A New Edition*, edited by Richard J. Finneran, © 1933 by Macmillan Publishing Company, renewed 1961 by Bertha Georgie Yeats. To The Women's Press for an excerpt from *Memoirs from the Women's*

Prison by Nawal el Sa'adawi. To Harper and Collins Publishers for an excerpt from *My Happy Days in Hell*, © 1962 by George Faludy. To Pantheon Books, a Division of Random House Inc. for an excerpt from *Discipline and Punish: The Birth of the Prison* by Michael Foucault, translated by Alan Sheridan, © 1977; and for an excerpt from *Shoah* by Claude Lanzmann. To Random House Inc. for an excerpt from *I, Pierre Riviere, Having Slaughtered my Mother, my Sister, and my Brother . . .*, edited by Michel Foucault, translated by Frank Jeelinek; and for an excerpt from *In the Belly of the Beast* by Jack Henry Abbott. To Telos Press Ltd for excerpts from 'Michel Foucault on Attica: An Interview', *Telos*, no. 19 (1974); and for excerpts from 'Intellectuals and Ordinary People' by Andrew Ross, *Cultural Critique 9* (1988). To Peter Murphy for excerpts from 'This Stors is written by me, PETER DEMITRO' by Peter Farrell, and to Peter Murphy and Janet Urquart for extracts from their 'Interview with Peter Farrell', *Prison Journal 7* (1988) and *Sentences and Paroles: Voices from the Pen* (Fifth House, 1990). To Oberon Press for excerpts from *A Book about Billie* and *The Rain Falls Like Rain* by David Helwig. To Allison and Busby for excerpts from *The Big Gold Dream* by Chester Himes. To Harcourt Brace Jovanovich for an excerpt from *Of Prisons and Ideas* by Milovan Djilas, translated by Michael Boro Petrovich, English translation © 1986 by Harcourt Brace Jovanovich. To Lawrence and Wishart Ltd for an excerpt from *Selections from the Prison Notebooks* by Antonio Gramsci. To Atheneum Publishers, an imprint of Macmillan Publishing Company, for an excerpt from *Hope Against Hope* by Nadezhda Mandlestam © 1970 by Atheneum Publishers. To Beacon Press for an excerpt from *Humanism and Terror* by Maurice Merleau-Ponty, translated by John O'Neill. To University of California Press for an excerpt from *Letters from Prison* by Adam Michnik, translated by Maya Latynski. To Prentice Hall Inc. for an excerpt from *Cell 2455 Death Row* by Caryl Chessman, © Caryl Chessman 1954, 1960, 1988. To Pan Books and Rosica Colin Ltd for excerpts from *The Prisoner of Love by Jean Genet*, translated by Barbara Bray, © Editions Gallimard 1986. To Curtis Brown Group Ltd, London for excerpts from *Bloody Murder* by Julian Symons, © Julian Symons, 1974. To Farrar, Straus and Giroux, Inc. and Faber and Faber Limited for excerpts from *Mouroir* by Breyten Bretenbach; for excerpts from *The True Confessions of an Albino Terrorist* by Breyten Breytenbach; and for use of the phrase 'From the Frontier of Writing', from *The Haw Lantern* by Seamus Heaney, as a chapter title.

Part I

THEMES

Prison Writing – Margin and Centre

I

Much of the influential literature of Judeo-Christian civilization was composed under conditions of incarceration or involuntary exile. Indeed, the Bible itself is a product of both prison and exile, and the Platonic dialogues, notably the *Crito*, the *Apology* and the *Phaedo* are centred around the trial, imprisonment and execution of Socrates. It is arguable that it is impossible to understand Occidental thought without recognizing the central significance of prison and banishment in its theoretical and literary composition. But it would be simplistic merely to classify the writing that owes something to imprisonment, to provide a natural history of the genres and to argue for the centrality of prison writing as a part of our literature, philosophy and anthropology. Such a system of classification would not help much in telling us how it is important or in what ways it might be read. Documenting volume is not the issue. This book is therefore an attempt at raising theoretical issues in understanding the forms that prison writing takes, its content and how the prison experience might be read.

At one level the book may appear to lean heavily towards those writers who were incarcerated for writing, or towards intellectuals whose incarceration came about for political or religious reasons. This bias is deliberate in that to understand prison as a centre of intellectual activity, it is necessary both to understand those ideas that have been nurtured by prison and to understand prison as a school for writers. And whatever the situation of writers in prison today, historically (in periods where the vast majority of prisoners were illiterate) the intellectual prisoner of conscience was the only figure who presented a continuous narrative[1] of incarceration. That narrative – which is not necessarily the narrative of other prisoners –

imposes its mark on how we all read prison, or how prison-as-writing comes to be part of our everyday world. Many images of prison have been used metaphorically to refer to many other features of life from language to sex, from the family to war. Certainly the metaphorical is a major feature of our understanding of ourselves and these images that have come to dominate our daily discourses, but to come to terms with prison as ideationally dominant it is crucial to begin with the prisoners' own texts.

The book therefore operates on three levels. The first is an attempt to understand the imprisoned intellectual as writing not only in a margin of the society that imprisons, but also in a margin of the prison itself. In this category I count such authors as Socrates, Boethius, Bunyan, Dostoevsky, Wilde, Breytenbach, Václav Havel. On the second level, there is the writer who operates directly out of a prison culture, whose messages and letters are as often as not forgotten, lost or destroyed. There are few names that are remembered, though Villon or Genet may claim to speak for many of the male writers. On a third level, the writings merge in a collectivity of epic and self-critical ur-epic[2] where the oral stories and songs become part of a folk-history of incarceration, exile and slavery. Sections of the Old Testament, the stories of the shtetl, the songs and stories of the American and Caribbean slaves, the accounts from the Gulag and Van Diemen's Land become part of the expression of collective resistance to oppression.

Taking the text as my theme – rather than simply writing a comparative history of incarceration using the texts as illustration – requires some explanation. Clearly we only know the past through the artefacts that have survived, and the most significant artefacts are our creative ones, notably language and the written word. We only know of oral history (until the invention of tape-recordings) through written accounts of what was said. To 'know' the past is ultimately impossible, but to read a pattern of connections is possible through text. For this reason text is central; but not for this reason only. Text, Foucault has argued in his various studies of social institutions, is also central to the ideas that form institutions. The history of Western civilization is the history of writing – the laws, edicts, manifestoes, theologies, verdicts that established codes of conduct, that patterned behaviour, that established prisons. The experience of being in those institutions is also in part contained in the writing. Thus the texts that frame dominant institutions and the countertexts that try to map routes out of them provide one of the central thematics of our culture, and also of this book.

All of this does not ignore the fact that texts – even the countertexts and this one – are subject to the production of translation, not only from foreign languages (and many of the texts quoted here are quoted as translations into English) but also from original contexts into other ones (including our own) and from one set of social and philosophical assumptions into another. But translation is in many respects the central theme of prison writing. Books were written in order to break through official barriers of definition and interpretation and to forge a means of communication where others had been denied. Their translation into other contexts and languages is thus an inevitable consequence of their original displacement and subsequent transmission. A large number of prison books were not published during the lifetime of the author and often, if published at all, lived a subterranean existence or were read in societies not their own.

Ultimately, what Walter Benjamin claims for sacred texts may also be claimed for much prison writing: 'Where a text is identical with truth or dogma,' he writes, 'where it is supposed to be "the true language" in all its literalness and without the mediation of meaning, this text is unconditionally translatable . . . For to some degree all great texts contain their potential translation between the lines; this is true to the highest degree of sacred writings. The interlinear version of the scriptures is the prototype or ideal of all translations'.[3] This plea for the 'potential translation between the lines' seems to be echoed in the work of Breyten Breytenbach, who writes: 'When you are interested in prison accounts as a genre you will soon see that prisons are pretty much the same the world over. It is rather the peculiar relationship of power-repression which seems immutable, wherever you may hide.'[4]

But this interpretation of translation provides, as it were, the apogee of the translatable. And it is perhaps no accident that Benjamin uses the sacred as the ultimate in translatability, just as Breytenbach uses prison or hell, since both search for the antipodean universal language which is ultimately rooted in the common source of everyday life. Hence translation is necessary but, except in the core that touches on the universal, impossible. The task of the translator is to liberate his own language in order to grasp 'the language of truth': 'It is the task of the translator to release in his own language that pure language which is under the spell of another, to liberate the language imprisoned in a work in his re-creation of that work. For the sake of pure language he breaks through the decayed barriers of his own language.'[5]

The textuality of the prison writer does, however, raise another issue of translation. Whether writing out of the culture of the prison or, even more, as a political prisoner, the author is both the transmitter and the translator of the oral culture of which he has become a member, and therefore the inclusion of aspects of this culture is necessarily a reinterpretation of what others have said and done. In discussing the work of E. P. Thompson – and in particular his essay on anonymous letters[6] – Michael F. Brown writes of the importance of such *sub rosa* activities and writing in understanding any form of social resistance:

> Thompson's discussion of the letters is not then merely speculative. Nor is it strictly speaking hermeneutical. It is constructive, an aspect of a project in which past and present must be shown as of the same order of human reality if the future is to be conceived as capable of 'production' through the actions of people. It attempts to *display* the fact that any account of class interactions and political life is 'complete' only when it takes account of the possibility of underground activity, inchoate resistance and the whole panoply of minor events and unregistered acts that must be a feature of any event or outcome if history is to have occurred and to have been part of our own history – if history is to be conceivable as human action such that we too could have acted.[7]

Perhaps this subterranean resistance is linked to (or is the same as) Benjamin's 'language of truth'. In any case its incorporation into tales and accounts of opposition must be an essential part of the exploration of prison writing, not only because of the articulation of the underlife of writing but also because of the further clarification of the modalities that comprise that ongoing prison narrative. The problems inherent in doing this are spelt out in the following chapter, but it must be noticed that the element of retrievability and translation is related here, much as it was for Benjamin, to the concern that the accounts of the past are important for understanding the present. Paradoxically, the challenge of retrieving the past is found in the ways in which it is presented to us: as a film which flickers by, or as Umberto Eco argues in *The Name of the Rose*, as names: *stat rosa pristine nomine, nomina nuda tenemus* ('the rose of former times is but a name: we hold mere names'). Otherwise it is present only in the accounts by others, constructing their own narratives.

The problematic of the text is therefore at the heart of this exercise in reading and theorizing. But what is the problematic of this book? As will have been deduced from the first paragraph of this introduction, the author regretfully accepts prison as an integral part of Western civilization. This is therefore not an emotionally or ideologically loaded book but an attempt to understand how the incarcerated imagination has become part of Western ideas and literature. In doing so it accepts the entire history of Western society as its provenance, though ultimately the twentieth century (which, as with scientists, has produced as many prisoners and prison writers as in the entire previous history of man) is the focus of attention. Thus it searches for motifs, forms, continuities, metaphors, engagements, displacements which characterize the incarcerated imagination. Unlike the activities of PEN (the international authors' rights group) or Amnesty International, which seek to rescue the incarcerated prisoner of conscience (an intervention which is moral, just and appropriate), the exercise here is to explore the discourses generated by prison literature and to understand, in some part, how prisoners, through writing, try to rescue themselves and us. Everywhere, across time and societies, prisoners are not expected to write. They are expected to be written for. What happens when the prisoner writes? The answer to this question requires a historical perspective, across societies, as well as specific in-depth studies of prison writing in particular contexts.

The answer also requires a study both of the relationship between prison writer and prison, and of that between prison writer and society. The first point is obvious enough, while the second needs a little further explanation. Prison writing within any particular society may (as it appears to be in Canada or Holland) be relegated to a backwater. The social ethic (masterminded by its own distributive system) conceives of its own tolerance as being of such a high order that prison writing is read as important only if it comes from prisons in other countries: prison writing from abroad is a confirmation of the tolerance of this society, setting a seal on its internal complacency. In Toronto and Amsterdam the bookstores are filled with prison writing from other societies, while that produced in Canada or Holland is instantly remaindered. Its own prison writing does not become part of its own literary or philosophical sense.

In other societies this is apparently not so. In Russia, for example, or France, or South Africa, writing from prison is of great importance: it is debated, censored, restored, downgraded, reappraised. The historical debate around Tolstoy and Dostoevsky in Russia, the romanticized sense of prison and values in France, from Villon to Genet, the self-appraisal of Afrikaans and Africans in South Africa are integral to understanding what those cultures are about, or what they see themselves as being about. It is *that* writing, ripped out of context, that becomes the reading material of the Dutch and the Canadians, enabling them to subscribe to *Index on Censorship* and become members of Amnesty International or PEN (along with their cousins in the United States, Germany, Australia and Britain). This book will be read largely by that same liberal bourgeoisie, but also, I hope, by those activists in the Third World and Central Europe (even Romania) who may receive it in samizdat; and the Gypsy prisoner in Hungary who wrote his poems 'in the style of' Villon; and the trucker, incarcerated in Laval Penitentiary in Quebec, who celebrated the Trans-Canada Highway in a Creative Writing course of which he was only half a member.[8]

There is a community of prisoners – across the centuries – of which we are all a part: the 'Canadians', the 'Dutch' and the liberal bourgeoisie by negative appropriation, but much of the rest of the world by positive involvement. This statement of comparative philosophy and literature is not new: it is as old as Aristotle and as recent as Milan Kundera. In trying to create a comparative framework for the literary philosophy of incarceration, this book leans heavily on a few people (some of whom were not incarcerated), who have tried to make sense of creativity both as opposition and as an aspect of our total incarceration: Boethius, of course, Dante, Cellini, Rabelais, Pascal and Dostoevsky; but ultimately for this century, the century both of incarceration and of freedom, Franz Kafka, Walter Benjamin, Frantz Fanon, Mikhail Bakhtin, Theodor Adorno, Michel Foucault and Albert Camus. And it is perhaps to Camus that one turns in the last resort. 'What matters here is not to follow things back to their origins, but, the world being what it is, to know how to live in it.'[9]

As regards knowing how to live in it, Camus is certainly correct. But, as it was for his so for our understanding, going back to the origins is central to knowing how to live and what the problems are.

II

One of the central tasks, then, of reading prison literature is to uncover the silences of those who do not write, and about whom no one has written. As Lady Philosophy says to Boethius while he is contemplating his fate as prisoner of King Theodoric of the Ostrogoths: 'Many men who were famous in their lifetime are now forgotten because no one wrote about them. But even written records are of limited value since the passage of time veils them and their authors in obscurity.'[10] The prison writer is one who seeks to preserve himself and others from the obscurity to which the law and the condescension of Letters has sentenced him or her and to overcome the many damnations to which he or she is subject – the damnation of crime, often of race, of class, sometimes of sex and certainly of the presumption to literacy. Prison culture is everywhere an oral one, and until this century prisoners who could read or write were few. It is thus impossible to consider the written work without considering the oral, impossible to take the text without taking the context and the practice of the speaker. Thus a purely semiotic analysis of prison writing makes no sense at all: we would have to string together the 'readings' of so many texts and come up with some kind of intertextual connectedness. Also, most writing out of prison is necessarily by privileged prisoners – not only are they literate but in a large number of cases they are there for political, religious or other ideological reasons which set them apart from the everyday criminal. They are as much interveners in the process as they are prisoners.

The reason why we read prison writing is much like that why we read any story. In lamenting the passage of the storyteller, Walter Benjamin argued that

experience which is passed on from mouth to mouth is the source from which all storytellers have drawn. And among those who have written down the tales, it is the great ones whose written version differs least from the speech of the many nameless storytellers. Incidentally, among the last named there are two groups which, to be sure, overlap in many ways. And the figure of the storyteller gets full corporeality only for the one who can picture them both ... The resident master craftsman and the travelling journeyman worked together in the same rooms; every master had been a travelling journeyman before he settled down in his home town or somewhere else. If peasants and seamen were past masters of storytelling, the artisan class was its university. In it was combined the lore of faraway places, such as a much-travelled man brings home, with the lore of the past, as it best reveals itself to the natives of a place.[11]

The prisoner, too, leaves home for a faraway place, and his writings return with a notion of that place, a place which is both of us and yet set apart from us. The writing of the prisoner, however it is cast, is neither novel, nor autobiography, nor epic. Benjamin makes the distinction between novel-writing and storytelling:

> What differentiates the novel from all other forms of prose literature – the fairy tale, the legend, even the novella – is that it neither comes from oral tradition nor goes into it. This distinguishes it from storytelling in particular. The storyteller takes what he tells from experience – his own or that reported by others. And he in turn makes it the experience of those who are listening to his tale. The novelist has isolated himself.[12]

The writer from prison, having been isolated from society, is thrown into the company of people who tell stories about themselves and others like them in invoking the ur-epic. His storytelling has many of the features of the shtetl or of Alcoholics Anonymous: the recounting of experiences which are at once mordant and ridiculous, flattering and moralizing, painful and uplifting, boastful and humiliating.[13] The writer overhears these stories and appropriates them to himself, urging them on their way.

The nature of the stories and the ur-epic to which they relate is suggested by Mikhail Bakhtin's writing on Rabelais and Dostoevsky and it is worth exploring the parallels. In his discussion of carnival as the popular cultural tradition of the Middle Ages, Bakhtin stressed that the 'world inside out' of carnival was legitimized by tradition, that it would be inconceivable to imagine the carnival without the tradition which it transgressed. The culture of medieval Europe must thus be seen as consisting of the official and the parodic, a parodic which had values and forms which appeared antithetical to the official.

> These forms . . . were sharply distinct from the serious, official, ecclesiastical, feudal, and political cult forms and ceremonials. They offered a completely different, non-official, ecclesiastical and extrapolitical aspect of the world, of man, and of human relations; they built a second life outside officialdom, a world in which all medieval people participated more or less, in which they lived during a given time of the year.[14]

Prisons anywhere do not offer a time-limited event in which the carnival parodies extracarnival life. For prisoners the 'carnival' is an episode in which the external power implodes, and the play one in which all prisoners are compelled to become actors. There are other major differences from Bakhtin's sense of the carnivalesque, and these are revealing enough to be considered at some length, before I can begin to develop a framework for reading prison literature. Bakhtin argues that medieval and Renaissance folk culture had three different manifestations – ritual spectacles (carnival pageants, comic shows), comic verbal compositions (oral and written) and various genres of billingsgate (curses, oaths, blazons). The pageants, feasts and comic shows stood, as we have seen, in juxtaposition to the solemnity of official culture and displayed a sense of laughter and liberation. The festivals, although taking place in a Christian society, retained elements of pagan religion, and maintained an ambivalence towards all religious belief. The laughter itself is a 'laughter of all the people'; it is 'directed at all and everyone, including the carnival's participants,' and it is 'ambivalent; it is gay, triumphant, and at the same time mocking, deriding. It asserts and denies, it buries and revives.'[15]

It will be immediately protested that prison culture is not festive and displays no laughter, that there are no carnivals nor even any ritualized events that could be seen as a substitute for carnival. All of this I concede. In fact, prison culture is the exact obverse of the carnivalesque: there is little or no spontaneity in the ritual, the social hierarchy is tightened, not relaxed, and if identities are sometimes played with they are more often negotiated. But the prison culture is in another sense a culture that is set apart from everyday culture, establishing a creative, experiential scheme in dealing with its own everyday world. In analysing the absorption of the 'fish' (the new-comer) into the life of the prison, Robert Gaucher has written:

> the prisoners' culture and interpretive scheme is a system constructed to handle the kinds of problems that arise in prison, and to act as an exigency for certain deprivations. It is a time-tested, historicized and institutionalized means of providing solutions. In short, the prisoner culture and interpretive scheme available to the fish is not shoved down his throat, caught like measles, or blindly accepted, but one which makes increasing sense and is of great utility. Thus he embraces it. But he embraces it not as a rigid, reified set of proscriptions and prescriptions for action, but as a culture system and interpretive framework which allows him to reinstate a degree of control over his situation, re-establish a self-conception and social identity which mirror his desired self, and in terms of these, deal with the problems encountered within the prison. This individual construction and ascription is not any kind of criminal or

antisocial scheme directed toward the establishment, maintenance, or perpetuation of a criminal or antisocial way of life, but
deals with the multitude of problems (radically different from
those he previously has encountered) produced by the prison,
and is relative to living life within the context of the prison.[16]

Gaucher also argues that the frame of such a culture is the staff's
imposed definition of the prisoner's action or words in any situation
which the prisoner must take into account when 'he makes sense of,
defines and acts in that situation'.[17] But if he is to survive, he can
only build his strategy within the community of fellow-prisoners.

The opposite of carnival is therefore the situation in which every
movement is circumscribed, every identity has to be negotiated, every
piece of space clearly defined, and laughter is forbidden. The ultimate
ritual in the non-festive community is the prison riot in which the
'culture' breaks down.[18] But even here group solidarity operates.

> The bingo had been under way for almost an hour, and a lot of
> guys were still occupied with smashing open the cell gates and
> also destroying the locking mechanisms so they couldn't be used
> against us again . . . Most of the prisoners were convinced that
> we were only being given enough rope to hang ourselves with,
> that the warden was bound to use his massive fire power to
> regain control of the prison, and that it would be accomplished
> by bloody day break. Although my numbered friends knew only
> too well that in any prison riot the convict ends up suffering the
> most, it didn't seem to matter at the time. Perhaps we all suffered
> from defective reasoning – we couldn't seem to apply past
> experiences to present reality. We had a paradoxical trust in
> each other, trust in the fact that at face value none of us could
> be trusted. That most of the rioters were desperate men was
> evident from the terrible destruction inflicted upon our dreaded
> bastion.[19]

In Bakhtin's second definition, of comic oral and written compositions, the prison culture provides a stronger affinity with the
medieval, but here again we have to be careful to define what we
mean. It is arguable that most prison stories are in fact parodies of
other stories, though in some cases not consciously parodic. The
culture of the oral experience in prison is such that experience is
transmitted by jokes, tales of exploits, songs, proverbs. Some of the
jokes and stories are adaptations of stories told on the outside, while

some are derived directly from specific prison situations. They include stories about local characters, escapees, stupid guards and clever convicts, sexuality, drink, drugs, religion, and the use of tools and equipment. These stories and jokes, which constitute what might be seen as the prison folklore, are in fact not the mimicking of the dominant culture but classically antagonistic to it. The stories of prison parody the stories told outside but also empty them of their hollow moralism to fill them with the vitalism of struggle. In this they are part of that process described by Frederic Jameson in *The Political Unconscious*, in which the social grounds of cultural opposition to dominant values are explored.[20] It is also the material, in anthropology, of examination of prison folklore as 'not only an expression of culture, but as a force operating on it'.[21]

The parody in prison involves many master-genres – from the Wild West story to the Bible, from Sweeney Todd the Barber to contemporary TV cops and robbers series, from soap operas to rock and country and western music. In contemporary Western society much of the media organizes its accounts both of 'news' and of dramatic entertainment by building on the stereotype of hard-headed cop getting ruthless killer or drug pusher. The novels of Mickey Spillane and Joseph Wambaugh and their filmed versions, the classic film *Dirty Harry* and the TV series *Kojak, Night Heat, Miami Vice, The Sweeney* and *The Equalizer* provide the points of departure for a parodic treatment by prisoners. The major film versions of prison life (there are few TV series set in prisons) all owe much to Paul Muni's *I Was a Fugitive from a Chain Gang* and its modernized version *Cool-Hand Luke*, which themselves build in the parodic, and hence provide us with an interesting problem in discussing the fictive accounts of literature which deal with prison itself.[22] (It is arguable that most contemporary writing about the prison situation itself is less parodic than some of these films and more concerned with producing a fictive or autobiographical documentary.) The existence of major texts, films, architectures which provide the superscription for our attitudes to crime is the occasion for the prisoner writing his counterinscription. The analogy from Bakhtin for considering the antagonistic text as parodic therefore provides an important point of departure for examining what it is that prisoners write and why they write it.

In the third element, Bakhtin refers to curses, oaths, 'blazons' as a form of billingsgate (the language of the market). In prison this can be easily identified with prison argot and with the transgressive use of external everyday speech. The major characteristics of this language are the disparaging designations for those in authority and their collaborators (bull, croaker, rat, goon squad, nark, stool pigeon, joint man), the precise designations for prisoners (can man, diddler, fish, pete man, sweet kid, tappers, wolf pack), and the nonchalant descriptions for situations (beef, cherub, digger, drum, jug-up, laying track, piped, stir-crazy). There is, however, a more serious issue here than the purely scatological and vernacular use of language, often used by writers who simply want to give a sense of 'penal colour' to their stories. The use of 'billingsgate' as invoked by Bakhtin does not merely refer to localized terminology but ultimately to conceptions of the body, to the uses of epithets, double meanings which together relate to a view of the world which celebrates the underworld, an alternative set of values and meanings which defy the superior inscriptions and perhaps even go beyond the parodic. The imagery of billingsgate in Rabelais is seen by Bakhtin as providing the basis for understanding a discourse that appears to owe nothing to official, public discourse, that is 'alogical' and which transgresses 'all distances between objects, manifestations and values', fusing and combining

> elements that the mind is accustomed to divide strictly and even to oppose to each other. In these unpublicized spheres of speech all the dividing lines between objects and phenomena are drawn quite differently than in the prevailing picture of the world. These lines seek as it were to reach another object at the next point of development.[23]

Bakhtin also argues that this medieval use of language is now scarcely to be found, 'and only in the lowest and most senseless comic verbal forms'.[24] Even so, this language might represent an ideal type of a language operating on points of dialogue at the extreme opposite pole to the official language, and its utility in examining prison language would have to convince us that such an alternative form of discourse, or something approximating to it, might be found anywhere. And of course its utility would relate not only to an abstraction of an alternative language but to the specifics of an alternative social context, which might be prison in general, but is more likely to be particular kinds of prison within particular social communities. As Bakhtin himself remarks:

> This Rabelaisian system of images, which is universal and all-embracing, permits and even demands both an exceptional concreteness and fullness; it looks for detail, exactness, actuality,

the sense of reality in the presentation of historical facts. Each of these images combines an extreme breadth and a cosmic character with an exceptionally concrete feeling of life, with individuality and a journalistic response to the events of the day.[25]

Thus the languages that we would investigate would not be some generalized prison alternative, but the language of the prisoners drawn from and in particular communities – the black slaves and convicts in the USA, the Indians in Canada and the USA, the gypsy in Hungary and Romania, the Irish working class in Britain and in Australia, the Ukrainian peasant in the USSR, the Bantu in South Africa. Bakhtin's use of language is an invitation to study the language of the world turned upside down.

From this mapping out of the potentialities of reading the prisoners' own creation we might begin to sketch what reading prison literature entails. The sweep of Bakhtin's formulation leaves untouched the issues of the moment of writing itself, or indeed the variations in the writing, although his studies of Rabelais and Dostoevsky provide the clues for connecting the writing with its context, for reading it against the context. It also raises the important question of dialogues that might exist across dialogues. To what extent, for example, in spite of the peculiarities of social situations, are there ultimate dialogues of commonality? Do the dialogues across the prisons of the world reveal what Breytenbach claims the writing displays, the same immutable 'relationship of power repression'[26] or what I have called the ur-epic? In searching for that and the interjection against it – Bakhtin's 'universal and all-embracing ... and an exceptionally concrete feeling of life' – we can make a beginning at sorting out the writing itself. We might, to start with, argue that the books coming out of prisons can be put into three categories: those written by long-time criminals, those written by long-time non-criminals (homicides,[27] political and religious prisoners) and those written by short-time criminals and non-criminals. This distinction is based on familiarity with the prison culture, with the internalization of the ur-epic, and it clearly affects both the ways in which the experience is transmitted and, in Benjamin's sense, the closeness to the 'nameless storytellers'. We might argue that the nearer the writer is to the ur-epic, the less his story will be about himself and the more it will be about the folk-memory of the collectivity, while the further he is from the collectivity, the more he will see the prison as alien and the story as his own or related to another (external) collectivity. But, notwithstanding this distinction, almost all prisoners write as if their stories were unique. Thus in stories as distinct as *A Book About Billie*[28] and John Bunyan's *Grace Abounding to the Chief of Sinners*,[29] the peculiarity of the author's plight is stressed throughout. Yet in both books the singular 'I' masks the collective 'we'. In Billie's case he claims as his own stories that are told about themselves and others by many prisoners, while in Bunyan's case the specifics of his present condition draw him closer to God and to the example of all those who have similarly been persecuted, 'of whom the world was not worthy'. The great mass of writing by prisoners is by people who have stumbled into prison because of drug offences or the murder of a member of the family, as prisoners of conscience or because of white-collar crimes. For many there is only one book – the shock of recognition of being in another culture, and, perhaps as a consequence of this, most books by those who are not famous for other reasons never get beyond the first printing.

The peculiar nature of the prison writer as hero is perhaps a consequence of this process. For there are prison writers who claim only to write about themselves, and where the writing – recalling Boethius' comments on obscurity – is a personal attempt at fame, an inscription against the prison walls. In retrospect, however, Lady Philosophy was right. Their work merges into that of other prison writings, and their personal survival can be related back only to the survival and elimination of others. The distinction between motives for writing and the effects of that writing can however be kept separate. The prison writer as hero is of far less significance than the inscription itself. And this is for the strongest of all reasons.

III

Prison writing is centrally about violence. The beginning of the sense of violence is the awareness of death. Prison writing, more than most, is contemplation of death, our own deaths, the deaths we impose on others, the deaths imposed on us by others, the great gamble between our deaths and theirs. It is therefore not for nothing that most of the theology of incarceration is coupled with the theology of the afterlife, that the concepts of heaven, hell and purgatory are bound up with our concepts of otherness, separation, discipline and judgement. The locations of our most powerful prison writings are precisely those where violence is a prominent feature of resolving social difference, 'riven situations' in Seamus Heaney's phrase,[30] where antagonistic states of mind are manifested in counter-brutalities. Violence as a way of life, death as a wager, hell as other people – these and metaphors like them recur in all prison writings.

The common point between the religious mystic incarcerated for being a heretic and the killer incarcerated for taking another life is not only that they are victims of institutional violence but that both must contemplate their own and other deaths. The absurdist argument – so carefully destroyed by Camus in *The Rebel* – that all murder, all death is a matter of existential indifference, melts away in the commonality of the cell where all death is real. What makes the death of the 'riven situation' sharper is that its very commonplace nature makes the issues involved seem clearer and more urgent. The masses of dead would seem to defy any expression, producing only inarticulate horror, the flat journalistic account. And yet it is from precisely these situations that the voices are loudest, and where the articulation of that life-that-would-be is most clearly heard. It has become commonplace in sociology – particularly that of education and culture in the West – to talk of 'symbolic' violence, that terror created to mould the individual into the structural and formal demands of prescribed order, and the work of Pierre Bourdieu in France is perhaps the most important testimony to this.[31] But such work borrows its terminology from a deeper and more powerful situation, as both Hannah Arendt and Maurice Merleau-Ponty stressed,[32] in which the struggle for human dignity is bound up in the relationships between man and nature, man and his fellow-men, where real violence has inscribed its mark on all communication.

The voices of those speaking out of the riven situations call clearly to those whose violence appears to be symbolic, and it is perhaps *that* dialogue which it is important to establish here, for the symbolic violence is part of a mechanism of real violence whose imperial extensions include maintaining the riven situations elsewhere. The symbolic violence of Western classrooms, the more evident violence in the American or British ghettos, the continual warfares in Ireland, Israel and South Africa all interconnect. But to stress the interconnections is not enough. Camus put the moral situation succinctly:

> It is a question of finding out whether innocence, the moment it begins to act, can avoid committing murder. We can only act in our time, among the people who surround us. We shall be capable of nothing until we know whether we have the right to kill our fellow men, or the right to let them be killed. Since all

contemporary action leads to murder, direct or indirect, we cannot act until we know whether, and why, we have the right to kill.[33]

Those who write in prison are not dead, though their lives are sharpened by the sense of death and the apprehension of violence. Their writing connects the reality of violence and the attempt to rearticulate humanity, re-establishing a bond between our sense of finitude and the infinity of our experiences.

Writing out of prisons is just such an attempt at rearticulation, and the privilege that this book accords such writing is precisely because of its attempt to overcome violence, stare death in the face and provide the basis for human affirmation.

> We all carry within us our places of exile, our crimes and our ravages. But our task is not to unleash them on the world; it is to fight them in ourselves and others. Rebellion, the secular will not to surrender . . . is still today at the basis of the struggle. Origin of form, source of real life, it keeps us always erect in the savage formless movement of history.[34]

The task of writing, like any other form of human creative endeavour, is fraught with problems, not least of which is the struggle between the authentic and the inauthentic, a problem which may lie in the writer, but lies equally in the reader. 'To tell one's own story,' writes Roy Porter in his *A Social History of Madness*, 'what could better establish one's own veracity, or provide more conclusive symptoms of utter self-delusion?'[35] Every prisoner's story is caught on the horns of that dilemma.

NOTES

1   The use of the term 'narrative' here owes something to the work of Frederic Jameson and even more to that of Mikhail Bakhtin.
2   By 'ur-epic' I mean the epic of the collective consciousness, not written but told. The prefix 'ur-' is used because it comes from the beginning of human history.
3   Walter Benjamin, *Illuminations* (London: Cape, 1970), p. 82.
4   Breyten Breytenbach, *The True Confessions of an Albino Terrorist* (London: Faber, 1984), p. 339.
5   Benjamin, *Illuminations*, p. 80. A fuller discussion, developed from themes

suggested by, among others, Benjamin, Hölderlin, Nietzsche and Quine, is found in George Steiner's *After Babel* (Oxford: Oxford University Press, 1975). But see also Linda Hutcheon, *A Theory of Parody* (London: Methuen, 1985) for a variation of this theme.

6   E. P. Thompson, 'The Crime of Anonymity', in Douglas Hay et al., eds, *Albion's Fatal Tree: Crime and Society in Eighteenth-Century England* (Harmondsworth: Penguin, 1975).

7   Michael F. Brown, 'History and History's Problem', *Social Text*, 16 (Winter 1986–7), pp. 158–9.

8   The last two references relate to a visit I made to the Youth Prison in Hungary, and to Nate Jones, 'Trans-Canada Highway Revisited: Holiday '72', *Canadian Journal of Political and Social Theory*, 10, 3 (Fall 1986), pp. 1–23.

9   Albert Camus, *The Rebel* (London: Hamish Hamilton, 1953), p. 12. Camus also said: 'But slave camps under the flag of freedom, massacres justified by philanthropy or the taste for the superhuman, cripple judgement. On that day when crime puts on the apparel of innocence, through a curious reversal that is peculiar to our age, it is innocence that is called on to justify itself' (ibid., p. 212).

10   Anicius Boethius, *The Consolation of Philosophy* (Harmondsworth: Penguin, 1969), p. 38).

11   Benjamin, *Illuminations*, p. 85.

12   Ibid., p. 87.

13   The oral–written culture of the shtetl is displayed in a marvellous collection edited and translated by Joachim Neugroschol, *The Shtetl* (New York: G. P. Putnam's Sons, 1979). An account of the storytelling at Alcoholics Anonymous meetings, which owes something to Walter Benjamin's perspective, is found in 'Elpenor', 'A Drunkard's Progress', *Harper's*, October 1986, pp. 42–8.

14   Mikhail Bakhtin, *Problems of Dostoevsky's Poetics* (Minneapolis: University of Minnesota Press, 1984), pp. 5–6.

15   Ibid., p. 12.

16   Robert Gaucher, 'The Prisoner as Convict: an Interpretive Study from a Canadian Penitentiary', MA thesis, Carleton University, Ottawa, 1974, pp. 223–4.

17   Ibid., p. 238.

18   A lively but tendentious account from the perspective of a psychiatrist is provided by George D. Scott, with Bill Trent, *Inmate: the Casebook Revelations of a Canadian Penitentiary Psychiatrist* (Montreal: Optimum Publishing International, 1982).

19   Roger Caron, *Bingo!* (Toronto: McGraw-Hill Ryerson, 1985), pp. 110–11.

20   The argument, derived from Bakhtin, Christopher Hill, Ernst Bloch and Eugene Genovese, is developed by Frederic Jameson in chapter 1 of *The Political Unconscious* (Princeton, NJ: Princeton University Press, 1981), especially pp. 83–93.

21   George Jackson, *Soledad Brother* (New York: Coward-McCann, 1970), p. 317.

22   A brief account of this type of literature and its ideological importance can be found in Gaucher, 'The Prisoner as Convict', pp. 61–9. But see also Stuart Hall et al., *Policing the Crisis* (London: Macmillan, 1978).

23   Mikhail Bakhtin, *Rabelais and his World* (Cambridge, Mass.: MIT Press, 1968), p. 421.
24   Ibid., p. 422.
25   Ibid., p. 436.
26   Breytenbach, *True Confessions*, p. 339.
27   Most homicides are not criminals in any accepted sense of the word. They are not in prison because of their membership in a criminal subculture, but rather because of a crime committed in passion or frustration. Their relationship to crime is akin to that of solitary domestic alcoholics to the bar scene, and derives from probably much the same reasons.
28   David Helwig, *A Book about Billie* (Toronto: Oberon Press, 1972).
29   John Bunyan, *Grace Abounding to the Chief of Sinners* (Grand Rapids, Mich.: Baker Book House, 1978).
30   See most of Heaney's work, but in particular *The Haw Lantern* (London: Faber, 1987), which draws on comparisons between Ulster and Poland.
31   See in particular Pierre Bourdieu, *Distinction: a Social Critique of the Judgement of Taste* (Cambridge, Mass., Harvard University Press, 1984) and Pierre Bourdieu and Jean-Claude Passeron, *Reproduction in Education, Society and Culture* (London: Sage, 1977).
32   Hannah Arendt, *On Revolution* (New York: Viking, 1963); Maurice Merleau-Ponty, *Humanism and Terror: an Essay on the Communist Problem* (Boston: Beacon Press, 1969).
33   Camus, *The Rebel*, p. 12.
34   Ibid., p. 268.
35   Roy Porter, *A Social History of Madness* (New York: Weidenfeld and Nicolson, 1987).

2

Framing the Subject

I

Prisoners, literate or not, are compelled by circumstances to try to come to terms with themselves and the world, with issues of personal responsibility and the framework of justice, with the violence of which they are a part. In one sense all prison writing is an expression of that reappraisal, but in another there are dominant motifs which impose themselves on or emerge from the prisoner's meditations, characterizing the thinking and marking it off as peculiarly carceral. Some motifs come from the presence of the carceral in our religious and social philosophies, but highlighted in a particular way to give important meaning to those in prison. Others are directly born of the experience of incarceration and are transferred to life in general. It is important to recognize the existence of a philosophy of incarceration which is specifically located in the experience of having been in prison.

I would like to approach this issue in two ways. The first is to indicate some key interpretations of the prison situation (whether they have been penned by prisoners or not) which are thematically important for considering prison philosophy. Broadly speaking, I am concerned not with philosophies of prison – though some of these are alluded to – but with philosophies which take the predicament of prison as having personal significance. My interest is not with how we rationalize having prisons, nor how prisons fit into a general conception of social order, but how, being prisoners, we come to terms with our own incarceration. It is important to do this partly in order to frame the discussion of prison philosophy, but also in order to create a dynamic tension between two kinds of thinking – one which might see a historical development in philosophy and one which sees none at all, where the philosophy is specific to the time and place within which the prisoners find themselves.

My second approach, in Chapter 3, is therefore to examine some of the major problems from inside prison of talking about 'philosophy'. I will do this initially by keeping as close as possible to the thematics of the approach in this chapter so that the differences, where they exist, will be all the more marked.[1]

II

That prison might provide a discipline which is conducive to clear thinking and internal control has been argued by many people, none more so than those religious writers to whom the practices of abstinence, self-mortification, poverty and hardship are virtues in themselves. The centre-piece of most religion involves the voluntary abdication of power to God:

> Make me a captive, Lord,
> And then I shall be free;
> Force me to render up my sword
> And I shall conqueror be.

The transference of the imaginary gaol to the real is not such a great leap; indeed, the justification of gaols as conducive to salvation is at the heart of most Christian theories of penology, and has also entered the folklore of literary criticism. Eli Mandel has argued that Oscar Wilde and Jean Genet 'needed' prison in order to write,[2] and a whole French intellectual tradition has been based on the romanticization of the cell;[3] the classic earlier romantic versions of this idea are to be found in the *Vita* of Benvenuto Cellini, who claimed, with some humour, that prison gave him both spiritual regeneration and the gift of writing,[4] and in the drama and poetry of Torquato Tasso, whose imprisonment in sixteenth-century Ferrara (apparently for the love of Leonora d'Este, the Duke's daughter) became the symbol of the poet *enchaînée*.[5]

The twin themes of prison as salvation and prison as happy creativity are paired with their opposites – prison as damnation and prison as the spiritual, creative void. The figure at the centre of this paradox in French writing is Pascal, whose work, like Kafka's, acts as a metaphorical reference point from outside prison of what incarceration might be seen to be about. But if Kafka defies the divine paradoxes, Pascal restates them. Both authors take prison to be the ultimate metaphor of life, but in Kafka the transcendental, the mythical, the haggadic is replaced by desire, the immanent search for being.[6] In Pascal, as in most other Judeo-Christian texts, desire is subservient to God, but it is a subservience that is dialectical:

> The true and only virtue is, therefore, to hate ourselves (for our appetites make us hateful), and to look for a truly lovable being, in order to love him. But we cannot love what is outside us, we must love a being that is within us and not ourselves, and this is true of each and every man. Now there is none like this except the Universal being. The Kingdom of God is within us, is ourselves and is not ourselves.[7]

And this state of tension can only be maintained by recognizing the importance of both mobility and immobility, of excitement and tranquillity, of being at an equal distance from extremes, of being separated from all that is not God in order to be closer to Him. The necessary solitude is without walls, poised between the finite and the infinite. And the problems of attaining this happy prison can be reduced entirely to being entrapped in another prison. In discussing the Wager, Pascal has his interlocutor give his reasons for not believing or accepting the Wager:

> 'My hands are tied and my mouth is gagged, I am forced to play, and I am not free. Something holds me back, for I am so made that I cannot believe. What would you have me do?'
> What you say is true. But at least be aware that your inability to believe arises from your passions. For your reason urges you to it, and yet you find it impossible. Endeavour, therefore, to gain conviction, not by an increase of divine proofs, but by the diminution of your passions.[8]

Desire is therefore entrapment, and release from this prison requires an imprisonment in the intersection between the finite and the infinite, a metaphysical cell where the human atom seeks to become part of the vast interstellar spaces.

This consciousness of existing between two prisons in order to discover the Hidden God calls for paradoxical and fragmentary writing. As Lucien Goldmann wrote:

> If Pascal is a great writer — as he is — it is first of all because he went against the aesthetic values of his sceptical and rationalist

contemporaries and was able to expoloit the two forms of literary expression demanded by his own philosophy. By giving the *Pensées* a paradoxical form, and by leaving them as fragments, he made them into a paradoxical masterpiece, complete by their very lack of completeness.[9]

Fragments, paradoxes are thus the essence of the tragic vision's inscription, and in some respects the nature of this enterprise is at the heart of understanding the problematic of accepting a theological basis for prison writing. But if the fragmentary and the paradoxical are at the heart of much prison philosophy, so are the definitive and the certain, and perhaps one of the tasks of contemplating prison writing is to come to terms with the fragmentary on the one side and absolute certainty on the other. The dilemma is there clearly enough, in John Bunyan's saga of the prison being merely a testing-ground in the long journey to the Celestial City, in Jean Genet's reversal of Christian and French symbolism in creating a counternarrative for the homosexual prisoner, and in the numerous accounts where prison becomes for the writer an arena in which the play of the world is acted out in a confined place.[10]

The Christian project specified the mapping of the regions of personal and collective relationship. By the time of the Reformation, across most of Europe the problematics of the human condition were rendered comprehensible within a code of language, prescriptions for daily living and a procedure for reading texts which apparently covered every contingency. The Reformation and the Renaissance fractured that wholeness of interpretation; and both Pascal and Bunyan, writing in the first century after the Reformation, provide dichotomous interpretations of the ensuing dilemma for the religious: on the one side the tragic vision of the twin prisons with its fragmentary explorations, and on the other the absolute certainty of salvation in a universe populated by personified virtues and vices.

In many respects these polarities reflect the dichotomous world Bakhtin saw, not only in Renaissance culture, but in all culture. The Renaissance and the Reformation (along with other historical moments of splitting asunder the existing fabric, such as the English, French, Russian and American revolutions)[11] brought to the surface man's encounter with his inner and outer space, and rethought the concept of both eternal and temporal punishment. Dante's neat structural resolution to the problems of social order and individual responsibilities had provided a dramatically symmetrical accommodation to the social system that he found about him. For in mapping out hell, purgatory and paradise he was, of course, also mapping the world of medieval Italy and classifying people (most of whom were still alive when he wrote) according to their actions. In addition, he was providing in allegorical form an elaboration of his political philosophy in which both reason (embodied in the Holy Roman Empire) and revelation (embodied in the Catholic Church) derived their power from God. Dante's journey through the various circles of hell, his explorations of the spiralling moralizations of purgatory, and his view of the visual splendours of paradise all testify to the ultimate way to God, uniting our wills by submerging them in the Universal Will. Against that might be set the Rabelaisian underworld where Dante's hell becomes a gay carnivalesque world, the isles of the Catchpoles, of Papimania, Popefiggery and Gaster, situated not on a vertical axis of ascent and fall but rather on the horizontal exploration of Jacques Cartier's North-West Passage. The joyous hell is Newfoundland, Greenland, St Pierre and Miquelon, not the mythical paradise of St Brendan's tenth-century Irish offshore islands. The search is for the 'Oracle of the Holy Bottle', not the Holy Grail.

The world of Rabelais released the genie in the bottle and freed hell from the 'hole of St Patrick'. For now hell could be associated with exploration, the joys of discovery, the hope of historical development. This explains Bakhtin's twentieth-century buoyancy at the discovery of Rabelais: the people, in spite of the strictures imposed on their lives by a verticalist religious and social structure, would triumph and the new means of communication were at the heart of their triumph. Such a sense of release, as Bakhtin himself pointed out, was not new. It originated with the Athenians, continuing through the last years of the Roman Empire and up to the present, represented for Bakhtin in the work of Dostoevsky and Joyce. Above all it emphasized the dialogic sense of human relationships, always at odds with a monologic authoritarianism, a collective open-ended vitality against unitary restriction.

Rabelais reintroduced the horizontal dimension to the vertical so that the two axes would thereafter continue to interplay in the interpretation of man's relations with others, with order and with death.[12] The philosophy of the prison is a philosophy that contemplates at once finitude and infinity, it is a philosophy of the carnal and the spiritual, of the violence of space, of the subterranean and the galactic, of the self and of the many. Above all it is a debate between the imposition of human controls and man's involvement in making those controls; and, because it is produced in the form of writing, it is an excursion into the limits and possibilities of inscription.

But because imprisonment itself takes place in the context of mechanized space, there is a further dimension, directly related to the mechanization of the body, of the senses and of human relationships. In the *Inferno*, Dante's sense of mechanized space is clearly medieval:

> We now were come to the deep moats, which turn
> To gird that city all disconsolate,
> Whose walls appeared as they were made of Iron.[13]

In Rabelais the use of terms like 'symmetry', 'portico', 'frieze', 'peristyle' all indicate an awareness of the architecture of the time, but they are set against the non-mechanized body which lives in its full naturalness, while Dante's bodies are themselves mechanized, compelled to exist in unnatural postures:

> They bump together, and where they bump, wheel right
> Round, and return, trundling their loads again,
> Shouting: 'Why chuck away?' 'Why grab so tight?'
> Then round the dismal ring they pant and strain
> Back on both sides to where they first began.[14]

This Dantean sense of mechanization is also found in Bunyan's *Pilgrim's Progress* in the Valley of the Shadow of Death, Doubting Castle and Vanity Fair. Thus the importance of the mechanistic, while present in all writing, is given different weights. The Dantean mechanism of the nether regions must be contrasted with the natural symbolism of paradise, where floral images of light, delicacy and translucency permeate a dancing galaxy. Not surprisingly, Bunyan's earthly mechanism is contrasted with the divine mechanism of the Celestial City which is paved with gold and populated by a mechanized orchestra and choir.[15] Pascal is well aware of the importance of the mechanistic but, as one suspended between two prisons, is conscious of its strengths and limitations ('for we must make no mistake about it: we are as much automaton as mind').[16] The mechanistic alone is slavery, the rational alone is self-deluding casuistry: 'We must therefore make both parts of us believe: the mind by reason and the automaton by habit.'[17] But ultimately, for Pascal, the physical, architectural prison is important only for its figurative value, and the mechanized stillness of the cell is death, for man is wholly animal and necessarily always in motion.[18] 'Infinite movement, ubiquitous point, moment of rest. Infinite without quantity, indivisible and infinite.'[19] For Pascal the mechanized is ultimately released from its space–time continuum, just as the mathematical inscription is released from the false sense of its own innate logic.

But if natural man and his mechanistic context is the primary focus of much of the Renaissance and post-Reformation debate, the conception of humanity as being freed altogether from transcendental concerns is the theme of much post-Enlightenment writing. The prison as a purely mechanistic institution, without even the redeeming feature of being restitutive or redemptive, is brought in forcefully in the late eighteenth century with the work of Sade. Both the standard Catholic interpretation of prison, as expressed in Dante, and the Puritan, as expressed in Bunyan, link it with the notion of external damnation, though purgatory in Dante and sojourns in such places as Doubting Castle in Bunyan provide alternative prison situations where restitution for sins might be made. With Pascal, prison is the metaphor of the world and also of the act of striving for salvation. This introduces the paradoxical situation of the prison metaphor permeating all of our existence. In a sense we understand ourselves through making these metaphors our own.

Rabelais' liberation of the idea of hell from the clerical writers is an important secularizing of sacred mythologies, grounding opposition to them in the everyday language and practices of the people and in their own search for secular pleasures; but it also creates the fear of anarchy and unlicensed naturalism. The major writers of political theory from Machiavelli to Marx can be seen as attempting to elaborate forms of contractual relations in order to create a social order that will tame desire, establish rights and obligations and provide a basis for moral actions. The distinctions among them – distinctions between collectivism or individualism, between ideal educational and economic systems, between what is appropriate to retain and what to abandon from earlier Christian or Hellenic systems – do not, in retrospect, seem as great as their common preoccupation with systems that, in attempting to tame the imagination and desire, also increased mechanization, violence, and incarceration.

The work of Sade must be seen in this context, written in French gaols while the ideas of the Enlightenment were being fought over in the streets outside. In *Dialectic of Enlightenment*, Horkheimer and Adorno whimsically linked together Kant, Nietzsche and Sade as the authors who reduced men to objects: Kant and Nietzsche as the scriptwriters and Sade as the accountant.[20] For the striking feature about Sade is not only his tedious catalogue of sexual antics, but his wish to achieve the perfect crime, where man becomes God and destroys himself. Sade's world is at once the world of absolute mechanism and the technologization of imagination and desire. Founded on the master-slave relationship, the Sadean world is a parody both of Christianity and of secular rationality, satirizing the social contract of Hobbes and Rousseau, and reifying the mechanization of the idea of desire. In Sade there are no real people; pure reason is at heart unreasonable, leading to the destruction of the subject. The logical consequence of rationality is not only complete mechanization, but mass-murder and mass-torture. The implication of the liberal theories of the Enlightenment was not freedom but the wholesale elimination of freedom. At one level it is possible to see all of Sade's work as purely parodic of the philosophies of rationalism and Christianity, of Gothic fiction, of liberal satire such as that developed by Diderot,[21] and thus to argue that Sade 'illuminates freedom through unfreedom'.[22] And many French authors have claimed as much for Sade: that he problematizes the importance of desire by overmechanizing it, that he turns the world back on his captors by making them act out a world of reason/unreason through a mechanized sexual slavery in a criminal republic.[23] Above all, as Roland Barthes has argued, Sade must be seen as a theatrical intervention in the play of the society he sees around him.

> Sade is boring only if we fix our gaze on the crimes being reported and not on the performances of the discourse. The function of the discourse is not in fact to create 'fear, shame, envy, an impression' etc., but to conceive the inconceivable, i.e. to leave nothing outside the words and to concede nothing ineffable to the world.[24]

It might also be argued that Sade's union of the rational and the mechanistic is also a direct parody of Pascal's happy prison.

The parodic and theatrical Sade is certainly there, and there is little doubt that the major intellectual effects of his writing have come from such a reading, but is also clear that his nihilistic and circular writing is directly a consequence of long periods in prison and mental institutions. As David Cook writes:

> The imagination is entrapped in the same way as Sade was in the Tower of Liberty in the Bastille. There was a price to pay for Sade and his work in the prolonged stays in prison. His imagination, as for example evidenced in the creation of the castle of Silling, ultimately did not go beyond the asylum of

Charenton where he spent his last days. Sade's prodigious effort to find reason, to find the intelligible order related to the sensible, never allowed him to listen to the unreason of his situation.[25]

Prison, in the long run, is not a place for creative dedication, but a cul-de-sac, and in this sense Sade's work is the ultimate embodiment of the horror of imprisonment.

But there is another aspect. If Sade is a parodist, this is a parody that consumes its own tail. The final impression left by Sade is that of the ultimate immoralist, the prophesyer and affirmer of wholesale destruction, positing, in the words of Georges Bataille,

> the necessity of . . . an anti-religious and asocial organization having as its goal orgiastic participation in different forms of destruction, in other words the collective satisfaction of needs that correspond to the necessity of provoking the violent excitation that results from the expulsion of heterogeneous elements.[26]

The mechanistic sadism of *The 120 Days of Sodom* becomes the gleeful mass-murder of Joseph Mengele, or, in literary terms, of Hitler's *Mein Kampf*.

There is, however, one further marker in the spectrum of prison philosophy, and this is perhaps best expressed in the work of Victor Serge, revolutionary extraordinaire and inhabitant of many prisons. The rethinking of social relationships from the Renaissance onwards did not involve only a debate with Christianity and the Enlightenment, and Sade cannot be allowed to stand as the typical representative of secularized penal philosophy. The multiple revolutions of the nineteenth and twentieth centuries have produced a large number of attempts to change society and, in their wake, a large number of changes which include displacement of populations, mass-extermina-tions, wars and civil wars, genocide and the ultimate mechanization of the disciplining process. One of the central figures in this process is the individual who has come to be called the 'prisoner of conscience'. In its wider form this term includes all those who are imprisoned because the government disagrees with their ideas, whether the ideas are evidently revolutionary or not. In its narrower form, however, it stands for those dedicated to transforming a system which they believe is corrupt and immoral and to speaking the truth as they see it. A historical list would include Socrates, Savonarola, Wycliffe, Hus, Antonio Gramsci, Leon Trotsky, Rosa Luxemburg and Dietrich

Bonhoeffer, all of whom were as much concerned with ethical conduct as with social order. Savonarola, Wycliffe, Hus and Bonhoeffer could appeal to a set of religious principles for their arguments and could also, as with Socrates, appeal for transcendental validation for their ethical stance. Gramsci, Trotsky, Luxemburg and Victor Serge could not. Their ethical position was based centrally on the social and the secular, and their imprisonment was related directly to their conception of democratic social action.[27]

Victor Serge holds a unique place in all this in that his stance was eclectically revolutionary, just as his nationality was eclectic.[28] He is described thus by Peter Sedgwick:

> Victor Serge, who was born in 1890 and died in 1947, was an anarchist, a Bolshevik, a Trotskyist, a revisionist-Marxist, and, on his own confession, a 'personalist'. Belgian by place of birth and upbringing, French by adoption and in literary expression, Russian by parentage and later by citizenship, he eventually became stateless and was put down as a Spanish national for purposes of his funeral documents. He was a journalist, a poet, a pamphleteer, a historian, an agitator, and a novelist. Usually he was several of these things at once; there were few times in his life when he did not combine at least two or three nationalities, ideologies, and professional callings.[29]

With Sade we discussed the ultimate in the mechanization of torture and murder, and with Bunyan (and to some extent Pascal) the concept of prison both as metaphor and as staging-post to another destination. There are indications of these in Serge, but in terms of prison philosophy there is very little of the allegorical, of the parodic, though there is much irony, and none of the transcendental. The terrain of Serge's life and writing is real prisons, real revolutions and real wars. The prison is not a byway of the social but the ultimate expression of the social, and the writer – particularly in *Men in Prison* – deliberately adopts 'I' in order to mean 'we' ('This book is not about me but about men.'[30] The author is a man of political action, participating in revolutionary activities in Russia, Spain, France and Belgium, but, as far as possible, maintaining a critical stance on behalf of the common people, because 'he who speaks, he who writes is above all one who speaks on behalf of all those who have no voice.'[31] In order to do this,

Writing becomes a search for a poly-personality, a means of living several destinies, of penetrating into others, of communication with them. The writer becomes conscious of the world he brings to life, he is its consciousness and he thus escapes from the ordinary limits of the self, something which intoxicates his spirit while enriching it and sharpening it at the same time.[32]

The prison itself, no longer in any way possessing the old religious justifications, is a machine of terror. Of his imprisonment during the First World War Serge wrote:

The French prison itself, organized as it is according to ancient regulations, is nothing but an absurd machine for breaking those men who are thrown into it. Life there is a kind of mechanized madness; everything in it seems to have been conceived in a spirit of mean calculation how best to enfeeble, stupefy and numb the prisoner, and poison him with an inexpressible bitterness; his return to normal life must evidently be made quite impossible. This end is attained by an organization impregnated with the penal traditions of the pre-revolutionary order, with the religious idea of chastisement (an idea which now, lacking any basis in faith, is only a psychological justification for social sadism), and with the footling detail of our vast modern administrations. The hotchpotch mixing of malefactors, semi-lunatics, and victims of all descriptions; undernourishment; the rule of complete and perpetual silence imposed at every moment upon all common activity; arbitrary punishments designed to humiliate, torture, and weaken; prohibition of any knowledge whatsoever concerning life outside, even if it be war, invasion, or national peril; the maximum possible deprivation of intellectual exercise, prohibition of study, even of reading more than one book a week, to be chosen from the idiotic novelettes of the prison library (fortunately it also contained Balzac). In the long run this treadmill turns out sexual inverts, cracked brains, worthless and depraved beings incapable of rehabilitation, dedicated in short to joining the ranks of tramps in La Maub; or else parasitical toughs, hardened by suffering, who keep up their own special tradition. Cynics, but loyal to one another, such men preserve their 'emancipated' dignity with no illusions about either society or themselves. From this class professional criminals are recruited.
Truly wonderful was the struggle waged by some there, a

pitiful minority, to preserve their capacity for living. I was very definitely one of these. For this purpose a considerable degree of a particular kind of will-power was necessary: passive to all appearance, yet artful and incorrigible.[33]

But the purpose is not made possible by an extraterrestrial salvation. Ironically he reflects on the hope:

A gleam of light was at last visible: this would be the beginning of everything, the prodigious first day of Creation. An end to deadlock! This huge gateway would be open towards the future. No more problems now about the aims of the struggle or the rules of life, for the Russian Revolution was calling from the heart of the future.[34]

What replaces Pascal's happy prison and the wager of eternal life is another wager. In 1943, after ten years in Siberia, Serge wrote: 'Behind us lies a victorious revolution gone astray and massacres so great in number as to inspire a certain dizziness . . . I have more confidence in mankind and in the future than ever before.'[35]

Serge's reflections on violence have similarities to both Sorel and Camus.[36] The machine of the prisons and the machines of war, concentration camps and treason trials were all cut of the same cloth, that is, they all stemmed from historically ingrained ideas of retribution and revenge, bureaucratic convenience, and a fear of diversity and freedom of thought. Faced with this, the principled man of action is caught between the consequences of his actions and his moral intentions. 'We revolutionaries, who aimed to create a new society, the broadest democracy of the workers, had unwittingly, with our hands, constructed the most terrifying State machine conceivable; and when, with revulsion, we realized the truth, this machine, driven by our friends and comrades, turned on us and crushed us.'[37] And yet the faith in the people and a just society lives on in opposition to the machines of violence. 'May the passion, the experience and even the faults of my fighting generation have some small power to illuminate the way forward.'[38]

Thus Serge offers us as the basis of prison philosophy the experience of political action, a comparative mapping of areas of violence (prison, war, poverty, revolution) and the persistence, against all odds, of a humanism based on 'social justice, rational organization, respect for the individual, liberty'.[39] Serge is the self-confessed personalist of the Enlightenment. It is important to recognize that, for Serge, these values are not realized in any one existing system: the wager involves the belief in the validity of the practice of struggling for them, but the dichotomy or paradox, if we follow the Pascalian analogy,[40] is between the Hidden God of Marxism which cannot be revealed in action without serious penalty ('I cannot help considering as a positive disaster that a Marxist orthodoxy should, in a great country in the throes of transformation, have taken over the apparatus of power') and the impotence of reason ('the role of critical intelligence has seemed to me to be dangerous and even useless'). Yet both must be struggled for: the Hidden God must be made manifest, or the whole exercise would seem to be fruitless; and 'I persist in regarding critical and percipient thought as an absolute necessity, as a categorical imperative which no one can evade without damage to himself and harm to society.'[41]

Prison itself, for the incarcerated revolutionary, becomes the ultimate test of the powers of resistance. It is not symbolic of anything but itself ('there is no novelist's hero in this novel, unless that terrible machine, *prison*, is its real hero');[42] but it becomes the sharpened projection of the outside world, and resistance to it provides the equipment for wider resistance. Because from prison most people do not emerge intact, the revolutionary must

> overcome this. I do not want to carry away with me any defeat. The Mill has not worn me down. I am leaving it with my mind intact, stronger for having survived, tempered by thought. I have not lost the years it has taken from me. We have committed great errors, comrades. We wanted to be revolutionaries; we were only rebels. We must become termites, boring obstinately, patiently, all our lives: In the end, the dike will crumble.[43]

III

The argument so far is that there are certain frameworks which, taken separately or in relation to each other, provide the basis for the prisoner's own philosophical debates. The major shifts over time in the perception of the dilemma of the prisoner involve the collapse of the medieval institutionalization of what is virtuous and vicious and a social order held responsible to God in both its secular and its religious aspects. The vertical organization of the Dantean allegory (already in question as it was written) is replaced by three options:

the Puritan allegory of a world which is entirely prison-like and from which all must flee or risk destruction; the Pascalian world of the gambler's choice between two prisons; and the Rabelaisian release of the damned into a voyage of happy discovery. In a largely secular world, there are two major images: the Sadean world of the ultimate mechanization of violence and desire, the Serge's resistance to that world in the interests of humanism and enlightenment.

If these are the nodal points in the framing of prison philosophies, it is now important to see in what ways the prisoners' accounts negotiate themselves within their contours.

NOTES

1 It will be noted that nowhere in this chapter do I discuss feminist writing in prison, nor black writing, nor any of the other more specific forms of prison writing. This is quite deliberate, because the logic of the chapter leads me to ask in what ways the philosophies explored here are appropriate for discussing these other situations.

2 Eli Mandel, *On Oscar Wilde and Jean Genet*, in The Literature of Prison and Exile Series (Montreal: CBC Enterprises, 1968).

3 See the superb account by Victor Bromberg, *The Romantic Prison: the French Tradition* (Princeton, NJ: Princeton University Press, 1978).

4 A rough translation of part of his long poem, the 'Capitolo', which appears in the centre of the *Vita*, reads: 'One day I decided that I would try to write ... Brushing my eyebrows, I searched my cell and found a crevice in the door, from which I took out a splinter with my teeth. Next I found a piece of brick on the floor, crumbled part of it into powder and formed a paste by pissing on it. Then Poetry with a loud noise came into my body, through exactly that part where shit normally comes out. It was as simple as that!' A more sedate translation is found in Benvenuto Cellini, *The Life of Benvenuto Cellini* (London: Heron Books, 1968), p. 256.

5 It is doubtful whether Tasso was in fact imprisoned for love of a woman of the nobility, and more likely that the Duke Alphonso II of Este certified him as mad because of his paranoid behaviour at court. This historical inaccuracy, however, did not prevent Byron, Goethe and Donizetti from composing poems and operas on the subject, and Tasso's own *Jerusalem Delivered*, an epic of the First Crusade, written while he was in prison, provided a chivalrous underpinning of the whole myth.

6 See chapter 4 below for a more detailed examination of Kafka. He is, incidentally dealt with there and not here because of the logic of my argument, which leads from the general to the specific. Kafka is primarily about the specific which deconstructs the general.

7 Blaise Pascal, *Pensées* (Harmondsworth: Penguin, 1966), p. 247.

8 Ibid., p. 158. Pascal's Wager was based on the sense that if God exists (which is probable precisely because it is unprovable) it would be unwise to

discount his existence – and therefore my future in the afterlife – by pretending that he is not a mathematical certainty. The gamble is on the sense that he is more than mathematics, that the unprovable is true, that there is a higher mathematics than the relative abstraction of mathematics as a science. But *that* gamble is conditional on knowing that this world (in which we are imprisoned) is less rational than revealing to ourselves the higher (happier) prison to which we all aspire. The Wager is dependent on knowing that there is a better world to which I aspire than the eternal doldrums of the present. In its twentieth-century sense, it implies a belief in more than technological (mathematical) rationality. It is the ultimate (Gnostic) version of us all being trapped in one world (the sense of the present as being all that there is) and reaching out for another one, wherever it is.

9   Lucien Goldmann, *The Hidden God* (London: Routledge, 1964).
10 The classic post-Enlightenment literary production from outside prison which attempts to combine these elements into a dramatic exploration of most of the salient issues is Peter Weiss's *Marat–Sade* (*The Persecution and Assassination of Marat as Performed by the Inmates of the Asylum of Charenton under the Direction of the Marquis de Sade* (London: Calder & Boyars, 1965)). The play should be read, however, in the context of de Sade's own writing, of some of the major commentaries on him, of Brechtian and Theatre of Cruelty debates, and ultimately of the issues raised by the relationship between hermetic thought and political action.
11 It depends, of course, on what we are looking for, but the English Revolution is there mainly because it realized the consequences of the Reformation, as the American Revolution realized the consequences of the English, while the Russian arguably realized the consequences of the French. The Industrial, Capitalist and Technological Revolutions cut across all of them.
12 Aspects of the intersection have been produced graphically by Mary Douglas in *Natural Symbols* (Harmondsworth: Penguin, 1973) in an exercise that interconnects with Pierre Bourdieu's graphology of culture in *Distinction: a Social Critique of the Judgement of Taste* (Cambridge, Mass.: Harvard University Press, 1984) and Basil Bernstein's graphology of the curriculum in *Class, Codes and Control* (London: Routledge, 1971). But Douglas's diagram is related to situating mental attitudes more in relation to power mechanisms than temporal or spatial ones, though it is suggestive for some of the ideas discussed here.
13 Dante Alighieri, *Inferno* (Harmondsworth: Penguin, 1949), p. 118.
14 Ibid., p. 111.
15 Christopher Hill, *A Turbulent, Seditious, and Factious People: John Bunyan and his Church, 1628–1688* (Oxford: Clarendon Press, 1988).
16 Pascal, *Pensées*, p. 274.
17 Ibid.
18 Ibid., pp. 238–9.
19 Ibid., p. 243.
20 See Max Horkheimer and Theodor Adorno, *Dialectic of Enlightenment* (London: Allen Lane, 1973), pp. 81–119.
21 In particular, perhaps, *The Nun*, which satirizes convents, and *Jacques and his Master*, where the servant is sharper, more intelligent than his lord.
22 David Cook, 'The Dark Side of the Enlightenment', *Canadian Journal of Political and Social Theory*, 5, 3 (Fall 1981), p. 7.

23   The list of authors is almost endless. But for some of the earlier ones see
     Mario Praz, *The Romantic Agony* (Oxford: Oxford University Press, 1933)
     and for some of the later, Cook, 'The Dark Side of the Enlightenment'. See
     also Georges Bataille, *Visions of Excess: Selected Writings 1927–1939*
     (Minneapolis: University of Minnesota Press, 1985), pp. 91–102, and
     Bataille, *Literature and Evil* (London: Marion Boyars, 1985), pp. 105–25.
     The major English versions of de Sade's writing published by Grove Press
     in 1966–7 include important essays by Maurice Blanchot, Simone de
     Beauvoir, Pierre Klossowski and Jean Paulhan.
24   Roland Barthes, *Sade/Fourier/Loyola* (New York: Hill and Wang, 1976),
     pp. 36–7.
25   Cook, 'The Dark Side of the Enlightenment', p. 13.
26   Bataille, *Visions of Excess*, p. 101.
27   They should be carefully distinguished from people who were imprisoned
     simply for advocating violence, or the overthrow of the existing system, or
     whose ideas of progress are so simplistic as to produce a logic that leads
     itself 'to mutilate man more and more and to transform itself into objective
     crime' (Albert Camus, *The Rebel* (London: Hamish Hamilton, 1953), p. 246.
28   In discussing Victor Serge, here and elsewhere in this book, I draw on his
     Memoirs of a Revolutionary 1901–1941 (Oxford: Oxford University Press,
     1963), *Destiny of a Revolution* (London: Hutchinson, 1937), *Men in Prison*
     (London: Writers and Readers Publishing Cooperative, 1977), *Conquered
     City* (1978), *Birth of our Power* (1977), *The Case of Comrade Tulayev*
     (1977), *If it is Midnight in this Century* (1979), *The Long Dusk* (1946), *The
     Year One of the Russian Revolution* (1972).
29   Serge, *Memoirs of a Revolutionary*, ix.
30   Serge, *Men in Prison*, xxv.
31   Ibid., p. xix.
32   Ibid.
33   Serge, *Memoirs of a Revolutionary*, pp. 45–6.
34   Ibid., p. 47.
35   Serge, *Men in Prison*, p. xviii.
36   See in particular Sorel's *Reflections on Violence* (Glencoe, Ill.: Free Press,
     1950) and Camus, *The Rebel*. The philosophical treatise which discusses
     the issue in terms closest to Serge's is, however, Maurice Merleau-Ponty's
     Humanism and Terror: an Essay on the Communist Problem (Boston:
     Beacon Press, 1969). See below.
37   Serge, *Memoirs of a Revolutionary*, p. 380. Before his death in Mexico in
     1947 Serge could say to Trotsky's widow Natalia Sedova, 'We are the sole
     survivors of the Russian Revolution here and perhaps anywhere in the
     world. There is nobody left who knows what the Russian Revolution was
     really like, what the Bolsheviks were really like – and men judge without
     knowing with bitterness and a basic rigidity' (Serge, *Men in Prison*, p. xx).
     Stalin had eliminated all the leading Bolsheviks. See Serge, *Men in Prison*,
     pp. 273–82.
38   Serge, *Memoirs of a Revolutionary*, p. 382.
39   Ibid.
40   Serge's writings also display a Pascalian predilection for fragments and the
     significance of the incomplete, though in part this is attributable to

circumstances (though circumstance – the circumstance of imprisonment – is precisely the issue).

> I knew that I would never have time to polish my works properly. Their value would not depend on that. Others, less involved in struggle, would perfect a style; but what I had to tell they could not tell. To each his own task . . . For in my books I adopted an appropriate form: I had to construct them in detached fragments which could each be finished separately and sent abroad posthaste; which could, if absolutely necessary, be published as they were, incomplete; and it would be difficult for me to compose in any other form. (Serge, *Men in Prison*, p. xv)

41 Serge, *Memoirs of a Revolutionary*, pp. 376–7.
42 Serge, *Men in Prison*, p. xxv.
43 Ibid., p. 250.

3

The Consolations of Philosophy

I

When Boethius debates with himself the meaning of life under the penal system of Theodoric of the Ostrogoths, he invokes as his Saviour not Christ, but Philosophy, that forerunner of Dante's Beatrice, born of Pallas Athene and Saul of Tarsus.[1] Lady Philosophy in Boethius is well travelled, the persona of a philosophy which knows itself through experience and learning. Having lived according to his lights and according to his beliefs, Boethius needs to know why he is now locked into this fatal space. It is not a simplistic belief in external salvation that will get him through, because the simplistic will only persuade him that he deserved to be here. (After all, is not guilt the ultimate Judge?) Boethius is innocent of the crimes for which he is accused, but he is doomed. What can he do? Repent? There is nothing to repent of. Can he possibly renege on his beliefs? But what sense would that be when he will be executed anyway? What value is there in talking about willpower when anyone who has willpower to survive the prison may also be doomed by the executioner? Boethius is the moral man on trial, caught up in the machinations of others, but ultimately doubting his own morality. This man, sick of his moral dilemmas, does not invoke Christ or Socrates to comfort him but she

of awe-inspiring appearance, her eyes burning and keen beyond the usual power of men. She was so full of years that I could hardly think of her as of my own generation, and yet she possessed a vivid colour and undiminished vigour. It was difficult to be sure of her height, for sometimes she was average human size, while at other times she seemed to touch the very sky with the top of her head, and when she lifted herself even higher, she pierced it and was lost to human sight. Her clothes were made of imperishable material, of the finest thread woven with the most delicate skill. (Later she told me that she made them with her own hands.) Their colour, however, was obscured by a kind of film as of long neglect, like statues covered in dust. On the bottom hem could be read the embroidered Greek letter Pi, and on the top hem the Greek letter Theta. Between the two a ladder of steps rose from the lower to the higher letter. Her dress had been torn by the hands of marauders who had each carried off such pieces as he could get. There were some books in her right hand, and in her left hand she held a sceptre.[2]

Boethius is the forerunner of Dante, Pascal and Rabelais, the 'last of the classicists and the first of the schoolmen'. His contribution is fundamentally as a translator – of Aristotle, of all the Greeks, of Livy and of Virgil – and his personality that of a mediator through the transition from the classical to the Christian period and, via the Dark Ages, to Christendom. Boethius is the man of the intersection, caught up in a world of thought dominated by the translatability of the messages of one set of arguments to other experiences. I argued earlier for the primacy of translation in prison literature: Boethius in prison has to confront his own translations. His personality is at once much cruder than that of Dante or of Pascal: he knows that he is the man who has been made by the translations. He has *become* the philosophy of virtue, but now buried in the carceral situation where virtue apparently does not matter. In *After Virtue*, Alasdair MacIntyre argues that the idea of the Aristotelian virtues was lost somewhere between the end of the Roman Empire and the beginning of the Reformation (a mere 1,000 years).[3] The culprit is perhaps Boethius, who as translator of the classical became the monitor of subsequent actions. Boethius, sick in gaol, needs his nurse to convince him of the validity of his translation, to turn him into the text that must be read by others. Our loss of the virtuous has somehow to do with Boethius' prevarications, his uncertainty between prudence (where moral actions are characterized by their battle with excess) and providence (the internalization of the divine). Boethius is closer to prudence and therefore Lady Philosophy, experienced and emanating from above, challenges him on his tendency toward excessiveness, his personal battle with the other whores, those muses who try to make him into a poet.[4]

As translator, Boethius is also parodist, self-consciously appropriating the original texts of his translations in order to make them his own. His sojourn in prison is an occasion for coming to terms with

their separateness from him, but also with their translatability into
his own concerns. In his use of their styles (in the first part of the
Consolation he appropriates Menippean dialogic satire in the style
of Martianus Capella's *Marriage of Philosophy and Mercury*, Plato's
Gorgias and the parable of the Cave from *The Republic*) he not only
sets up the stylistic as the pro forma of his own debate with himself,
but also connects their stylistics with their content. An open-ended
discourse, with all the textual references and parameters on the table,
will surely influence its direction. In Boethius – as in Plato or Capella –
the discourse appears to be open, but it is clear that with Boethius a
closure is imposed by the prison within which he writes. With Plato
and Capella the prison is clearly metaphorical, but with Boethius it
is real and final. As Lady Philosophy sings to him:

> His neck bends low in shackles thrust,
> And he is forced beneath the weight
> To contemplate – the lowly dust.[5]

Of course, the metaphorical prison and the real prison are ultimately
one and the same, but where is the closure of this debate? With Plato
and Socrates we know the closure: it is both death and the closure
of the sense of interpersonal dialogue. Death and imprisonment is
the point at which I switch from the obvious to the hidden, from
what is displayed to the gameplaying behind the obvious. As in
any posthumous biography (or autobiography) I move from the
presentation of self to the secrets of the self. I reveal the hidden self
and ultimately the hidden god.[6] I also point beyond self and the
present to the self-consciousness of the philosopher who, because he
is self-conscious, is 'aware of man's place in the cosmos which
presupposes a Rational vision of cosmos, of man and of man's
relationship to cosmos (and the relationship "internal" to man
between pleasure and Reason within his soul.)'[7] The closure of the
debate is a recognition of a future of which I will not be a part.

Philosophy is therefore the act of taking the ideas and the works
of others in order to relate them, through me, though incarcerated in
this silly but final resting place, onwards. The dialogue is therefore
about the apprehension of the posthumous. 'He being dead, yet
speaketh . . .' Boethius, the translator of the other dead, very conscious
of the deadness of his own interpretations, may only transmute those
dead into the newness of oncoming life. The presence of Lady
Philosophy, invented by Boethius in order to give presence to the
collective dead wisdoms, becomes the incarnation of the parodic, the

mimetic who becomes the figura, dancing through all eternity. The clue is surely found in the banning of the muses in Book I of the *Consolation* because they trade only in passion, and in their partial resurrection in Book III when Lady Philosophy poetically retells the story of Orpheus' descent to the underworld, but largely in order to teach Boethius the vanity of having any consort with the powers of darkness. It is not simply that Orpheus went down to hell to reclaim his loved one, or that he looked back, but that desire has its own law which does not respect that of providence. Desire is passion and love as we know it: providence is the Kingdom of God within, it is, of course, Lady Philosophy herself, and ultimately Dante's Beatrice. The muses are banned because they represent the apparent randomness of fate, and to celebrate this apparent randomness is to fail to encounter the inner meaning of providence, the beauty of which is so clearly displayed in Lady Philosophy, who, 1,300 years later, could appear both in Shelley's 'Hymn to Intellectual Beauty' as her 'to whom I would dedicate my powers' and in Keats as 'La Belle Dame Sans Merci'. She is perhaps also Robert Graves's 'White Goddess'[8] to whom the poets would thereafter dedicate their powers, unless, of course, they married her incarnation, in which case they would be back with the Boethius of Book I, tormented by the women of desire on the one hand and the women of 'beautifully activated reason' on the other.

But Boethius, twisting on the racks of pain so conveniently provided for him by Theodoric of the Ostrogoths, is not discussing these issues with real women. They are the dancing figurae of his imagination, the realization of his translation, the images of the others – outside – to whom he must relate both by the knowledge that he will not be able ever to relate to them again, and by the knowledge that he has always related to them through the translations and the imagination. As he contemplates whether only the good are rewarded, where is the validity of the claim that the evil have their just deserts, what is the justice of the virtuous man being incarcerated, and what do memories matter when you know you have to die, Boethius can only console himself, by inventing figurae out of his translations, that there is only posthumous hope when the present is found wanting, that virtue is enshrined in the contemplation of the posthumous realization of translatable beauty.

In Aristotle the idea of the virtues was socially grounded, albeit in an aristocracy of the Macedonian marabout who congregated round the Athenian polis. With Boethius – and perhaps already in Socrates – the virtues were transformed into the imaginary other, the ideal type personified in those who would perform on a stage where the fates and desires and providences would act out the play we would like to see as part of our own action. Aristotle tried to reclaim the virtues for the pathetic fallacy of the ungrounded Plato, placing it in a real tug-of-war between ideas and practice. Boethius, caught in the trauma of the cell, and also as the translator who tried to place the translation at a point where we could appreciate the meaning of the dead texts, pushed mimesis to the point of no exit. Because his exercise was guided largely by his translations, reifying them into beings which dominated our sense of ourselves for over 1,000 years and beyond, he projected our perception of our relationships with each other by turning the virtues into personifications, ultimately reversing the anthropomorphism of Greek theory, and translating it into the objectivism of the Platonic Cave. If the virtues of Aristotle were grounded in real people and in real societies, through the writings of Boethius they became imaginary people in imaginary situations. Boethius' battle with himself and the figurae which dominated his imagination resulted in the reinvention of the virtues only to turn them into an abstract female, and therefore nothing.

It is possible, of course, that the virtues would have been destroyed in any case by other events, and therefore Boethius' personification of them and the vices was a holding operation which kept the idea of morality going for another 1,500 years. But this is not our issue. Incontestably, through prison Boethius created the image of the reified virtue, the personification of the idea turning the subject into a thing. With Boethius there are no people, only thing-like ideals, the ultimate degradation of the subject. In spite of the importance of the subject being virtuous (after all, he wants to be known as being good for himself), Boethius, in probably the greatest Menippean discourse, finally decides that he can only *be* (let alone virtuously) through the persona of her who will dance against desire and through providence. It is the ultimate retreat. With Boethius the Oedipal urge becomes in time directed towards the Virgin Mary (though Dante's presentation of Beatrice is a final medieval fling against this iconic tradition of the virginal), and all virtues are subject to the incarnate other who would kill off the father. Sex is denied and mind is the idealization of gender. We have, in Boethius, the consummate imprisonment both of sex and of mind.

But if Boethius presents us with the ultimate problem in the message of the incarcerated writer, it is as translator that he also provides the notion of the messenger, the carrier of messages from the one who was, through the interpretation of others' writing, to those who will be. He does not see himself as being on trial by the real Theodoric, who as the Gothic Christian is responsible for his present plight, but as the figura of the transmitter of the symbols of messages. Boethius' whole discourse is symbolic, and thus he presents us with the fiction of the dancer who plays with the translatable images that bounce off his prison walls. This is his strength and his weakness. His strength is that he can act out philosophy, dancing to the repertoire of the images and, because of his sense of the infinite, not caring whether the images come to rest in a real world with real people with real sexual crises and a real sense of closure. In this sense he dances to us, as do the book in his translations, providing for us the flickering images that play out of the gaol to the infinite beauty of the Madonna, the pure unsullied Blessed Damozel that would keep all of us sane. His weakness, of course, is the weakness of refusing to confront the real and the self-evident, the rejection of desire which is surely the basis of our experience in the everyday prison that all of us encounter. For in the end, Lady Philosophy does not come to us 'penetrating heaven' but displaying gnarled hands, or as Dante put it (though from hell) with

> . . . the face
>
> Of that uncleanly and dishevelled trull
> Scratching with filthy nails, alternately
> Standing upright and crouching in the pool.[9]

Confronting the everyday and translating it into a language that makes sense is a problem that remains, and much of the language of prison philosophy is therefore a debate with the translatable, not only of what must be translated but also for whom it should be translated. Boethius' mistranslation of philosophy, history and women has a long legacy, almost all of it disastrous. By avoiding Aristotle's empirical sense it projected a conception of providence that, by idealizing Woman, ignored women. From Boethius' idealization of woman as Lady Philosophy to W. B. Yeats denouncing Con Markievicz as 'dragging out lonely years, conspiring among the ignorant' runs a straight line.[10] Con Markievicz was not the Lady Philosophy that Yeats thought she might have been: the image of woman from Boethius onwards was torn between Beatrice on the one side (ritualized as the Virgin Mary in Catholic inconography) and the harlot, the strumpet on the other. The Con Markieviczes, the Rosa Luxembourgs and the Emma Goldmanns did not fit. They could only be seen as

Lady Philosophy turned whore. Their moment might be consigned to the flames:

> Arise and bid me strike a match
> And strike another till time catch;
> Should the conflagration climb,
> Run till all the sages know.[11]

The missing part of all this is real bodies with real struggles in real situations. The virtuous are not entirely virtuous; the feminine personification of virtue, never.

II

The philosophical debate within prison literature is often about sexuality and revolution and violence and community. Frequently all four go together. Most writings that use parody, metaphor and allegory are debates with these concerns. Similarly, all discussions that invoke space, technology, writing as specific tools of articulation, are machines for collecting together the fundamental themes and the modes of speech. Boethius, like Pascal, Bunyan, Dante, de Sade, imposes the modes of speech on the themes in such a way that the themes become less and less connected with the basic question of how we struggle with the modes of speech. We are trapped in the prisonhouse of language and are concerned primarily with the nuances of an overarching narrative (including parodies of these narratives – though these are essential for creating counternarratives because we can never wholly escape the prisonhouse). By the time we reach de Sade, where the mechanization has reached absurd but terrifying limits, we need a Kafka to rethink the modes of speech in order to deconstruct the machines and to get back to the basic themes. The following chapter, using space as the overarching framework, addresses strategies by which this is possible. Here it is important, following the discussion of Boethius, and the issues raised in the previous chapter, to raise some of the important themes from contemporary prison writers which ask the central question: 'how then do we live?'

   At the very least, Boethius provides us with some major clues. These might be summarized. First, by accounting for self in relation to others, virtuous and not, he asks the central question 'what did I do wrong?' Secondly, he asks 'how, as translator of those who defined me and others, have I contributed to the knowledge of this whole process?' Thirdly, in relation to sexuality, he asks how desire and the human urges relate to living the virtuous life. Fourthly, he recognizes the importance of parody in his own writing as a debate between that which has been written before, that which is written now and that which will be written into others' practices and actions. Fifthly, in the discussion on the relationship between providence and fate (borrowed in large part from Plato and Augustine) he raises the very important issues of personal responsibility in the (apparently) deterministic scheme of things, otherwise known as free will and predestination, or individual creativity and social determinism. Finally, he raises the issue of membership in a community as a basic issue of the prison dilemma.

My disagreements with what he did with these issues is of less significance than his laying the ground for what a prison philosophy would entail, and in this respect his relationship to prison writing is of the same status as Marx's to twentieth-century politics. Most subsequent writers approached similar issues from different vantage points, and it is their writing that we now address. It is of course also important to recognize that most prisoners have not served their sentences simply for falling out of favour with an invading monarch (though Boethius' crime was seen as high treason): they have been imprisoned for everything from murder (political, domestic or related to property), to other crimes against the body, property crimes, all manners of fraud and crimes of conscience or simply for being black, gay or Jewish. All these crimes are in one sense an inscription against the system that ultimately incarcerated them, whether they knew they were potential prisoners or not. But all prisoners bring with them their works of translation (of laws, norms, religious beliefs, etc.) which are necessarily reviewed in prison. The creation of a prison philosophy is thus necessarily a translation of ideologies through personal experiences in an attempt to inscribe a new way of thinking about narrative.

One important point of departure is to consider the situation where the crime and its inscription are seen together as constituting a whole. The most vivid example of this is provided by Michel Foucault and his colleagues in their presentation and analysis of the triple murder by Pierre Riviere.[12] In this nineteenth-century French case, Pierre Riviere, a Norman peasant 'barely able to read and write' murdered his mother, sister and brother, and, in gaol, wrote a memoir justifying the act. In analysing the case, Foucault concludes that the text provided by Riviere must be read not merely as an adjunct to his crime but as integral to it. Although in no way could it be argued that Riviere killed his family in order to protest against a social and legal system, still it can be seen that Riviere, both by murder and by writing the memoir, wanted to accomplish a 'historical murder'. The entirety of the events surrounding the murder constituted a theatrical intervention, in which Riviere read the family situation, his work, the legal process and the popular culture that attended the crime, and tried to impose his own stamp on it. As Foucault notes,

> Riviere, there is little doubt, accomplished his crime at the level of a certain discursive practice and of the knowledge bound up with it. In the inextricable unity of his parricide and his text he *really* played the game of the law, the murder and the memoir which at this period governed a whole body of 'narratives of crime'.[13]

Thus Riviere plays out his theatre in relation to the texts as he understands them. His theatre of cruelty seeks an end to representation as theatre: it projects into the everyday world the theatricality of the early parricides and in so doing tries to cry halt to their representationality. The parents, their siblings, the judges, the local popular balladeers, Riviere himself – all are interwoven into a text of which Riviere is author. The play and its text are for real and all the actors play out their expected parts with Riviere himself finally achieving his glorious final death. The murderer/narrator has produced the consummate play. But Foucault argues that, perhaps because he had written his own script, Riviere's final execution was not as glorious as he had wished, because 'a newspaper informs us that in his prison he considered himself already dead'.[14] Thus, although Riviere succeeds in not being declared insane, in the end he does not succeed in being the triumphant hero of his own play. His script wins out.[15]

The implications of such an analysis for understanding what we mean by prison philosophy are important. With Riviere, the memoir in gaol might appear to bear sharp contrast with Boethius. The 'crime' and the scripting of it would appear to be antithetical: Boethius is imprisoned for a politico-religious crime, Riviere for killing his mother, his brother and his sister. Boethius does not mastermind his crime and the subsequent course of events, Riviere does. And so on. But it is important also to note that neither of the works is a confessional – both are justifications. Boethius has indeed masterminded his crime as much as Riviere, and his Menippean dialogue is a carefully organized set of arguments that pull together the validations of his actions, urging him not to falter in his beliefs nor to be surprised that he, of all people, should be treated in this way. Boethius, of course, did not *expect* to be imprisoned, but, once he has been, his entire previous history must be rewritten to accommodate the fact, so that we are convinced that that previous history was a progression to this glorious moment. Theodoric, the Roman legal system, the guards, the Catholic Church and the whole of classical philosophy then become actors in the play that Boethius has constructed. Similarly with Riviere: the family history is rewritten to show the inevitability of his crime and all the actors become actors in his play. In both, however, the text becomes more significant than the play itself, and the justification is a posthumous one.

The differences are striking too. Although both writers are conscious of authorship, for Boethius it is a theological authorship 'dominated by speech, by a will to speech, and by the layout of a primary logos which does not belong to the site and governs it from a distance'.[16] For Riviere it is a non-theological but parodic authorship ('I wished to defy the laws, it seemed to me that it would be glory to me, that I should immortalize myself by dying for my father.')[17] For Boethius, the vindication is necessarily posthumous; for Riviere it is conceived of as being immediate, though for his father it follows on Riviere's death. ('I thought to myself he will hold me in such abhorrence that he will rejoice in my death, and so he will live happier being free from regrets.'[18] And finally, the sense of community for each author is quite distinct. For Boethius the community is an abstract one: the philosophers, the Church, the virtuous. For Riviere the communities are also abstract – he compares himself to those historical figures who died for noble causes and he positions himself to join the community of all murderers – and yet for Riviere those abstractions are related to dying very specifically for one man, and to a very specific dramaturgy in the judicial process.

There is, however, a commonsensical distinction which affects my decision to contrast the two cases, and which in doing so provides the polarities necessary to tracing prison philosophy. In *The Rebel* Camus distinguished two major types of literature: the literature of consent and the literature of rebellion.[19] He argues that the first characterizes all literature prior to the end of the eighteenth century, and the second – exemplified in the novel – all that has been produced since. The distinction is historically too clear-cut, as I suggested in the previous chapter, but the two cases just described bring it into sharper focus. For the major distinction made in academic professional reading of prison writing has been precisely between writing reflecting a prison philosophy (in which the gaol becomes an occasion for contemplating the nature of the world) and that embodying an anti-philosophy, in which the experience of being a criminal and of being in prison creates a reversal of the universality aspired to in the first. Thus the two kinds of writing are necessarily negatives of each other. On the one side sits Boethius; and on the other, say, Genet, whose extolling of the 'penal fraternity' and the 'divine' criminals creates a world of fantasy and dream in which the world's values are upturned. But the dichotomy is solipsistic. As Elissa Gelfland puts it:

> This solipsism, by which the material aspects of the prison experience are absorbed into and transcended by the author's spiritual response, is one example of the hierarchy that has underlain all judgements of literature. Prison works, like literature in general, have been viewed through an ideological prism that dichotomizes the spiritual and the material, then sees the spiritual as governing. What is more, the spiritual has been made synonymous with 'universal'.[20]

If the dichotomy is to hold, it is not Genet who should be seen at the polarity, but rather Riviere; because with him we have not the successor of Sade, but a new type of prison philosopher who chooses murder, dramaturgy and suicide expressed in a text in order to explore his own psychosis. For Riviere belongs not in Genet's fold at all, nor in the cul-de-sac of French rational romanticism, but among those uniquely twentieth-century manifestations of terrorism on the one side (the televisual, theatrical display of violence for a cause) and the suicidally willed execution on the other.[21] Genet's romanticism of prison life must be set against the integrated drama of violence as public spectacle. And this new form of prison philosophy at once subverts the work of a Serge as it extends that of a Riviere.

One other major feature of Riviere is the actual nature of his crime. He murdered his mother in order to vindicate his father. No amount of romanticizing of a penal spiritual homosexual community will eliminate the basis for examining the precise interpersonal sexual situations that give rise to crime, and which ultimately affect the philosophy that is constructed around it. What Riviere does with all this is to vindicate the father by killing everyone off who seems to be in the way. Thus his answer to the question 'how then do we live?'

is 'we allow Oedipus room to move by eliminating the rest of us.' The primacy of the patriarchal situation is maintained.

III

What has been said so far will offer no consolation to anyone seeking a philosophy in prison writing. And this is for good reason. I have deliberately offered two contrasting cases which provide the extremes of the ideal/rational on one side and violent interventionism on the other. They serve their purpose, however, in drawing us back from the romanticism of the cell that has marked so much other writing on prison creativity. The inscription into and out of prison walls cannot be decontextualized, and although certain operating themes and modes of expression can be deduced from decontextualization, the 'philosophy', if it is to have any meaning, must come from the examination of the particular. Romanticism in prison writing is almost always an imposition from outside prison, a projection of those who, having failed to find sufficient validity in their own experiential symbols, search for them behind prison walls. The prisoner must escape from this over-writing as much as from any other: in Genet's case, and others, it might be argued that he accepted it as his own in order to subvert it, but also in order to be heard.

Two themes are sufficient here in order to indicate the nature of the problem and set the tone for the rest of the book. The first is that of community; the second is that of revolution. The two themes generate sometimes contrasting and sometimes overlapping issues.

Community has already come up as an essential factor if we want to know for whom, as well as against whom, the prisoner thinks he is writing. It is clear that for most prisoners there is no simple answer to these questions; indeed, in a large number of cases the answers are bound up with the question of *from* whom they are writing. The prison writer is generally unsure of his readership and therefore his perception of his audience, though important, is frequently a shot in the dark at posterity. What is clear is that, contrary to claims by non-prison writers, prisoners do not write for writing's sake and their inscriptions in the cage are inscriptions meant to have some effect on someone, somewhere. The earlier work of François Villon is important in setting the tone for much subsequent writing in this respect. For the legacy of Villon combines a number of motifs in one figure: as bandit, prisoner, lover, troubadour he can encapsulate important elements of the imaginary romantic prisoner. He is the man on the run who prides freedom above the restraints of society; he is the poet who unflinchingly criticizes the evils of his society; he is the literary outlaw who chooses not to be co-opted. His experiences in and out of prison bring him face to face with death, hunger, cruelty and fear, and highlight concerns that others in his society had with the organization of the Church and the family and with war, death and poverty. His dual role as criminal in this society and supplicant in the next gives him a unique voice. In fact, for most of history Villon has become the epitome of the literary bandit, assured of fame in this world and in posterity.

Villon is an impressive metaphor for community, speaking to the oppressed members of his society and to all of us subsequently, yet maintaining his own independence and desires. The idea of bandits as heroes has other resonances in history, as E. J. Hobsbawm has recorded, because they 'belong to remembered history, as distinct from the official history of books. They are part of the history which is not so much the record of events and of those who shaped them, as of the symbols of the theoretically controllable but actually uncontrolled factors which determine the world of the poor.'[22] And yet we remember the bandit because he has been intellectualized and has been translated into other contexts by film-makers, novelists and political journalists. He has become a symbol of something else.

Villon, by being a writer, has in a sense been spared this co-optation. His texts are available to be read and placed in our lives as we see fit. And yet – in spite of that – in literary discourse he has been adopted as part of a specific community. In her major study of writing in French prisons, Françoise d'Eaubonne places him at the beginning of a tradition of French writing that leads through André Chenier (beheaded in 1794, he consciously sought a dramatic literary presence), Sade, Paul Verlaine (imprisoned twice for attempting to kill Rimbaud and his own mother) and, finally, to Genet.[23] Thus the poetic bandit Villon is ultimately made a spokesman for the male penal 'fraternity', where crime becomes noble and of the highest philosophical order. According to this tradition it is impossible to read Villon without seeing him through a lens which has been ground by Sade. But, as I have argued above, there is not one tradition in prison literature but many, as in any other form of literature, and the question of 'community' as being identical with 'tradition' requires some consideration before we proceed further.

Writers as distinct as Breyten Breytenbach, Jean Genet, George Jackson, Eldridge Cleaver, Victor Serge and Alexsandr Solzhenitsyn all make claims to there being a common culture of prison. In fact, one of the great organizing principles of most prison writing is to assume this commonality. As Genet writes in his introduction to Jackson's *Soledad Brother*, the common ground among prison writers is that 'starting in search of themselves from the ignominy demanded by social repression [they] discover common ground in the audacity of their undertaking, in the rigour and accuracy of their ideas and visions.'[24] Genet makes a number of assumptions based on his own experiences – but primary among them is that his cultural attitudes and Jackson's are fundamentally the same. From this it would follow that there is a common prison philosophy that is 'universal'. Breytenbach begins to make his claim but then backs down, recognizing the importance of the unique cultural community from which he comes against all the apparent universals. And Solzhenitsyn, though claiming universals, systematically knows that he is only writing about the Gulags – indeed, that he cannot write about anything else. The idea of a Solzhenitsyn, a Breytenbach, a Jackson and a Genet being able to hold a conversation that lasted longer than half an hour is risible – though Serge would have made a good chairman.

What I think we can agree on is that there are common points of discourse and that there appear, in the articulations, to be certain features with which most of the participants seem to be in agreement. The idea of community therefore cannot be imposed on this debate – as Genet attempts to do by co-opting Jackson to his own solipsistic position – but is in reality a problematic behind all prison writing. For even if we could agree on, say, the commonality of certain cultural features inside prison, this would by no means apply to the contexts within which prisons were located or the backgrounds from which prisoners came. Two examples will precisely express what I mean and what is the central issue when we talk about prison 'philosophy'. These examples, writing by blacks in American prisons and writing by women from prison in France, Britain and the USA, will be looked at in contrast to each other.

The history of writing in American prisons is closely bound up with the history of slavery, of the chain gangs, of the penitentiaries. In fact it is difficult to conceive of any study of American prison writing which did not recognize that the country was founded on convict and slave labour, and that even the founding fathers were fugitives from justice in England. The writing by blacks out of modern penitentiaries therefore comes out of a long tradition of an enslaved people, and this tradition has been expressed in song, music, ballads, 'narratives', 'confessions', autobiographies, poetry, stories and novels. From the earliest days, the use of biblically-derived allegories of captivity in Egypt acted as a framework for a black culture and until recently it was difficult, if not impossible, to distinguish between collective and individual authorship. The gist of this culture was an account of oppressed conditions coupled with hopes and plans for liberation, religious and secular symbols being closely interwoven. The use of allegory in black music and literature is strong and powerful and provides the basis for much of the most serious discussions of the appropriation by a subjected people of the culture of their masters in order to reverse its implications and give meaning to their own lives. In many respects it can be seen as a fertile ground for Marxist theoretical interpretations of culture and social action, and the most forceful research has come from that quarter.[25]

The history of black imprisonment in the United States is therefore part of a process of economic control and cultural dominance, and to read the texts independently of the context of *that* development, as Genet apparently did, is to risk intellectual triviality. To read the prison philosophy without an understanding of its narrative form and its specific continuities and discontinuities is to risk trivializing the experiences of those blacks who articulated them. And finally, to read the literature from American black prisons as a contribution to the philosophical–spiritual penal nostalgia of Western 'culture' is totally to misunderstand that literature and to fail to recognize its opposi-tional, aggressive stance.

Similar concerns are raised if we deal with women's writing from prison. Though based on a much wider geographical and social terrain than black American writing, and with a less articulate and cohesive cultural movement behind it, women's writing again warns against universalizing from specific and unique experiences. For what is noticeable here is not the uncommonality of the experiences and the writings, but rather the commonplaceness of the experiences and the paucity of the writings. For women, as Elissa Gelfland has pointed out in her excellent study of French women's prison writings, have had to endure a triple damnation – as criminals, as women and as writers – and the writings that emerge have been neither 'transcenden-tal' nor rebellious. 'There is little evidence . . . of a will to dominate or possess; there is at best a sense of weakness inverted into irony or solitude glorified as martyrdom.'[26] The subversiveness of women's texts lies in quite other directions: 'the female tradition, deemed "particular" because its authors apparently affirmed their personal conformity, ultimately shows how women exploited and manipulated prevailing social and criminological discourse to counter myths about women criminals . . . [and thus] collectively undermined the cultural imagery that led to their damnation.'[27] The woman writing in prison has thus not had the indulgence of being consoled by a universalistic Philosophy (who would presumably have to appear in male form), but has rather had to construct a practical philosophy from the materials that lie around her cell.

There are therefore important social (and hence epistemological) distinctions to be made between prison philosophies; the contrast between black American and women's writing suggests perhaps the most important divergences from those traditions discussed in chapter 2. From this contrast we can see that community can mean a baseline of cultural solidarity which encompasses the prison and out of which individual and collective works might emerge, or it can mean the apparently personalized accounts of specific experiences which articulate the problems of an evidently wider community. The tensions that these processes create are of far-reaching importance for thinking about the philosophies of prison writing.

In conclusion, it is worth suggesting just how fruitful this tension might be by considering the revolutionary woman in prison. The black prison tradition suggests the importance of collective servitude and the development of a culture of resistance in understanding the nature of articulation by writers in prison. The black prison culture is, in Bakhtin's sense, part of the culture of the carnivalesque which stands in opposition to the officially sanctioned culture: the carnivalesque is parodic of the official and uses official symbols in order to mock them. In Marxist terms, the class culture and the political coalesce in a definition of a counter-hegemony: the prison experience is the ultimate attempt by the dominant class to break the potentially revolutionary nature of the oppressed, though for blacks it may be precisely the locus where the sense of alternative political potential is forged. Thus the personal experiences (as in Bunyan and Boethius) are by way of clarification of the ultimate political/religious philosophy.[28] Women's writing, I have suggested, works in precisely the reverse direction, where the personal experiences may ultimately feed into a socio-political movement which emerges slowly out of gender conflicts.

Marxist revolutionaries in prison provide yet a third category of prisoners, suggested in part by the example of Victor Serge in chapter 2. Here, of course, the prisoner is part of a revolutionary movement which *may* represent 'community' in the black sense, but is more likely to be an organized political party which might, in fact, be elitist and intellectual, even though it may enjoy wide popular support.[29] The relationship between prison writer and revolutionary movement is an age-old one, but, in virtually all cases, prison or exile has provided the opportunity for the reformulation of ideas in such a way that they had profound implications for the direction of the political movement.[30] The relationship of prison writing to revolutionary movement is thus a crucial one. But what happens when women revolutionaries are imprisoned?

Several prominent women revolutionaries have been imprisoned and they have left an important body of literature.[31] What is striking about this literature is the strengthening of revolutionary resolve by the authors as well as the emphasis on the person as a whole, as Peter Nettl wrote of Rosa Luxemburg, 'protest no longer consisted in *doing* but demanded *being*; individual gestures of protest lost their significance and perhaps did more harm than good.' Prison provided 'a whole process of deliberate self-examination . . . turning inward on herself all her formidable tools of analysis which could not now be deployed upon a society from which she was cut off'.[32] It involved a deliberate choice of friends and correspondents, a repudiation of much of the triviality of everyday revolutionary activity, a cultivation of a garden in the prison grounds, and a clarification of the issues in political life.

> 'Every act and interest became life writ large, and took its place in the composite but vital business of living. This was the message of optimism which poured out of prison at her friends. Cut off from the collective life of the community, the individual, instead of shrinking, had to grow large enough to speak not only for itself but for everything. Things had to be substitute for people – plants, flowers, animals, large and small. The old fortress of Wronke became a universe with its own laws and purposes, strong enough to reach out into the consciousnesses of all Rosa's friends. They must have rubbed their eyes over the morning mail and wondered whether they were not the ones cut off from reality.'[33]

In other cases, as in that of Constance Markievicz, prisons were less comfortable than Wronke was for Luxemburg; yet the striking feature of Markievicz's prison life was again the organized sense of purpose coupled with personal self-discovery. In Mountjoy prison in the late 1910s and the 1920s she helps to focus on the new generation of women organizers, teaches herself Marxism and studies the Russian

Revolution, and actively advises on the battles being fought between the Republicans and the army of the Irish Free State. Markievicz, though certainly much less of a theorist and an intellectual than Luxemburg, is ultimately concerned with using the prison to pull together her commitment as a revolutionary as well as to tighten her sense of herself.

But what of their conception of the role of women in society? If we refer back to Gelfland's observation that women writers in prison deal with the specifics of their own situation, but neither generalize from them nor attempt to argue for a universalism of the prison condition, we see something different when we read the letters from Luxemburg and Markievicz.[34] The external cause for which they were in prison is seen as bigger than woman's inequalities. But, on the other hand, both of these authors argue that the status of women will only change after the revolution if women become actively involved in the process. Each, in her letters, documents specific problems for women in prison and in society, and their correspondence is a specific way of creating a revolutionary basis for feminist activity, though they stop short of advocating anything like a feminist strategy. Some of the most regular correspondents of both women were leading feminists. As with Victor Serge, the crucial thing is not to lose hope; but also, more than that, to develop a set of networks from within prison that will expand the idea of the 'political' while at the same time creating a set of confidantes who will have been radicalized, activated precisely because of their experience in prison. Thus the women revolutionaries in many ways combine elements of the patterns we have seen in relation to both black and women prisoners. The experience of being a woman in prison is fed back into a carefully selected community so that prison, far from being a disadvantage, becomes an asset in the future of the movement.

IV

We have come full circle. The Boethius who contemplates his fate in Theodoric's prison has been replaced on the one side by mass repression and collective action from American black prisons and on the other by the clear call to organization for revolutionary activity from Wronke and the Berlin Alexanderplatz. The change is noticeable: the philosopher who would save himself and justify his own activities to himself has been replaced by a prisoner whose anger and whose sense of the collective is organized from within the cell. Reflection has been replaced by a commitment to an active holistic being. It is impossible to use philosophy to console self, except on the grounds of pure indulgence. And although they often sound alike in their denunciations, Lady Philosophy denounces the man in the cell, Rosa Luxemburg those outside. Lady Philosophy was the fiction of a tormented imagination. Rosa Luxemburg was a real person. Boethius and Luxemburg were in the end both killed: Boethius by Christian executioners, Luxemburg by police assassins. But if their writings explore the polarities of practical political philosophies, Riviere compels us to contemplate a philosophy that is purely subjective, where actions are tied up in a sense of personal theatricals and therefore ultimately (though lethally) meaningless.

NOTES

1   For the importance of Boethius in Dante see the introduction to Dante, *The Divine Comedy: Paradise* (Harmondsworth: Penguin, 1962).
2   Anicius Boethius, *The Consolation of Philosophy* (Harmondsworth: Penguin, 1969), pp. 35–6.
3   Alasdair MacIntyre, *After Virtue* (Notre Dame, Indiana: University of Notre Dame Press, 1984).
4   The Platonic influence is evident:

> At the sight of the Muses of Poetry at my bedside dictating words to accompany my tears, she became angry. 'Who', she demanded, her piercing eyes alight with fire, 'has allowed these hysterical sluts to approach this sick man's bedside? They have no medicine to ease his pains, only sweetened poisons to make them worse. These are the very women who kill the rich and fruitful harvest of Reason with the varren thorns of Passion'.   (Boethius, *Consolation*, p. 36)

But see Iris Murdoch, *The Fire and the Sun: why Plato Banished the Artists* (Oxford: Oxford University Press, 1977) for a discourse on Plato's relationships with the artists.
5   Boethius, *Consolation*, p. 37.
6   For a suggestive analysis of this as a possibility, see Alan Blum, *Theorizing* (London: Heinemann, 1974), pp. 119–27.
7   Blum, *Theorizing*, p. 119.
8   Graves does not refer to Boethius but his study is resonant with the mythical interpretation of women in poetry. See Robert Graves, *The White Goddess* (London: Faber, 1952).
9   Dante Alighieri, *Inferno* (Harmondsworth: Penguin, 1949), p. 184.
10 Yeat's poem 'In Memory of Eva Gore-Booth and Con Markievicz' is perhaps the ultimate male statement of the dismissal of women as activists. It is reproduced here in full:

The light of evening, Lissadell,
Great windows open to the south,
Two girls in silk kimonos, both
Beautiful, one a gazelle.
But a raving autumn shears
Blossom from the summer's wreath;
The older is condemned to death,
Pardoned, drags out lonely years
Conspiring among the ignorant.
I know not what the younger dreams –
Some vague Utopia – and she seems,
When withered old and skeleton-gaunt,
An image of such politics.
Many a time I think to seek
One or the other out and speak
Of that old Georgian mansion, mix
Pictures of the mind, recall
That table and the talk of youth,
Two girls in silk kimonos, both
Beautiful, one a gazelle.
Dear shadows, now you know it all,
All the folly of a fight
With a common wrong or right.
The innocent and the beautiful
Have no enemy but time;
Arise and bid me strike a match
And strike another till time catch;
Should the conflagration climb,
Run till all the sages know.
We the great gazebo built,
They convinced us of guilt;
Bid me strike a match and blow.

(W. B. Yeats, *The Poems: a New Edition*
(New York: Macmillan, 1983)

11 Yeats, *The Poems* p. 264.
12 Michel Foucault, ed., *I, Pierre Riviere, having Slaughtered my Mother, my Sister, and my Brother . . .: a Case of Parricide in the 19th Century* (New York: Pantheon, 1975).
13 Ibid., p. 209.
14 Ibid., p. 212.
15 For a suggestive essay which explores the implications of the Theatre of Cruelty, see Jacques Derrida, 'The Theatre of Cruelty and the Closure of Representation', in Derrida, *Writing and Difference* (Chicago: University of Chicago Press, 1978), pp. 232–50.
16 Ibid., p. 235.
17 Foucault, *I, Pierre Riviere*, p. 105.
18 Ibid., p. 106.
19 Albert Camus, *The Rebel* (London: Hamish Hamilton, 1953).

20   Elissa Gelfland, *Imagination in Confinement* (Ithaca, NY: Cornell University Press, 1983), p. 109.
21   Norman Mailer, *The Executioner's Song* (New York: Warner Books, 1979).
22   Eric J. Hobsbawm, *Bandits* (Harmondsworth: Penguin, 1972), p. 133.
23   Françoise d'Eaubonne, *Les Ecrivans en Cage* (Paris: André Balland, 1970), which, together with Victor Brombert, *The Romantic Prison: the French Tradition* (Princeton, NJ: Princeton University Press, 1978) and Gelfland, *Imagination in Confinement*, provides the most important introduction to French prison writing.
24   George Jackson, *Soledad Brother* (New York: Coward–McCann, 1970), p. 2.
25   See in particular Eugene Genovese, *The Political Economy of Slavery* (New York: Random House, 1967), Francis Newton (alias Eric J. Hobsbawm), *The Jazz Scene* (Harmondsworth: Penguin, 1959) and H. Bruce Franklin, *Prison Writing in America: the Victim as Criminal and Artist* (Westport, Conn.: Lawrence Hill, 1982).
26   Gelfland, *Imagination in Confinement*, p. 20.
27   Ibid., p. 29.
28   To some extent this was borne out in the 1960s and early 1970s when the emergence of a number of movements and individual writers (Malcolm X, Eldridge Cleaver, George Jackson) from prison indicated the potential within the US penitentiary for revolutionary action.
29   I try to spell out the relationship between revolutionary movement and political writing in chapter 7 below.
30   The most dramatic case is that of Antonio Gramsci, General Secretary of the Italian Communist Party, who was imprisoned by Mussolini in 1926 and remained there almost up until his death in 1937. See chapter 7 and the appendix.
31   In particular there are Emma Goldman, Angela Davis, Elizabeth Gurley Flynn, Sylvia and Emmeline Pankhurst, Constance Markievicz and Rosa Luxemburg.
32   Peter Nettl, *Rosa Luxemburg* (London: Oxford University Press, 1966), p. 670.
33   Ibid., p. 664.
34   That I have a different point of view from Gelfland must be obvious, even though I accept certain of her premises regarding women writers. Her wholesale appropriation of the notion, derived from Lucy Irigaray and Hélène Cixous, that all women's work is politically decentree and necessarily non-authorial is suspect in the extreme. See Nancy Fraser and Linda Nicholson, 'Social Criticism without Philosophy', in Andrew Ross, ed., *Universal Abandon* (Minneapolis: University of Minnesota Press, 1989), pp. 82–104 for some suggestive points in this direction.

4

Violent Space

I

To understand prison writing it is important to understand space and the reading of that space, and if possible to dispute the validity of the distinction that Gaston Bachelard is careful to make in his discourse on space and the poetic imagination, where he argues that the habitable spaces of the poetic image are spaces that attract, spaces that have been lived in 'with all the partiality of the imagination'.[1] In contrast, he dismisses 'hostile space' of 'hatred and combat' as capable of being studied only 'in the context of impassioned subject matter and apocalyptic images'. The space in prison is of a different order, being, in Bachelard's sense, both familiar and hostile, and its understanding requires not the formalization of ethnographic or poetic dichotomies but the metaphor and allegory of inscription and sight and voice.[2] For space is not physical in the sense that Bachelard uses it, where places become images, but physical in a quite different sense where the interplay between the biologically physical (the tactile, the audible, the visual) and the graphic is assembled in the context of higher voices, eyes, inscriptions by being forced into the voiceless, sightless readability of a mechanized physical structure. What I mean by this is that it is impossible to conceive of space without an architectonic of space and the hierarchy of that architectonic. We do not only inherit space, but we live through a space which brings with it its own structuring of use into which we inject our own kinetic sense. To study space is initially to study the eye, the voice, and the hand, and at the same time to conceive of other voices, eyes, hands reworking the space. The old dichotomies of public and private space, which have characterized much writing in sociology, while useful as a metaphorical starting-point for the study of the problem, must ultimately be discarded because of their inability to grasp the interstitial nature of a territoriality which is at once biological, material and political.[3] It is not so much that the public sphere (the prison) dictates the private (the personal everyday sense of ourselves), though it appears to do so, but that in the organization of space the centripetal and the centrifugal coexist, so that the exits and entrances are contiguous, and while there is the illusion of total power there is, in fact, the two-way mirror of total mistrust by each of all.[4]

The language of prison space is therefore one in which eyes, voices, limbs interact in a moving out from the cell with its definite physical contours and back into the cell from the more obvious dimensions of the power/ideology that attempts to control. Victor Serge provides a classic description of the relationship between the graphology and kinetics of the cell:

> The walls also speak with voices of the present.
> The guard has scarcely made his round when a faint noise, a mouselike scratching, makes your ears perk up. Three discrete little taps, a pause, three more taps. A man is calling me from the other side of the stone wall. I answer: three, pause, three. Then, coming regularly now, the taps are spaced out evenly in long series. As many taps as are needed for each letter of the alphabet: 16, p; 9, i; 5, e; 18, r; 5, e. The tapper's name is Pierre. It takes a great deal of concentration to avoid making a mistake counting up these hasty little taps to which you must listen with one tuned to the noises of the corridor so as to avoid getting caught. After long minutes, 'Pierre of the Gang of the Four' managed to tell me:
> 'Hello. Sent down for murder. And you?'
> Personally I have nothing to say to Pierre of the Gang of the Four. This conversation made up of mouse noises and alphabetical additions wearies me. I tap: 'Goodbye!'
> And I fall back into my silence . . . To work.[5]

And yet in this description the 'I' of the prisoner is more like the 'I' of the television viewer. When he has had enough, he switches the set off, whereas the regular reality is that of the 'I' cohabiting with his own body and his own memories. Horst Bienek, a Polish playwright and poet sentenced to forced labour in Siberia in the 1950s, wrote in *The Cell* of his first encounter with this space:

> I stood in the cell leaning against the iron of the door, I felt the coldness taking possession of my palms and spreading through

my whole body, I walked two steps and found myself in the middle of the cell, around me there was air and emptiness and stillness and the smell of sweat and chlorine and urine, I stood and waited for fear . . . suddenly I wished they would come and torture me, for I wanted to scream, but nobody came, I remained alone, alone in the cell, alone in the white foamy darkness; I knew the moment would come when I would throw myself on the pallet and stretch my body into the world, so far that I'd touch the edges of this city with my hair and reach far into the country with my feet, and then I shall gaze at the ceiling, which at first will confuse me with its whitewashed narrowness but which then I shall accept in its minute infinity, I shall lie there, pull the underpants which they left me over my belly, perhaps I shall scratch my neck, perhaps I shall smell my left armpit, perhaps my right hand will touch my genitals – and I'll spread the blanket over me, slowly, it won't quite cover me, I shall fall asleep and wake up, and then be again in the cell: an age without miracles! I did not stir, I stood waiting in the middle of the cell, I listened, my ears were still filled with the sound of the shutting of the cell door: I shall never forget it. I took another step and was up against the wall, therefore the crossing of my cell from door to wall took three steps, then I set about measuring the distance between the other two walls, I went back again to the middle of the cell, then to the left up to the wall, I turned around, leaned against it heavily, it took only two little steps to the cot at the opposite wall, I stood and looked around: the floor grey-black, made of cement, the door painted blue, an iron door, a window in one wall, I called it window wall, a bucket on the other wall, I called it bucket wall, the cot on the third wall, I called it cot wall, and above the cell door in a niche a searchlight behind wire mesh: this was the cell, they had assigned it to me, and I was busy taking possession of it, taking possession of it.[6]

This 'I' establishes first the contours of his own physique, and of the physical inscription of the cell. The cell written all around him forces him to make his own inscriptions:

I went to a corner of the cell, placed my finger into the join where bucket wall and window wall met, I wanted to feel the two walls touch, with the tip of my index finger I made a quick stroke downwards, felt the fingertip burning, I did it once more reaching further up, I wanted to have as long a stroke as possible, and when I made a second finger stroke downwards I knelt and brought my finger down to the floor where the two walls and the cement floor formed a triangle, the triad, the *trinity*, in which now, in my fifty-eighth year, I had to believe, for this was one of the few things which I saw, sensed, experienced with my body . . .[7]

And in South Africa, Breyten Breytenbach is compelled to write his way into and on to his imprisoned space:

Writing becomes for me a means, a way of survival. I have to cut up my environment in digestible chunks. Writing is an extension of my senses. It is itself a sense which permits me to grasp, to understand, and to some extent to integrate that which is happening to me. I need it the same way the blind man behind his black glasses needs to see. But at the same time I soon realize that it becomes the exteriorization of my imprisonment. My writing bounces off the walls, the maze of words which become alleys, like sentences, the loops which are closed circuits and present no exit, these themselves constitute the walls of my confinement. I write my own castle and it becomes a frightening discovery: it is unbalancing something very deeply embedded in yourself when you in reality construct, through your scribblings, your own mirror. Because in this mirror you write hair by hair and pore by pore your own face, and you don't like what you see.[8]

But, in many political prisons, to form any counterinscription is itself a crime against the cell's prior inscription. The Women's Prison in Cairo in the early 1980s was no exception, as Nawal el Sa'adawi recounts:

Still holding the sharp bit of rock between my fingers, I was inscribing letters and meaningless words in the dirt, my handwriting awkwardly crooked as it was when I was a child . . . The *shawisha*'s [guard's] eyes, as she reclined there, followed the movement of my hand over the dirt. She shook her head. 'If the Internal Security police officer were to show up right now in the courtyard and see from a distance that you are writing, he'd think you have some paper and pen. Nothing on his mind but pens and paper . . . One written word in the political cell is more serious than having a pistol. Writing is more serious than killing, doctor . . ."[9]

Similarly, in Kamiti prison near Nairobi, Ngugi wa Thiong'o describes a search:

Suddenly the sergeant saw piles of toilet-paper and pounced on them. Then, as if delirious with joy and triumph, he turned to the presiding officer and announced: 'Here is a book, sir, on toilet-paper.' 'Seize it!' the officer told him, 'the whole lot! Who told you to write in prison?' the officer said, turning to me.[10]

Even the graffiti is ultimately eliminated. Bienek again:

Even in the corridor I noticed that a change must have taken place in my cell, but not as usual when they rummaged through my pallet and pushed the bucket away from the wall, that didn't count, that often happened; this time, I felt at once, it also concerned me, I smelled paint even before the guard unlocked the door for me, for a moment I thought that, during my absence, they had painted the floor, it was of a blackness I had never seen before, I placed my foot on it almost hesitantly but when I saw that they had whitewashed the walls, they were still grey with moisture, spongy white patches spread out here and there, especially in the corners. My diary was gone, my calendar likewise, all inscriptions were erased: that was the change. Up to now, through all the searches, they had left me the signs I scratched on the wall, now they had taken away even that, this discovery stunned me or was it the smell which hung in the room and filtered into me, dark and crackling, through my nose, mouth and ears, and through my skin, I felt it thickening in my head and beginning to graze my brain cells, that hurt, I went to the cot and lay down on the pallet, spread my arms wide at my side and, motionless, watched from my place as the spongy clouds slowly spread more and more across the walls, I hoped I would rediscover at least part of my notes once the cell was dry.[11]

These are the more obvious cases of inscription/erasure where the writer, compelled by his own hand to rewrite the prison by writing himself on to it, in turn finds his writing eliminated. But the dominant space may also degrade his graphology by compelling him to write in order then to mock him by destroying or distorting what he has been compelled to write. George Faludy, the Hungarian poet, describes such an occasion when he was incarcerated by the AVO (the Hungarian secret police). After signing a false confession ('there was no point in not signing. There was no point in signing after two months of torture'), and after a vain attempt to leave a message on toilet-paper written with broom-bristle and blood (it said: 'Arthur Koestler was Right: I was guiltless'), Faludy is compelled to write his own autiobiography, several times:

> On the second day he ordered me to write my autobiography in at least thirty pages. Two days later, when I had finished, he read it carefully, then declared that if what I had written were true I should be decorated and not imprisoned. Then he called me Orwell's dirtiest disciple and spat into my eyes. During the following two days he made me tell him about every love-affair I have ever had, down to the smallest detail. It seemed as though he were simply passing the time of day until they had finished searching my room and collecting data and evidence against me.
>
> During the following week, after he had made me write two more autobiographies, had torn them up and flung them in my face, I at last discovered what he wanted. I understood from certain remarks he made that they had not searched my room, knew nothing about my past activities and, what is more, were not even interested in them. They wanted nothing but that I should furnish, or to be more exact, invent, the proofs supporting the eight false charges against me. I had to realize that AVO were not investigating, not examining, not proving and not reading. According to communist logic the very fact that they omitted to search me although they were accusing me of preparing an armed uprising, demonstrated that they were preparing to stage a show-trial. My remaining doubts were dispelled by Napoleon himself who, reminding me that I was a poet – a man of imagination – encouraged me to write a 'really beautiful and credible confession'. He said that if I refused he would have me taken to the cellar and beaten so thoroughly that they would have to take me out of the building in a dustbin. However, apart from a few slaps, he did not hurt me.
>
> Finally he declared that he would write my biography in co-authorship. He sat down to the typewriter and I dictated. But when he handed me each finished page it turned out that he had typed something entirely different from what I had said.[12]

The only solution to such double-crossing graphology may be a mental and verbal one:

> Learn this poem of mine by heart,
> You may not have the book for long.
> If you lend it, you will not get it back,
> the Hungarian borderguards will seize it,
> in the public library it will disappear . . .[13]

II

If proof were needed, these examples illustrate not only the inter-penetration of the idea of space by the significance of writing, but also the impermanence of a writing which is inserted against the superinscribed prison. But here it is important to consider the ways in which this writing exists at all and how the writing might be read. Michel Foucault wrote of the idea of the mechanized prison, tracing its architecture to Jeremy Bentham's *Panopticon*:

We know the principle on which it was based: at the periphery, an annular building; at the centre, a tower; this tower is pierced with wide windows that open onto the inner side of the ring; the peripheric building is divided into cells, each of which extends the whole width of the building; they have two windows, one on the inside, corresponding to the windows of the tower; the other, on the outside, allows the light to cross the cell from one end of the cell to the other. All that is needed, then, is to place a supervisor in a tower and to shut up in each cell a madman, a patient, a condemned man, a worker or a schoolboy. By the effect of backlighting, one can observe from the tower, standing out precisely against the light, the small captive shadows in the cells of the periphery. They are like so many cages, so many small theatres, in which each actor is alone, perfectly individualized and constantly visible. The panoptic mechanism arranges spatial unities that make it possible to see constantly and recognize immediately. In short, it reverses the principle of the dungeon; or rather of its three functions – to enclose, to deprive of light and to hide – it preserves only the first and eliminates the other two. Full lighting and the eye of the supervisor capture better than darkness, which ultimately protected. Visibility is a trap.[14]

This mechanization of the space requires a double interpretation. On the literal level the Panopticon was never realized effectively anywhere, though perhaps with the perfecting of electronics it may become possible. But it became the image of the ideal prison, the space that was all eyes, and hence may yet be for the prison what Dante's Inferno was to the concentration camps. As George Steiner argues,

> The concentration and death camps of the twentieth century, wherever they exist, under whatever regime, are Hell made immanent. They are the transference of Hell from below the earth to its surface. They are the deliberate enactment of a long, precise imagining. Because it imagined more fully than any other text, because it argued the centrality of Hell in the Western order, the Commedia remains our literal guide-book – to the flames, to the ice-fields, to the meat-hooks. In the camps the millenary pornography of fear and vengeance cultivated in the Western mind by Christian doctrines of damnation, was realized.[15]

In this sense the abstract mechanism of the designing board, the prefiguring theological torment, the construction of the law or the intentions of a Manichean political ideology provides the superordinate narrative of that which might be, an allegory that defines the real meaning of the mechanistic structures, the prisons, which by themselves are mere spaces incoherent and senseless.[16] If by themselves they are meaningless, the structures are brought into meaning by the abstract mechanism so that they appear to become instances of growing realization, incomplete but given meaning by the whole to which they aspire.

On the other hand, the abstract mechanism would be quite ridiculous unless it related to structures that took it seriously, which developed its grotesque ideas in such a way that the design was tested and even enlarged. As with the hegemonic culture of any society, the dominant ideas are constantly being remade or they cease to be dominant. At this point the prisons cease to be empty vessels which receive the abstract mechanism, and become the critical locus of their own abstractions. The meaningless nature of daily tasks, relationships, symmetrical shapes provides both a quotidian logic and its own transcendence, so that the abstract mechanism looks concrete by comparison. For if the prison is an unrealized or incomplete version of the abstract mechanism, its own self-justification becomes an abstraction which only the higher abstraction can justify. Thus the everyday behaviour within a prison may operate for years, with its own inbuilt normative structures, having no direct relationship to the procedure of law that called it into being. A riot, however, will immediately call into question those everyday practices and bring into force both the law and the abstract mechanism of the ideal panopticon. In this sense the eyes have it: the clear vision of what should be is brought to bear on what is, and the abstract mechanism – which was thought to have been transcendent – is revealed in all its immanence. New prisons will be built and they will be stronger, safer . . .

But the riot is the most extreme case of attempting to redraw or rewrite the space, and all the spaces can be seen as gradations on the route to the realization of the ideal, the absolute abstraction made concrete.[17] But just as there is no completed ideal, there is no completed writing, because the writing is necessarily an insertion, an interjection into the specifics of a particular space against the apparently competing claims of the abstract mechanisms. For abstract mechanisms, although they often appear to speak with one voice, in fact conceal their contradictions: law which seeks to punish but claims to rehabilitate; architecture which searches for the ultimate mechanism to control, neutralize, eliminate; theology which desires simultaneously restitution, salvation and damnation; and politics which seeks for the ultimate professionalism of order. The writer frequently appeals to one, forgetting or not knowing about the claims of the others, but, not only this, he may fail to see that the overlapping architectural sites to which he is subject are the product of competing laws, competing politics, competing theologies.[18]

Thus in the abstract mechanisms there are also, as it were, parallel abstract architectures which inform the specific realities of the prison into and against which the prisoner writes. Deleuze and Guattari argue in relation to Kafka's work that the conception of such architectural sites is built into Kafka's strategy for writing and that his own writing therefore becomes the pro forma for continuous, incomplete writing. The central issue in Kafka (and one must add that it must also be central in reading prison literature) is that the abstract mechanisms must be deconstructed, must be stripped of their teleological and transcendental significance if there is to be any serious writing at all. The abstract mechanisms together are the harbingers of guilt, and guilt is precisely what is absent in Kafka. It is not the transcendental abstractions that matter (they are the superficial apparatuses that must be dismantled), it is the immanent ones, those which are assembled in the courts, the prisons, the ante-rooms, the offices ('writing machines'), those that produce and reproduce themselves. It is against those assemblages that the continuous, never-ending writing must be inscribed.[19]

This argument provides the clue for understanding the nature of prison writing, and also for non-writing, for understanding the repetitions, recalls, interruptions, the urge to stop writing. As Bienek remarks in the middle of his book:

> at last I should call it a day, there are only stories left, old stories, repetitions, nothing else, if I am not repeating my own story, I repeat those of others. I remember a story by a Spanish author, or he might have been a South American . . .[20]

III

Having said all that, there are different spaces and those writing from prison define them for themselves in such a way that the particulars become important. Bienek's concern about repetition ('Well now: no repetitions, let's have done with old stories')[21] is another graphology that the prison writer has to write himself into and out of, but it is a triumphant Lazarian graphology. At one level the sepulchre is a dominant motif ('In this room the corpses are taken to the father's for embalming'),[22] but at others it is life triumphant ('I refuse obeisance to the King of hell or to any of his analogates and I believe in the Resurrected One and all his analogates').[23] This introduces in an important way the problem of the space of the theological abstract mechanism which appears to give the specific prison both its moral *raison d'être* and the means of resistance. The Bible itself provides both sets of imagery: the wicked are tortured and damned, but also the good are persecuted and imprisoned. The higher punishments are reserved for the wicked and the lower for the good (see Hebrews 11: 32–40, and II Corinthians 4: 8–10) and, notwithstanding Kafka, it is central to our understanding of prison to recognize the significance of the religious sense of space for the strategies of survival. If Kafka provides the ultimate materialist basis for deconstructing the space, many prison writers operate on a double level of imagery. The materialist is absorbed in the religious–mythical, as if the material cannot be understood without writing it through the religious. In a later chapter I consider the religious issues in some detail but here, as an illustration of the problems of reading space, I would like to use the religious in terms of the immanent and the transcendental, of reterritoriality and deterritoriality.

The central problem of the religious conception of imprisonment is guilt, and a sense of guilt which in many respects can only be coped with by making a distinction between the good and the bad, the 'sheep and goats' of the Bible. It is a problem that is well articulated by Foucault in a comment on a conversation he had with Genet:

> During the war he was in prison at the Santé and he had to be transferred to the Palais de Justice in order to be sentenced; at that time the custom was to handcuff the prisoners two by two to lead them to the Palais de Justice; just as Genet was about to be handcuffed to another prisoner, the latter asked the guard, 'Who is this guy you're handcuffing me to?' and the guard replied: 'It's a thief.' The prisoner stiffened at that point and said, 'No, I'm a political prisoner, I'm a Communist, I won't be handcuffed with a thief.' And Genet said to me that from that day on, with regard to all forms of political movements and actions that we have known in France, he has had not merely a distrust but a certain contempt . . .[24]

The religious or political prisoner can only make sense of his predicament by appealing to a higher order of things. He is, after all, by his own definition, not a 'criminal', he is a 'prisoner of conscience'. His appeal is to a higher court than that which currently exists in the society which imprisoned him, and his relationship to the other prisoners is, in the first instance, clearly a descent into hell. As Psalm 22 indicates, there is an ambiguity in his relationship to self: ('but I am a worm, and no man: a reproach of men, and despised of the people' (v. 6); to God: ('My God, my God, why hast thou forsaken me?' (v. 1); to the other prisoners: ('for dogs have compassed me: the assembly of the wicked have enclosed me,' (v. 16); and to his guards: 'strong bulls have beset me round; they gaped upon me with their mouths, as a ravening and raging lion' (vv. 12–13). Thus there is the internal sense of failure, the questioning of the Oedipal God: 'but thou art he that took me out of the womb: thou makest me hope when I was upon my mother's breasts' (v. 9); but ultimately there is the hope of deliverance: 'O Lord, my strength haste thee to help me' (v. 19) and the restoration of Oedipal power: 'all ye the seed of Jacob, glorify him, and fear him, all ye the seed of Israel' (v. 23). The apparent senselessness of imprisonment is made one with the continuity of the species as a testimony to the Oedipal God's power: 'Him shall they worship, Him only that are laid to rest in the earth, even from their dust they shall adore. I, too, shall live in his presence and beget children to serve him' (vv. 29–30).[25]

This series of transcendental/subterranean/reproductive motifs acts as a powerful focus for the prisoner's attempt at coming to terms with his incarceration. This is not only true of such obvious cases as Boethius, Bunyan or Bonhoeffer but is generally true of the most varied cases of prison writing, including, for example, convicts being deported to Australia, where Psalm 88 was a particular favourite ('I am counted with them that go down into the pit'),[26] with Dostoevsky ('In the mire I comforted myself with the idea that the rest of the time I was a hero, it was the hero who was wallowing in the dirt: for a ordinary man, I felt, it is shameful to roll in filth, but a hero is above really becoming filthy, and so I can let myself experience the dirt')[27] and even with Bienek ('I shall tell him . . . as unknown and yet well known as dying and behold we live/As persecuted as cast down as patient as blamed as chastized as forgotten will that ever stop').[28]

The self-confident arrogance of the political or religious prisoner is soon broken down so that in most cases his predicament is shared with that of his fellow-prisoners. He may of course want to convert them to his own set of beliefs, as Bienek half-heartedly contemplates converting his cell-mate Alban: 'perhaps I should even try to persuade him to convert to Catholicism, let's see if the force of conviction still lives within me';[29] or, as Charles Colson more assertively decided, 'as the weeks passed, my conviction deepened that God had indeed given me a vision for a new work in the prisons . . .'[30] But in general the transcendental symbols become deprived of their externalizing and internalizing power, the political prisoner is a prisoner like anyone else and the relationships he forms, the enemies he makes, and the spaces he inhabits have little to do with the higher abstract mechanisms and more to do with the assemblages that he finds around him. To understand his use of the transcendental symbols, therefore, primarily requires an understanding of these assemblages, and a distinction to be made between belief in the symbols in and for themselves and the symbols as metaphors for the actual conditions with their immanent messages.

Two exercises are necessary here. The first is the more general one of realizing the importance of philosophy in interpreting the prison condition, which is the theme of other chapters in this book, and which needs no particular elaboration here.[31] The second, however, involves a complex problem of the use of metaphor in understanding the prison condition. This question cannot be avoided in proceeding with this chapter, for in one sense the very word 'space' here has been used metaphorically, as have 'God', 'Oedipus' and 'mechanism'; and ultimately the word 'prison' is used metaphorically in many contexts, though it is itself frequently referred to metaphorically as 'hell'. The distinctions to be made in the understanding of metaphor are founded not in the sense that metaphor is denominative (i.e., in the classical rhetorical sense, merely 'naming' something, either because no name existed for a new thing or because of a need to decorate discourse), but in the sense that metaphor is predicative: it involves the whole sentence, that is, the relationship between a logical subject and a predicate.[32] Further, the study of metaphor necessarily shades into the study of cognitive models: the precise use of a term is evocative of another contextual use of the same term, and whenever metaphor is used it calls into play what Roman Jakobson called the 'split reference', in which the primary reference renders the secondary one ambiguous.[33] Metaphor in its imaginative use seizes on this 'split reference' and addresses the moment of commonsensical reference by projecting new possibilities of describing the world. Thus, when Breyten Breytenbach writes 'But this wild beast of expectation is entirely caged in',[34] his secondary references are of course to the prison and to himself, while his primary ones are to zoos and to the animal in a state of nature, thus evoking an alternative form of captivity and an alternative form of being. Further, desire ('expectation') is dramatized both by the use of the adjective 'wild' and by the verb 'caged'. Thus in one extended metaphor we have encapsulated the captivity that is the prison, an alternative social context and a cognitive dichotomy. The metaphor works by the dichotomous appropriation of another context.

In this sense the use of metaphor does not obscure the nature of the present situation, but rather heightens our perception of it by contrast (Breytenbach is not saying that he would like to be a wild beast in the jungle). But take another example. In *Grace Abounding*, John Bunyan writes of his prison experience:

I have had sweet sights of the forgiveness of my sins in this place, and of my being with Jesus in another world. Oh the mount Sion, the heavenly Jerusalem, the innumerable company of angels, and God the judge of all, and the spirits of just men made perfect, and Jesus, have been sweet unto me in this place.[35]

In this, as in other accounts of his stay in Bedford Gaol, Bunyan conveys little of the nature of 'this place', but rather uses an elaborate metaphor to contrast with it. Although elsewhere he itemizes some of the inner tensions that affected him while in gaol, these appear to be all cerebral and in no sense do the metaphors relate to particular experiences of guards, physical closure or the regimen of the prison. The reason is clear.[36] Bunyan's entire work is an exercise in metaphor and allegory, and prison is merely an instance of a much more important story.[37] In the introduction to *Pilgrim's Progress* he offers a long 'apology' for the use of parables, allegories and metaphors:

> But must I needs want solidness, because
> By metaphors I speak? Were not God's Laws,
> His Gospel-laws, in olden time held forth
> By Types, Shadows and Metaphors? Yet loth
> Will any sober man be to find fault
> With them, lest he be found for to assault
> The highest Wisdom . . .[38]

It is therefore not surprising that in his autobiography Bunyan is little concerned with the details of prison experience and much more with seeing it as a testing of his wider commitment. In the *Pilgrim's Progress* this assumes a full-scale allegorical form, and prison situations are used directly to provide object lessons in Christian's advance to the Celestial City.

The force of Bunyan's use of metaphor is therefore of a quite different order to Breytenbach's. In the one, the prison is absorbed into an ongoing allegory (whose properties are closely related to those in Psalm 22, discussed above); in the other, a particular sequence of experiences within prison invokes other situations in order to sharpen the urgency of this moment, at this time, even though the images invoked may suggest a common pattern for other such prison experiences. Bunyan's prison images involve stereotyping (for example, the Man in the Iron Cage as opposed to the Pilgrims in the Cage at Vanity Fair) in order to convey the stages of spiritual progress.

In both cases metaphor involves the assertion of a personal quality, but in Bunyan's case that quality is absorbed into the will of the Oedipal absolute who alone will give power to overcome the present. In Breytenbach all absolutes are oppressive: the metaphor is invoked to give expression to 'freedom, the minotaur outside the walls'.[39] The spaces are therefore quite different: Bunyan's is a road leading over mountains, plains and swamps, through castles and fairgrounds, from the City of Destruction to the Celestial City, with dungeon, cells, cages as punctuation. It is a route populated by personified virtues and vices, though all speak with the language of the common man. (Only Christian speaks the language of the Bible.) Breytenbach's space is composed of mirrors, mazes, rooms, corridors, colours, noises, rhythms, zoos, General Stores, smells, bodies; it has entrances and exits, it is populated by guards, left- and right-wing terrorists, thieves, murderers, pimps, coloureds, whites, blacks, drifters, cockroaches, priests, who speak in many voices or none. It is an account which 'is neither objective nor complete'.[40]

These two metaphorical ranges provide the scope within which prison space is conceived and experienced. In Breytenbach the prison is embodied, materialized, sensed, negotiated. In Bunyan it is asserted and made metaphorical. While the object in both cases is to survive, and while in both cases survival involves recognition of personal nothingness, the strategies adopted are diametrically opposed to each other. With Bunyan the Word of God is the leveller and saviour, but with Breytenbach it is the naked self:

> But it is important to know that you are nothing. And to search without stopping, be you awake or withdrawn into the wakefulness of sleep, for the hairline cracks, for the gaps and the unexpected moments of deep breathing, for the space which is created by alleys and by walls . . . prepare yourself for the interstices of freedom.[41]

Thus the prison is deterritorialized for Breytenbach, so that it ceases to have effective power. ('Power is a totalitarian concept. To realize that you are marginal is of itself a way of making distance your own.')[42] For Bunyan the prison is reterritorialized: it becomes an adjunct of the abstract mechanism, a function of the higher power. For all his metaphors and allegorical writing, Bunyan's prison is naked and brutal. As the Man in the Iron Cage put it: 'God hath denied me repentance: his word gives me no encouragement to believe; yea, himself hath shut me up in this Iron Cage; nor can all the men in the world let me out.'[43] John Bunyan is Breytenbach's gaoler.[44]

IV

The violent space of the prison is thus one which is constructed out of the ideologies of confinement. The interaction among architecture, ideas and relationships reads like a perversion of that sense of unity that we find in some poets. In the young Rilke, for example, the 'God' of *The Book of Hours* is an artistic co-operative creation:

> We are all workmen: prentice, journeyman,
> or master, building you – you towering nave.
> And sometimes there will come to us a grave
> wayfarer, who like a radiance thrills
> the souls of all the hundred artisans,
> as tremblingly he shows us a new skill.[45]

In another poem Rilke sees God as living in a cell next to his:

> Give but a small sign.
> I am quite near.
>
> Between us there is but a narrow wall,
> and by sheer chance; for it would take
> merely a call from your lips or from mine
> to break it down,
> and that all noiselessly.
>
> The wall is builded of your images.
>
> They stand before you hiding you like names . . .[46]

And in yet another, he sees that God will be impoverished by the poet's death:

> What will you do, God, when I die?
> When I, your pitcher, broken, lie?
> When I, your drink, go stale or dry?
> I am your garb, the trade you ply,
> you lose your meaning, losing me.[47]

Even if this is a simplified vision of ecological interdependence, joy, artistic wholeness (uncomplicated by the terrible Angels of the Duino Elegies, where there is the possibility that we are here for mere 'saying'),[48] it represents a vision of wholeness which is a far cry from the totalitarian inscription of the prison, where the concrete God was erected by other hands, and where it is *my* drink that goes stale or dry. In terms of game theory, prisons are conducted on the basis of a zero-sum game: *either* the prisoners win, *or* their guards win. In terms of Rilke's poetry, there is the possibility that relationships might be environmentally co-operative, that the textuality of violence might be overturned by other texts.

Two texts, one mathematical and the other dramatical, suggest a route out of this impasse. Both assume the violence of the spaces we all inhabit, but provide a rereading of the texts that led us here. The first is the mathematical game known as 'The Prisoner's Dilemma' and its various developments, including 'Tit-for-Tat'. The second is Sartre's playlet *Huis Clos* (*No Exit*), which establishes a situation of interpersonal contest among three people who find themselves together in a room which they have been led to believe is hell.

Both of these exercises take the form of abstract mechanisms: they do not relate to realistic situations. They are not descriptive and yet they both suggest alternatives to the mechanistic inscriptions of everyday life by, in a sense, speaking out of them. The problem with any mechanization is surely the inbuilt foreclosure of alternatives which zero-sum games, with their Calvinstic parameters, build into our architectonics. In structuralist terms (directly paralleling computer language), the binary codes are dichotomous. But as Edmund Leach argues when discussing the work of Claude Lévi-Strauss:

> Because he takes his cue from Jakobson-style linguistic theory and the mechanics of digital computers, Lévi-Strauss tends to imply . . . that the whole structure of primitive thought is binary. Now there is not the slightest doubt that the human brain does have a tendency to operate with binary counters in all sorts of situations – but it can operate in other ways as well. A fully satisfactory model of the human mind would certainly contain many analog features which do *not* occur in digital computers.[49]

In his collection of essays on aspects of mathematical logic, aesthetics, game theory and their social dimensions, Douglas Hofstadter discusses a series of games which evolve from a central game known, curiously enough, as 'The Prisoner's Dilemma'. In the basic game two accomplices (who have no particular concern for each other) are being held in separate cells, without any chance of communicating with each other. The proseccutor offers each of them, separately, the same deal: the state has enough circumstantial evidence to convict both of them. If both claim innocence, both will be sentenced to two years. If one admits guilt, making it easier to convict the other, he will be released, while the other will get five years. If both plead guilty, both will get four years. The tendency would be to go for broke and turn the other man in, even if this raised the near-certainty of a four-year sentence.[50]

In an extended version of the game (known as the iterated version), the dilemma is not a once-only decision, but a recurring one. Hofstadter gives the example of two people who have agreed to exchange, on a regular basis, something that the other very much wants, without knowing anything about the other, nor seeing them. At a given location they exchange bags. Do they each provide full bags or empty ones? Assuming that both exchange full bags on the first encounter, at which point will one of them break the agreement (defect)? What does the other one do? How long can the exchange go on? With what rules?

In a series of tournaments between mathematicians, political scientists, psychologists, biologists and military strategists, various programmes were devised to establish whether 'totally selfish and unconscious organisms living in a common environment [could] come to evolve reliable co-operative strategies'.[51] In doing so what clearly mattered was not so much whether one programme 'won' in the short run, but which programme, over time, could successfully demonstrate its superiority in co-operative terms against those strategies which set out to maximize victory. The superior programme proved to be the shortest. It was submitted by Anatol Rapoport from the University of Toronto and was called 'Tit-for-Tat'. Its tactic was simple:

co-operate on move 1;
thereafter, do whatever the other player did the previous move.[52]

Hofstadter, echoing Robert Axelrod of the University of Michigan, concludes that the reason this programme won was that, unlike most participants, Rapoport realized the importance of initiating co-operation. The final lesson of the tournaments was to 'Be nice, provokable and forgiving.'[53] Thus, although the tournament was played in typical computerized binary fashion, the logic of the game was that zero-sum encounters might show success in the short run, but in the long run it was a cummulative alternation between co-operation and firmness that guaranteed survival. Once the other programmes encountered Tit-for-Tat they were compelled to co-operate with it.

What this suggests for the interpretation of violent spaces is that the logic of violence is not pre-ordained. Tit-for-Tat accepts violence as part of its logic but not as its end result. Equally it accepts that, in the short run, people may act for egotistical reasons, but that in the long run a greater logic must prevail if the egos are not to self-destruct. What it misses, however, because it is locked into the mechanized language of computers, is the interaction of people for whom the zero-sum is necessarily a game of appearances, a face-saving device, one which must be abandoned if the space is to lose its aura of violence. Such a realization is contained in Sartre's play *Huis Clos*.

The 'hell' to which Sartre introduces his three characters is a sparsely furnished 'Second Empire style' drawing room. The characters, in order of appearance, are Garcin (a philanderer, deserter and failed revolutionary), Inez (a lesbian and a murderess) and Estelle (a 'good-time girl' whose lover committed suicide after she killed her child). Each attempts to cover up his or her crimes to the others by putting on a face-saving image. Together they break down these defences until, as Inez says, 'Well, Mr Garcin, now you have us in the nude all right. Do you understand things any the better for that?' To which Garcin replies, 'Alone, none of us can save himself or herself; we're linked together inextricably.'[54] As the characters talk to each other through the play, they are able to see the activities of the people they have left behind, the total effect of which is to show them how excluded they are, and consequently how the 'life' in the room is the only life that remains. Each of them in turn tries to form a relationship with one of the others, only to find that the presence of the third party makes this impossible. The violence of the space, the primal therapeutic space, tears out of each of them the last shred of internal violence. Three pairs of X-ray eyes strip them down to the ultimate search for individual and collective authenticity.

Each of the characters plays, in turn, a zero-sum game, but individually the sum is an illusion in this world where only the collectively authentic can win. In terms of The Prisoner's Dilemma, what has been added is the sense of knowing in interpersonal detail everything about the other, and that the iterated game has no conclusion. If, as Sartre makes Garcin say, 'hell is – other people', it is a hell which is a necessary route to the authentic, co-operative heaven, a therapeutic purgatory.

In both Hofstadter's games and Sartre's play, the masterminders of the tournaments are relatively benign, in that they allow the participants to come to terms with their own violent proclivities. The violent space that they inhabit is one which allows the participants to work out their relationships with each other against a mechanized text which is recognized as a human construct, rather than as a mechanized form of writing which is purely abstract.

To return to Bachelard and to Deleuze and Guattari, we have to recognize that *all* spaces are violent and all are therefore somewhat hostile. Prison, because it is the encapsulation of violence in spatial, ideological and interpersonal terms, is the epitome of violence, coming close to the ultimate violence of total annihilation. And yet the game strategies of the machine are predicated on death, either collectively or individually or, frequently, both. If we are all compelled to come to terms with death as our ultimate strategy, even more so is this the game plan of prison. The cracks that we would make through the edifice that the machine has constructed may sometimes be individual cracks, but, as both sets of games show, the effective cracks would be collective ones. Home is where we co-operatively gather ourselves.[55]

NOTES

1   Gaston Bachelard, *The Poetics of Space* (Boston: Beacon Press, 1969), p. xxxii.
2   Much of what I have to say here owes something, at least, to the work of Giles Deleuze and Felix Guattari, notably to their books *Anti-Oedipus: Capitalism and Schizophrenia* (New York: Viking, 1977) and *Kafka: Toward a Minor Literature* (Minneapolis: University of Minnesota Press, 1986).
3   Owing much to anthropological studies of territoriality, this concern with space dominated much sociological writing in the 1960s and 1970s, and with the dramaturgical metaphor was central to Erving Goffman's analysis; it also, to a large extent, provided the framework for C. Wright Mills's political sociology. See John O'Neill, *Sociology as a Skin Trade* (New York: Harper and Row, 1972), pp. 20–40 and Stanford M. Lyman and Marvin B. Scott, *A Sociology of the Absurd* (New York: Appleton-Century-Crofts, 1970), pp. 89–110 for suggestive explorations in this genre. Fundamentally, the work of Michel Foucault (by incorporating knowledge as a dynamic factor) and Deleuze and Guattari, following Lacan (tracing that graphological as an element of the sexual) put an end to all that. Space is imagined, put into place, and resisted. The meaning and use of space are everywhere subject to strategic negotiation.
4   In their study of Kafka, Deleuze and Guattari indicate how in Kafka's world 'each block-segment has an opening or door onto the line of the hallway – one that is usually quite far from the door or the opening of the following block – it is also true that all the blocks have back doors that are contiguous' (Deleuze and Guattari, *Kafka*, p. 73). And Foucault, in his discussion with Baron and Perrot, notes of the Panopticon: 'You have an apparatus of total

and circulating mistrust, because there is no absolute point. The perfected form of surveillance consists in a summation of malveillance' (Michel Foucault, *Power/Knowledge: Selected Interviews and Other Writings* (New York: Pantheon, 1980), p. 158.

5 Victor Serge, *Men in Prison* (London: Writers and Readers Publishing Cooperative, 1977), pp. 38–9.

6 Horst Bienek, *The Cell* (Santa Barbara, Cal.: Unicorn Press, 1972), pp. 24–5.

7 Ibid., p. 30.

8 Breyten Breytenbach, *The True Confessions of an Albino Terrorist* (London: Faber, 1984), p. 155.

9 Nawal El sa'adawi, *Memoirs from the Women's Prison* (London: Women's Press, 1986), pp. 72–3.

10 Ngugi wa Thiong'o, *Detained: a Writer's Prison Diary* (London: Heinemann, 1981), p. 164.

11 Bienek, *The Cell*, p. 55.

12 George Faludy, *My Happy Days in Hell* (Don Mills, Ontario: Totem Press, 1985), pp. 283–4.

13 George Faludy, *Learn This Poem of Mine by Heart* (Toronto: Hounslow Press, 1983), p. 113.

14 Michel Foucault, *Discipline and Punish* (New York: Vintage Books, 1979), pp. 200–1.

15 George Steiner, *In Bluebeard's Castle: some Notes towards the Re-definition of Culture* (London: Faber, 1971), pp. 47–8.

16 My debt to Foucault and to Deleuze and Guattari will be evident, though I have incorporated into my interpretation both the idea of a hegemony which constantly has to recreate itself (see Stuart Hall et al., *On Ideology* (London: Hutchinson, 1980) and Ernesto Laclau and Chantal Mouffe, *Hegemony and Socialist Strategy* (London: Verso, 1986), as well as Nietzsche's conception of the gay science.

17 In some aspects Attica prison in New York State provided for Foucault the closest to the realization of the ideal of the abstract machine. After a visit in 1972 he commented:

> At Attica what struck me perhaps first of all was the entrance, that kind of phony fortress à la Disneyland, those observation posts disguised as medieval towers with their machicoulis. And behind this rather ridiculous scenery which dwarfs everything else, you discover it's an immense machine. And it's this notion of machinery that struck me most strongly – those very long, clean heated corridors which prescribe, for those who pass through them specific trajectories that are evidently calculated to be the most efficient possible and at the same time the easiest to oversee, and the most direct. Yes, and all of this ends in those huge workshops, like the metallurgical one, which are clean and appear to be close to perfection. A former Attica prisoner whom I saw the day before yesterday told me that in reality those famous workshops that they display so willingly are very dangerous, that a lot of people are hurt in them. But actually, at first sight you have the impression that you are visiting more than just a factory, that you are visiting a machine, the inside of a machine.

So the question one obviously asks is what does the machine produce, what is that gigantic installation used for and what comes out of it. At the time of the creation of Auburn and of the Philadelphia prison which served as models (with rather little change until now) for the great machines of incarceration, it was believed that something indeed was produced: 'virtuous' men. Now we know, and the administration is perfectly aware, that no such thing is produced. That nothing at all is produced. That it's a question simply of a great trick of sleight of hand, a curious mechanism of circular elimination: Society eliminates by sending to prison people whom prison breaks up, crushes, physically eliminates; and then once they have been broken up, the prison eliminates them by 'freeing' them and sending them back to society; and there, their life in prison, the way in which they were treated, the state in which they come out insures that society will eliminate them once again, sending them to prison which in turn . . . Attica is a machine for elimination, a form of prodigious stomach, a kidney which consumes, destroys, breaks up and then rejects, and which consumes in order to eliminate what it has already eliminated. You remember that when we visited Attica they spoke to us about the four wings of the building, the four corridors, the four large corridors A, B, C, and D. Well, I learned, again, through the same former prisoner, that there is a fifth corridor which they didn't talk to us about, it's the corridor E. And you know which that one is?

SIMON: No.

FOUCAULT: Ah, well, it is quite simply the machine of the machine, or rather the elimination of the elimination, elimination in the second degree: it's the psychiatric wing. That's where they send the ones who cannot even be integrated into the machine and whom the machinery cannot succeed in assimilating according to its norms, that it cannot crush in accordance with its own mechanical process. Thus they need an additional mechanism. (Michel Foucault, 'On Attica: an Interview', *Telos*, 19 (Spring 1974), pp. 155–6).

18 Deleuze and Guattari, in their study of Kafka, expand on the concept of the abstract mechanisms in relation to Kafka's writing, seeing them as both forms of social order and of architecture. See Deleuze and Guattari, *Kafka*, p. 75.
19 Deleuze and Guattari, *Kafka*.
20 Bienek, *The Cell*, p. 59.
21 Ibid., p. 9.
22 Breytenbach, *True Confessions*, p. 151.
23 Daniel Berrigan, introduction to Bienek, *The Cell*, p. iv.
24 Foucault, 'On Attica', p. 159.
25 In this last quotation I have used the Knox versions as a neater translation of what the King James (Authorized Version) more clumsily puts this way: 'All they that be fat upon the earth shall eat and worship: all they that go down to the dust shall bow before him: and none shall keep alive his own soul. A seed shall serve him, it shall be accounted to the Lord for a generation.'

26   Robert Hughes, *The Fatal Shore: the Epic of Australia's Founding* (New York: Knopf, 1986), p. 467.

27   Fyodor Dostoevsky, *Notes from the Underground and The Double* (Harmondsworth: Penguin, 1972), p. 59. This schizoid interpretation of himself is, of course, related to a gnostic reading of the Bible, and is at the heart of Dostoevsky's own theological paradoxes.

28   Bienek, *The Cell*, p. 83.

29   Ibid., p. 82.

30   Charles Colson, *Life Sentence*, p. 43.

31   See chapters 3, 'The Consolations of Philosophy' and 7 'Riven Situations'.

32   The discussion of metaphor here relies in large part on the distinctions made by Paul Ricoeur in *The Rule of Metaphor* (Toronto: University of Toronto Press, 1978) and Max Black in *Models and Metaphors* (Ithaca, NY: Cornell University Press, 1962). A summary discussion of the issues is found in Sheldon Sacks, ed., *On Metaphor* (Chicago: University of Chicago Press, 1979).

33   Referred to by Ricoeur in Sacks, *On Metaphor*, p. 151.

34   The full title of *Pilgrim's Progress* reads: 'The Pilgrim's Progress for this world to that which is to come, delivered under the Similitude of a Dream, wherein is discovered the manner of his setting out, his dangerous journey and safe arrival at the Desired Country.' Then follows the legitimizing quotation: 'I have used similitudes' (Hosea 12:10).

38   Bunyan, *Pilgrim's Progress*, p. 4.

39   Breytenbach, *True Confessions*, p. 27.

40   Ibid., p. 338.

41   Ibid., p. 309.

42   Ibid.

43   Bunyan, *Pilgrim's Progress*, p. 37.

44   This hyperbole has respectable scholastic antecedents. See Michael Ignatieff, *A Just Measure of Pain: the Penitentiary in the Industrial Revolution* (London: Macmillan, 1978), pp. 44–79.

45   Rainer Maria Rilke, *Poems from the Book of Hours* (London: Vision, 1957), p. 27.

46   Ibid., p. 13.

47   Ibid., p. 29.

48   'Are we, perhaps, *here* just for saying: House, Bridge, Fountain, Gate, Jug, Fruit Tree, Window, – possibly: Pillar, Tower? . . . But for *saying*, remember, oh, for such saying as never the things themselves hoped so intensely to be?' (Rainer Maria Rilke, *Duino Elegies* (London: Hogarth, 1952), p. 85.

49   Edmund Leach, *Lévi-Strauss* (London: Fontana, 1970), p. 88.

50   See Douglas Hofstadter, *Metamagical Themas: Questing for the Essence of Mind and Pattern* (New York: Basic Books, 1985), pp. 715–34.

51   Ibid., p. 720.

52   Ibid., p. 721.

53   Ibid., p. 725.

54   Jean-Paul Sartre, *No Exit and three other Plays* (New York: Vintage, 1955), p. 29.

55   The British television series, *The Prisoner*, comes closest to portraying in film what I am trying to say here, though by centring on the individual who tries to resist the violence of the machine, it consumes itself in the image of

its own disappearing tail. The collective sense is present in several of the episodes (notably 'A. B. and C.', 'Free for All', 'Checkmate' and, ultimately, 'Fallout', but ultimately the series is concerned with zero-sum games and their tragic hyperreality. Even when the series attempts interpersonal encounters, they are not based on threesomes but are always one-to-one (see, in particular, 'Once upon a Time'). For all this, however, *The Prisoner* is one of the few television programmes to attempt to portray the seriality of violent space in such a way that the interpenetration of mechanized texts calls into play the possibility of an emancipatory resolution. For a guide to the series, see Matthew White and Jaffer Ali, *The Official Prisoner Companion* (New York: Warner Books, 1988). The intrinsic significance of the series lies, of course, in the fact that the subject is not in a prison for criminals, but a prison for spies, and thus, in Foucault's terms, a prison within which those who have become the penetrating eyes against the public are themselves exposed and laid bare.

Part II
NARRATIVES

5

Text / Anti-Text

I

Not even among those who are literate is all the telling done by writing; and for most, who are illiterate, the telling is done themselves, in story and song. Jack Goody's work has been centrally concerned with establishing that the language of written texts is quite different from that of spoken utterances,[1] and much of the current work on oral language has emphasized the cultural and political implications of such a distinction (even if, as with Jacques Derrida's massive interventions into the debate, to argue that the spoken is an enunciation of a text, that there is no oral exterior to textuality).[2] The most significant conclusion that Goody makes, for our purposes, is that literacy of itself carries power, not just because those who can read and write have a cognitive advantage, but also because they have the power to re-create (and imprison) oral narratives. The problem can be expressed in this way. Prior to literacy, stories might be told (and changed) as the situation demanded. The incorporation of these stories into a dominant narrative was the task of the writer (the Bible is perhaps one of the best examples of this process at work, though the debate in India on the Rig Veda and in classical Greek scholarship over the Homeric legends leaves the door slightly ajar to an alternative interpretation).[3] With the advent of supernarrative (or the Great Code, in Frye's terms), the relationship of oral transmission to storytelling changed. A small group of literati possessed the true story, while the illiterate public were taught to memorize and recite it, or parts of it, orally. The everyday stories of the people were necessarily embroideries around the Great Code, politics legitimized itself in its name, and the literate could choose to decide which literature could be transmitted and which kept secret. The advent of the printing press, by making more literature available, increased the number of the literate and, as European and Chinese history showed, made the power of the keepers of the literary tradition less absolute. The writing of Rabelais appears at just such an interjunction, when the carnivalesque laughter of the people established itself in parody of the Great Code and its servants. Although dependent on the Code for its point of reference, at the same time it provides the grounds for undermining it.[4] Equally importantly, the language of this counter-culture does not depend wholly on that of the Great Code, but also on alternative expressions of experience which developed in counterpoint to it, based on jokes, dramatic performances, storytelling and other forms of oral narrative. The structural relationship between the framework of the Code and the counterthrust of the carnival is an uneven one. As Bakhtin notes on the use of quotation:

> Is the Author quoting with reverence or on the contrary with irony, with a smirk? Double entendre as regards the other's word was often deliberate . . . The role of the other's word was enormous at that time: there were quotations that were openly and reverently emphasized as such, or that were half-hidden, completely hidden, half-conscious, unconscious, correct, intentionally distorted, deliberately reinterpreted, and so forth. The boundary lines between someone else's speech and one's own speech were flexible, ambiguous.[5]

All of this is contingent on literacy and an assimilation of texts into everyday language, and assumes a set of received texts that can be played with in the street, in the home, in the work-place, in prison. But the majority of prisoners in North America and Europe are barely literate. Does this mean that they are textually illiterate? All of us are influenced by textuality, as Foucault was at pains to display. The split between the deliberate parodying of text, which Bakhtin analyses, and the apparently inchoate expressions of experience do, in a post-Gutenberg and post Marconi/Baird world, requires a rethinking of Bakhtin, in so far as he deals with parody, satire and the oral.

The prisoner is surrounded by attempts at embodying text in 'helpful' practices. As Gertrude Katz writes in her study of prison literacy in a Montreal penitentiary,

> Correction in penal institutions, to a great extent, is on a do-it-yourself plan framed within punishment and questionable rewards of relaxed restrictions. Most of that period in prison is spent just gathering time for release.

Prisons are peppered with a curious lot of rehabilitation 'experts'. For example, there are the noted professionals like sociologists, psychologists, criminologists – they look down from their gilded cages of learning, and with textbook patterns before them, juggle types into already tabled slots. Clergy of all denominations – each with his personally spirited formula for salvation and cure faithfully make the rounds (reminiscent of mission impossible). 'AA' sponsors weekly club meetings where sober testimonials are encouraged from memory – very much like a starving society forming a gourmet's club – if there's nothing to eat at least it's a place to talk about indigestion. And there's our own organization, Creative Awards, with instructors in the arts who must sometimes appear like refugees from *Alice in Wonderland*'s Mad Hatter tea party.[6]

Thus, in terms of received texts, prisoners not only have to contend with the institutionalized texts that placed them here and framed their place of sojourn (mainly legal, architectural and economic); they also have to contend with the texts that purport to help them out of their misery. Their choice of which of these intermediary texts makes sense may have more to do with interpersonal relations in and out of the prison than with the internal coherence of the text itself. As Eldridge Cleaver wrote:

The reason I became a Catholic was that the rule of the institution held that every Sunday each inmate had to attend the church of his choice. I chose the Catholic Church because all the Negroes and Mexicans went there. The whites went to the Protestant chapel. Had I been a fool enough to go to the Protestant chapel, one black face in a sea of white, and with guerrilla warfare going on between us, I might have ended up a Christian martyr – St Eldridge the Stupe.

It all ended one day when, at a catechism class, the priest asked if anyone present understood the mystery of the Holy Trinity. I had been studying my lessons diligently and knew by heart what I'd been taught. Up shot my hand, my heart throbbing with piety (pride) for this chance to demonstrate my knowledge of the Word. To my great shock and embarrassment, the Father announced, and it sounded like a thunderclap, that I was lying, that no one, not even the Pope, understood the Godhead, and why else did I think they called it the mystery of the Holy Trinity? I saw in a flash, stung to the quick by the jeers of my fellow catechumens, that I had been used, that the Father had been lying in wait for the chance to drop that thunderbolt, in order to drive home the point that the Holy Trinity was not to be taken lightly.

I had intended to explain the Trinity with an analogy to 3-in-One oil, so it was probably just as well.[7]

And clearly, if positioned in a situation in which other intrusive aspects of life are denied, any of us may take the 'text' of this enclosed situation as all-important; as the definition of our 'problem'. We are at fault because we were drunk, on drugs, were not Christian enough, had problems with our parentage, with our neighbourhood, even our own chemical balance – almost any of which may be intrinsically correct, but which contain a mere segment of the overall conditions: we were also poor, black, Indians, Chicanos, Irish, gypsies, the products of broken or no families, were immigrants, illiterate, and so on. The tendency of the interventionist 'text' is always to read the individual as part of a subset of problems which, if cured, could 'reintegrate' the prisoner into the wider society. The success rate of this imposition of text is not good. As George Jackson wrote:

> Penologists regard prisons as asylums. Most policy is formulated in a bureau that operates under the heading Department of Corrections. But what can we say about these asylums since none of the inmates are ever cured? Since in every instance they are sent out of the prison more damaged physically and mentally than when they entered. Because that is the reality. Do you continue to investigate the inmate? Where does administrative responsibility begin? Perhaps the administration of the prison cannot be held accountable for every individual act of their charges, but when things fly apart along racial lines, when the breakdown can be traced so clearly to circumstances even beyond the control of the guards and administration, investigation of anything outside the tenets of the fascist system itself is futile.[8]

II

And yet these are not the only texts. In addition to the framed texts of religious belief, academic discipline, social do-gooding, there are also the twentieth-century electronic media:

One of the first things I discovered when I entered the B.C. penal system was that most of the prisons are swamped with radio. Each cell and/or corridor is fitted with well-grated speakers, very occasionally flanked by a volume control but never a kill button. We were, in other words, obliged to listen to rock music from 7.00 a.m. to 10.30 p.m., and no place to hide. In Oakalla the situation was even worse in that the bottom tier of cells, generally inhabited by older inmates consigned to do their entire time in maximum security, had the odd television set and private radio as well, so that at any given time we stood a good chance of being attacked by three radio stations, two television soundtracks and the public address system to boot.[9]

The electronic media do not, of course, consist only of competitive, insistent, meaningless noise. They have their own texts which frame the activities of the inmates. The texts, in general, are somewhat dramatized versions of those which brought the inmate to the prison cell in the first place. As we noted in chapter 1, the tendency of most television entertainment, in so far as it deals with prisoners, is to stress the pursuit of the criminal, to emphasize the strategies employed by law enforcement agencies to catch their man (or, occasionally, their woman). A detailed investigation of this form of textual framing is quite beyond the scope of this book, but one or two observations might be called for in so far as the texts provide the basis for a counter-reading by inmates. In most European and North American societies, the media provide three quite distinct images of the prisoner. The first (with very many nuances on the nature of the pursuit)[10] is of course about the search for the 'criminal'. In this the struggle to preserve law and order is paramount: the 'criminal' is either killed in the course of the hunt or ultimately sent to his just deserts (very rarely specified). The 'criminal' is largely stereotypical as befits the nature of the story built around thh 'hunt', and his/her cowardly/treacherous/mean attributes are generally similar to those associated with animal hunts or cowboys and Indians sagas, to which they bear an unsurprising resemblance. The 'heroes', also unsurprisingly, are not the 'criminals' but the pursuers. (In some stories – notably by Conan Doyle, Dashiel Hammett and Chester Himes – the criminals and pursuers are on an almost equal footing, in that law and order is itself problematic. In general, however, it is not law and order that is problematic, but rather the relationships between the different law-enforcing agencies and individuals: the state police versus private police.[11]

The second is the approach which, for want of a better term, centres on the 'good' criminal, the bandit or the leader of a movement which has been sanctioned by the media as being morally OK. In general those prisoners are not American or Canadian or British or French (depending on which country produced the film). They are other people's prisoners: prisoners of war, people suppressed by other political regimes, prisoners (even if they were criminal in their acts) who could be designated prisoners of conscience. Thus Spartacus and Robin Hood and Nelson Mandela and Leadbelly are all right as themes (though it gets more difficult as we get nearer to the present, as Lenny Bruce observed).[12] Basically, 'Hollywood' – and its equivalents in other countries – appropriates selected heroes to its ongoing concerns. The Dream Factory invents the heroes and situations of other wars, other battles, in order to validate the central significance of the present moment, the violations of whose harmony can be confirmed by appealing to other situations where things apparently are or were worse, but whose heroes confirm the rightness of our present engagement with ourselves. They become our heroes, fighting our wars in a strange country. (In Hollywood most of the directors and producers who portrayed the 'American Dream' were German and Russian Jews who invented America as the world which offered the freedom they felt they had missed in the real terror of their home countries. Their dream-world was an imposition on living Americans, formed with a bile directed against those from whom they had apparently escaped. It also simplified world history to a point where it could only become a legitimizing aspect of contemporary ideology. Tradition, in Hobsbawm and Ranger's sense, has to be invented in order to be useful.[13]

The third kind of media treatment of criminals – and by far the least important by volume – is the film or television series that attempts to deal with situations inside prisons in America, Canada, Britain, France, etc. From *20,000 years in Sing Sing* and *I was a Fugitive from a Chain Gang* to *Cool-hand Luke, Papillon, Loneliness of the Long-distance Runner* or *Kiss of the Spiderwoman*, there *are* films which have imaginatively tried to come to terms with the experience of incarceration (even when, as with *Papillon* and *Kiss of the Spiderwoman*, they are set in other people's prisons, they are recognizable as ours). The debate between self and collective solidarity in prison films, however, gets nowhere on television where, apart from emasculated reruns of films and some documentaries, very few attempts have been made to treat prison life as a suitable theme for comedy or drama. The British produced two series: *Porridge* (a situation comedy based on a medium-security prison) and *The Prisoner* (Patrick McGoohan's drama of a prison for spies). The Australians tried *Caged Women*, a rather banal attempt at enclosing women in prison in order to show the inanity of feminist politics, which was imitated (badly) by a series of the same name in the United States. Otherwise, televisual representations of prison are reduced to moments in the county gaol in *Hill Street Blues* or half-hour stints of vagrants on *Barney Miller*. Probably the only film that attempts to portray a contemporary penitentiary is *Weeds*, though McGoohan's *The Prisoner*, in spite of its exotic setting in Portmeirion, West Wales, probably comes closest to capturing the claustrophobia of prison, mainly by emphasizing the circularity of social space, visual entrapment and the symbolic relationship between them, selecting not only out of the texts that are evidently there – because they constantly bombard the prisoner with messages – but also choosing texts which are not provided. For most of us this is a problem (even with our computers, libraries, newspapers, magazines). Even if the prisoner, comes in with prior experience of literary possibilities, an attempt to eliminate the redundant texts and noises might be made as Andreas Schroeder tried to do:

> I finally concocted an absurd Tower of Babel by jamming a towel-filled hard hat (from the mill) against the speaker, holding that up with a broom which was supported by a chair which stood on a card table I'd placed on the floor directly beneath the speaker. The whole arrangement tottered uneasily but it held, and the sound was reduced to almost silence. Blessed relief. Everyone cheered *sotto-voce* and tiptoed back to their bunks since any sudden vibration would have been fatal to the stability of our volume control tower.[14]

Or the prisoner, as Victor Serge argued, might try to acquire the texts that are known to exist but which are absent from this place.

> The administration tolerates the study of foreign language on the condition that it remains purely mental: owning a pencil is forbidden. In my fifth year of imprisonment, I applied for permission to acquire Pascal's *Pensées* and Marcus Aurelius' *Meditations*. Refused . . .
>
> Pascal and Marcus Aurelius nonetheless entered our jail: Jean Fleuriot from Rue Aubry-le-Boucher (known as 'One Eye', having left the other on the point of a knife in a Constantine

gin mill-burglary, six years) was released, and made a trip to Paris, risking the loss of his parole, just to get them for us. And the lamplighter, accompanied by an affable guard who had been paid fifty francs, picked up a package wrapped in rags behind the prison wall – the 'came' – containing (a treasure for which any man would have done thirty days in the hole without hesitation) three packets of tobacco, two copies of *Le Matin*, three chocolate bars, a postcard representing a nude from the Salon Automne (at the express demand of Guillaumet), Pascal, and Marcus Aurelius.[15]

If he has no prior experience of alternative texts, the prisoner may have to learn by group activity, by political action, by appraising his own situation in the face of repeated frustrations:

Up until now, the prospect of parole has kept us from confronting our captors with any real determination. But now with the living conditions deteriorating, and with the sure knowledge that we are slated for destruction, we have been transformed into an implacable arm of liberation. The shift to the revolutionary anti-establishment position that Huey Newton, Eldridge Cleaver, and Bobby Seale projected as a solution to the problems of Amerika's black colonies has taken firm hold of these brothers' minds. They are now showing great interest in the thoughts of Mao Tse-tung, Nkrumah, Lenin, Marx, and the achievements of men like Che Guevara, Giap, and Uncle Ho.[16]

Much of prison literature is created by people who tried to read against the imposed texts, in some fortunate cases assisted by creative writing workshops, but in most by their own efforts, cutting against the grain of the plethora of texts that would define them out of existence. The real issue of writing in prison, for those who never wrote before, concerns that point at which the writing began, and what the act of writing meant. The transition from the oral experiment to the literary is a savage one. Two stories – both about gypsies – illustrate the problem. The first is from Hungary, where I visited a Borstal outside Budapest largely populated by gypsies and Transylvanian Hungarians. I asked around if I could see some writing by the inmates. An officer in charge of the creative writing workshop showed me a number of things that I had never seen in England, Canada or the United States, the most significant of which was the library, which included Hungarian translations of Hugo (*Les Misérables*), Genet

(*The Thief's Journal*), Villon (*Collected Poems*), Baudelaire (*Fleurs de Mal*), Dostoevsky (*Notes from the Underground*) and Rabelais (*Pantagruel and Gargantua*). And then she showed me her *pièce de résistance*: a collection of poems composed by a gypsy boy from the Hungarian/Romanian border. It consisted of a series of adaptations of Villon's *Epitaph*.[17] The first page displayed an exact copy of Villon's poem in Magyar, transcribed from the library copy, and signed François Villon. On subsequent pages he changed one line on each page until at the end of the book he had composed a new poem, by rethinking each line as it related to him. The poem (in my free English translation) went as follows:

> Comrades you live because we're dying,
> So don't impose your lives on us.
> Karl Marx might pity you for lying,
> But would he sanctify your lust?
>
> The five of us who dangle here, thrust
> Into view to feed your greed
> for vengeance, are torn apart
> by moral stabs that burn and bleed.
> Would you forgive a gypsy heart?
> Oh, please remember what Marx said!
>
> Comrades we swing to justify
> Your sense of violent rectitude
> And yet you know we typify
> The stubbornness of gypsy blood
> Have we not something that is good?
> Our only hope is that your heads
> As we are twisting on this hill,
> Have moral pangs of Marxist will.
> Our dying may not make you brood
> But please remember what Marx said!
>
> The little huts we lived in, dried
> Our souls and left them bare.
> The winds laughed through the void
> And burned our cheeks and tore our hair.
> Our bodies travelled everywhere
> New Budapest, Arpad, Szeged
> But when our travelling was dead
> You strung us up on this bleak space,

> True comrades of the human race.
> O please remember what Marx said.
>
> All holy Lenin, Kadar, Grosz,[18]
> You only know what troubles us,
> But nothing that we say can plead
> That death was not becoming us.
> O please remember what Marx said!

The Hungarian gypsy, because he had all the necessary books at hand, became, slowly, a translator. He had appropriated the best of the poet with whom he felt a close affinity and made Villon's words his own. He became (for himself) the Villon of Hungary, even if his poem was for a time buried in a psychiatric file.

My other gypsy story is based on a different dynamic. It is drawn from a magazine, *Prison Journal*, published in Vancouver. The gypsy there is also semi-literate, but though he has no Villon or Hugo to draw on, the catalyst of his own oral and interpersonal experience is faced with the need to be literally assertive. Here is an example of such writing:

> This stors is written by me
> PETER DEMITRO
> (the master)
> of modern mystery
> (by hook or by crook)
> or by me

> it all started in 1987 form vancouver b.c. too montreal.
> the gypsy had there hand's in toever thing form telling
>   card reading to steeling money form old man and all
>   of the above, but that wasn't good enough for them,
> they wanted it all , like running all the afterhour's in the
>   city's, so
> that they could sail all the hot good's to mark's and
>   sucker's , , , , , ,
> and that is waer I come in to this story baby?,
> Iwas to sat every thing up for the family's in these city's ,
> and Idid with no problems from the pig's in these city's
>   because the family's waer giving me the money to pay
>   them off and go about my bussiness,
> and they had on problems with taking the money,b ecause

they waer just has happy to see me has Iwas to see
   them.
but it didn't matter to me any way because Ihad a degree
   in murder to go.
murden against the grain. murder makes the wheels go
   round.

the only trouble Imight have was from the bishop family,
but I could control these greedy and deadly family,
nick bishop was the first one for me to get out of the
   picture and then work up form there,
it wasn't going to be easy to get this guy,so I calld my
   friend,.paul gooday.

he would do the job with no questions asked about it,and
   thats what I liked
about him ,
wellafter I'd talk to him he told me that it would take
   three days' to do the job and that would be the end of
   it.
but paul didn't make out has will has he might have if he
   didn't get a killed
by nich bishop
any way people, Idesided too do the fucking thing my self
   ,and do it rigth,
once and for all.

nick didn't know me so it would be easy to get him,
by the way i'm bug's bunny
and when Iseen nick in the plag ets after hours nigthculb
   I waited out side
for him

and when he came out Ilet him have it three times in the
   head,
and then lift the seen ....

like a good little bunny.
                              the end
                              Peter Farrell[19]

But from what did this come? Clearly not from imitating Villon,
appropriating him and transcending him. Peter Farrell (allowed to
talk, as the Hungarian gypsy was not) makes an important sense of

experience in relation to writing. His writing is based on a substitution for the activities that are part and parcel of his everyday life. Three passages from an interview suggest the interconnections of oral and written authorship. The first extract goes like this (PM is the interviewer):

PM: You were obviously taught certain things about stealing. But you weren't taught how to write or read?

PF: No. They don't like to have anything to do with the white race too much. Because they feel that it's a bad environment. In other words, it messes up their culture trip.

PM: So, literacy is not good for stealing? I mean, you could become a highly successful thief without it?

PF: Well, you gotta understand the stealing part in the gypsy way of life is basically pickpocketing, manipulating, fraud, body work, roofing, ceilering. Body work is what we are doing with the work on cars with cheap bundle. Sometimes we don't even use the bundles. It all depends on what race you are. There is about like twenty different races out there. Initially, the one that does the worst work would be the Mexic guy and those are from Mexico. And they use plaster in bundle and make the first bump in the head and the plaster comes up.

PM: To be a gypsy – as you have described it so far – means that, in addition to the thieving, you also do a lot of straight jobs like roofing and body work.

PF: That's how you get the connections. Like for instance, when I was in Montreal and they have these big parties for the gypsies, you see like four or five police. They are detectives that would be in charge of like the vice squad and they pass up the summons as in fortune telling. And you see them there sitting with the elders and taking like a big bottle of Crown Royal and 200–300 under the table. So me, myself, I don't like that shit. I think a crooked cop is worse than a harnessed cop.

PM: Gypsies have to be on the move all the time and don't send their children to school. Are you told stories by your parents or elders? Is there a literature – not written down – a body of stories that all of you could be told?

PF: Stories consist mostly of the old country and of things that matter in this world. Like spirits running up against some kind of person who you feel is not totally all there. You know, stuff like that. Stories of great gypsies that had wealth — unbelievable wealth — and yet, you know, when they died they hid it so no one else would get it. Stuff like that. Myself, the only stories I was ever told were from my grandfather because the way it goes it's families from one race stay together. They don't like to puck into the family for the simple reason — it's like the Italian thing now. Everybody is dropping diamonds to get rid of their problems quicker. You see, what I'm saying it's a lot quicker to drop diamonds than to kill them.

PM: Drop a diamond?

PF: Yes, in other words, call the cops and straighten it up that way.

In the second extract, Peter Farrell talks about writing:

PF: The way I see my writing — all it does for me in my background is it points out the corners of players, a sucker, an eligible mark and a potential friend until it gets out of the pocket. In other words, what I mean about getting out of pocket is backstabbing, telling somebody else your business.

PM: You see your writing as basically trying to explain things to yourself that happened before or is it just a way to get your mind off things?

PF: It's just a way to keep my mind off the penny shit that goes on in here. But when I do write, some of it is true but I don't say which is true because if I was to do that, I'd get stinged from my family if I was to write about everything that happened in my life.

PM: You didn't learn how to read or write until quite recently?

PF: Yes.

JANET URQUHART (*his teacher*):   He's just finishing up Adult Basic Education Level One. When Peter came to class, he had very strong verbal skills and a really strong memory and so he got in there and made something happen to the language — he knew how to use it. And there was a sense of frustration because he knew a lot of words and was trying to guess which one was on the page. You started using the language in a really fresh way. All of sudden you had this tool that you suddenly got to use.

PF: Well, it could be that but I just think it's this. You see I'd got into so many different situations, Janet, out on the streets and suddenly trying to put them on paper, I'd never do that. I just ... stored them back in my mind. And now that I am dealing with this – and you keep asking me for stories – it just leaves me to think, 'Well shit, I don't wanna write about this because this here is negative as far as I am concerned.' So I'd rather write something positive, yet negative, and it all works out in the end for somebody in here. If you try and work something out it never does work out for the right.

In the final section of the interview Peter Farrell discusses storytelling at home:

PF: Story telling in my family consists of this: of some middle-aged man who knows everything and there is no way to pull the wool over his eyes. And he may tell you stories of how he sent his two sons to break the farmer's buckets one day and the following day sent the sons back to that same area to fix the farmer's buckets. Stuff like that. But they are very religious people because they believe in the spirits a lot and that's the only kind of stories I've ever heard. Like when my grandfather was in Romania. One time, you know, he was sitting near the campfire and at the time my grandmother was in the tent. And I don't know, there came this guy, his exact duplicate and said, 'I'm here to take you.' And you could see the horse behind him galloping and, you know, I found it kind of hard for me to believe the scene, you know, being raised in New York or going to all these fancy cities and getting all this game on me. And I say to myself, 'OK, this old man is lying to me'. But then I pull him out of the pocket. I'd say, 'Hey you, are you being honest with me?' And he'd just say, 'I'd never lie to you'.

JU: But women tell stories, they tell fortunes?

PF: You know what kind of stories those are? Of making money, of how they got a sucker in this town and that town.

JU: Are these stories also passed on?

PF: Yes. Only to be learned by. I'd say, you learn by your past, you know. I mean, the best story I've ever heard came from Uncle Joe. And that was when he swindled all these gypsies in the United States. He went to Venezuela and, before he came back, he went and had blueprints figured out. And he got bank certificates from Shell and Gulf and that was a goldmine. And him and this other guy by the name of Archie Wilson, which was another gypsy, they decided, 'OK. We got a scam here. We'll go and dress with suits, with the big containers, with the blueprints, little certification tickets.' And they came to stuff both Shell and Gulf. And these gypsies are gonna think, 'Hey man, let's lick it because look at these stamps, look at these blueprints, the containers. This gotta be 100% white business.' And they got sucked in.[20]

So translating others' printed texts or transmitting oral history, via selective reading of media texts, becomes the focus for the emergent author. Both are, in different ways, parodists, but the Hungarian gypsy accepts the framework of the original text as his own while Peter Farrell tells his own story but by injecting aspects of media images into it ('by the way I'm bugs bunny'). The Hungarian parody is, of course, ultimately very precisely political, while the Vancouver one is political in the sense that the media convey a second-order literacy and Farrell pierces through this in order to create a poetry based on direct experience. The parody in Farrell is produced by allusions to other texts and by a constant surprise that he has recreated them in terms of his own story. With the Hungarian gypsy we are pleased with how he has reinterpreted a particular form (a pleasure that we also get from Robert Lowell's version of Villon, which was also written as a result of a prison experience). The Hungarian *updates* Villon while Peter Farrell *replaces* Bugs Bunny. But both gypsies see their predicament as part of a collective experience, whereas Villon and Lowell try to assert individuality against collective appropriation of them. And yet, again, the act of writing is itself an act of individualism, and in prison particularly so; but this individualization might be seen as an attempt either to re-establish the self or to place self as the spokesperson for others. In the most impressive literature both of these aspects are combined, but *how* they are combined in relation to the oral narratives is examined further below.

III

This returns us to the nature of the oral and the means by which we can make sense of oral narratives in their own terms; and how such narratives become the basis for written texts. In examining Peter Farrell's poetry above it is clear that he was drawing not only on a 'second-order literacy' derived from the media but also on the oral narratives of his relatives. Oral tradition for him and for many prisoners is one which has been formed by legends, beliefs, rituals which are part of an ongoing folk culture and thus of what Derrida calls *writing*, even if in many cases this culture is shot through with aspects of first- and second-order literacy. There are many ways in which we might examine this process, but here – partly because it provides the most impressive counterthrust to the dominant texts of Western society, but partly also because its documentation can be checked back against my own account – I want to address the evolution of American black expression in juxtaposition with an imprisoned oral tradition.

The oral tradition was imprisoned, first by slavery, next by the convict-lease system, and more recently by the penitentiary. Its parameters were laid down by an economic/political system which saw the blacks not only as property and free (or at best cheap) labour, but also as fundamentally not people, rather as beasts of burden salvaged from the Heart of Darkness. The development of black expression was contingent on second-order literacy, on being able to create an oral tradition out of the remnants of African ritual, music and legend and out of those elements of Western belief systems which seemed to make some sense in understanding the situation of slavery and imprisonment. The transmittable elements of this tradition took the form of music which emerged initially because, like (to some extent) religion, and unlike architecture, sculpture or even political systems, it could survive without artefacts. Even with an imperial language, the nature of the music could become part of a tradition that could be passed on.[21] The obvious major factor in appropriating Western culture was the adoption of elements of Christianity, which brought with it an aspect of literacy. This was a Christianity which owed more to the Old Testament than to the New, mainly because the collective experiences of Jews in captivity suggested a close parallel with those of the blacks; but it was also influenced by the idea of the Holy Spirit:

'Getting the spirit,' 'getting religion' or 'getting happy' were indispensable features of the early American Negro Church and, even today, of the non-middle-class and rural Negro churches. And always music was an important part of the total emotional configuration of the Negro church, acting in most cases as the catalyst for those worshippers who would suddenly 'feel the spirit.' The spirit will not descend without song.[22]

Between them, the Judaic and the spiritual or emotional elements of black Christianity re-created the idea of Christian music, but based on 'rhythmic syncopation, polyphony, and shifting accounts, as well as the altered timbral qualities and diverse vibrato efforts of African music'.[23] The major element of black religious music was thus a composite of parodies – parody of the African rhythms, and parody of the biblical stories. This shifting parody sometimes had a long history. In *Blues People*, Leroy Jones (Imamu Amiri Baraka) discusses the case of the well-known spiritual, 'Swing Low, Sweet Chariot':

Early observers also pointed out that a great many of the first Negro Christian religious songs had been taken almost untouched from the great body of African religious music. This was especially true of the melodies of certain black Christian spirituals that could also be heard in some parts of Africa.

Maude Cuney-Hare, in her early book *Negro Musicians and Their Music*, cites the experience of a Bishop Fisher of Calcutta who traveled to Central Africa: '. . . in Rhodesia he had heard natives sing a melody so closely resembling Swing Low, Sweet Chariot that he felt that he had found it in its original form: moreover, the region near the great Victoria Falls have a custom from which the song arose. When one of their chiefs, in the old days, was about to die, he was placed in a great canoe together with trappings that marked his rank, and food for his journey. The canoe was set afloat in midstream headed towards the great Falls and the vast column of mist that rises from them. Meanwhile the tribe on the shore would sing its chant of farewell. The legend is that on one occasion the king was seen to rise in his canoe at the very brink of the Falls and enter a chariot that, descending from the mists, bore him aloft. This incident gave rise to the words "Swing Low, Sweet Chariot," and the song, brought to America by African slaves long ago, became anglicized and modified by their Christian faith.'

It would be quite simple for an African melody that was

known traditionally to most of the slaves to be used as a Christian song.[24]

But the growth of black American music felt other influences too, although the religious were frequently the most dominant. Early (i.e. late eighteenth- and early nineteenth-century) secular music developed the 'holler', a work-song based primarily on West African rhythmical chants, though progressively adapted to slavery conditions in America. Attached to folk tales, riddles and proverbs, 'hollers' were an essential part of black education in the work-place, much of them depending on antiphonal singing techniques in which a leader sang the main theme and a chorus of workers answered him. Although the content of these songs changed to reflect the altered conditions of work, the form persisted, and was used in relation to work and domestic conditions (which of course interrelated with each other). With the abolition of slavery and the convict-lease system the work-song became a significant part of black culture, telling the stories of captivity, imprisonment and forced labour. The evolution of the 'John Henry' work-songs provides an important example. The bare story is that John Henry, appalled at the possibility of the steam-drill replacing human labour, worked his hammer harder than anyone else in driving steel in the building of the Big Bend road tunnel in West Virginia in 1870. It is said that as he hammered away to his death, John Henry was singing an old Alabama work-song:

> Take my hammer,
> Carry it to the captain,
> Tell him I'm gone,
> Tell him I'm gone,
> If he ask you was I running,
> Tell him no,
> Tell him no.
> Tell him I was going across the Blue Ridge Mountains
> Walking slow, yes, walking slow.[25]

This song and many others like it was used in building railways or roads, digging in mines or working on plantations. Their transformation into legend and ballad is part of the transformation of working conditions. As Bruce Franklin wrote:

> The ballad versions of 'John Henry' are of course more elaborate than the versions used as hammer songs. Printed, oral, and

recorded poems telling of John Henry include almost countless stanzas. Taken together, they comprise an epic of the Black worker who died transcending the machine that took away his livelihood. A version that includes the most common stanzas was sent to Guy Johnson by a prisoner in Ohio State Penitentiary who found that 'it was necessary to interview a number of Old-Timers of this Penitentiary to get some of the missing words and to verify my recollections.' Some of these stanzas are:

> When John Henry was a little boy,
> Sitting upon his father's knee,
> His father said, 'Look here, my boy,
> You must be a steel driving man like me,
> You must be a steel driving man like me.'
>
> John Henry started on the right-hand side,
> And the steam drill started on the left.
> He said, 'Before I'd let that steam drill beat me down,
> I'd hammer my fool self to death,
> Oh, I'd hammer my fool self to death.'
>
> The steam drill started at half past six,
> John Henry started the same time.
> John Henry struck bottom at half past eight,
> And the steam drill didn't bottom till nine,
> Oh, the steam drill didn't bottom till nine.
>
> John Henry said to his shaker,
> 'Shaker, why don't you sing just a few more rounds?
> And before the setting sun goes down,
> You're gonna hear this hammer of mine sound,
> You're gonna hear this hammer of mine sound.'
>
> John Henry hammered on the mountain,
> He hammered till half past three,
> He said, 'This Big Bend Tunnel on the C. & O. road
> Is going to be the death of me,
> Lord! is going to be the death of me.'
>
> John Henry hammering on the mountain
> As the whistle blew for half past two,
> The last word I heard him say,
> 'Captain, I've hammered my insides in two,
> Lord, I've hammered my insides in two.'[26]

This evolution of the work-song was also accompanied by the development of blues and jazz, and if we are to discuss the total black tradition forming prison literature in the USA it is important to bear this in mind, though I think it is clear that the growth of jazz – and its subsequent appropriation by white America and the world – is an indication of a process that runs parallel to incarceration. By this I mean that if prison songs and prison literature are essentially about the dark side of humanity, the subterranean text that runs underneath the dominant one, jazz was the triumph of a popular form of expression, even though – and perhaps because – it drew on the subterranean. This point is well made in Francis Newton (E. J. Hobsbawm)'s *Jazz Scene*:

> The English language provided the words of Negro speech and song, and in it coloured Americans have created, with the jazz idiom, the finest body of English folk-poetry since the Scots ballads: the work-song, gospel song, and secular blues. The secular music of the colonists – perhaps mostly the Scots–Irish poor whites of the South – provided a mass of songs many of which, taken up and modified by the Negro travelling minstrels, entered the jazz repertoire. 'Careless Love', the Kentucky mountain ballad, or 'St James' Infirmary', whose derivation from an early English original A. L. Lloyd has traced, are examples. After 1800 religion – more especially the 'great awakening' which swept the Southern and frontier poor, coloured and white, into a frenzied, egalitarian, democratic Protestant sectarianism – provided the musical framework. The harmonies of the blues, as distinct from semi-African melodies and rhythms, are those of Moody and Sankey's type of hymn. But perhaps more important than the juicy harmonium chords, which were thus later to be so strangely adapted to jazz, was the fact that the 'great awakening' achieved the first systematic blending of European and African music in the USA outside New Orleans. Moreover, since this was not the imposition of organization and orthodoxy from above, but a largely spontaneous mass conversion from below, the two were equally blended, the African component not being subordinated to the European. More: it did not even subordinate European folk-music to European art-music. Culturally the 'great awakening' was the counterpart to the American War of Independence; or perhaps more precisely, to the rise of Jacksonian frontier democracy. It ensured that religious music, white and coloured, should remain

a people's music. From our point of view the important thing about this was that even Negro music thus won its right to independent development.

For the crucial factor in the development of jazz, as of all American popular music, the factor which more than any other accounts for the unique American phenomenon of a vigorous and resistant folk-music in a rapidly expanding capitalist society, is that it was never swamped by the cultural standards of the upper classes. English musical working-class culture in the nineteenth century consisted of a patently dying rural and pre-industrial folk-music, a musically extremely shoddy music-hall song, and the twin pillars of organized working-class music, the classic oratorio and the brass band. But however admirable the Messiah or the test pieces at the brass-band festivals, they are working-class conquests of orthodox culture, not independent folk-music. American popular and folk-music in the nineteenth century retained the initiative, and its persistent supremacy over Britain, even in the field of commercial pop music, derives largely from this.[27]

The importance of the blues, in particular, as integral to the development of black prison culture is, however, strategic as an extension and development of the prison experience.[28] The blues singers, whether they had been in prison or not (and many had been) sang to all features of incarceration. Many of their songs emerged from these experiences and, as blues translated from the South to the major cities of the North, it became crueller, more bitter as the urban situations revealed not only the slick grimness of urban violence but the atomization of social life and the dominance of the penitentiary as an occupational hazard.

In all of this, the transformation of forms and content can be seen by the shifting social context within which American blacks moved. (One of the shifts is the marked abandonment of the term 'negro' for 'black' to account for the interpretation of that experience.)[29] The continuing feature is that those contexts built on an oral expression which was drawn from the language of exclusion and suppression. If the songs and the music were progressively drawn into the religious and popular culture of the white Americans, another form of expression has, from the earliest times, had to contend with constant attempts to appropriate it to the general assumptions of white American culture. That form was the slave/convict 'confession', and it is perhaps with this that a chapter on the rediscovery of voice and text should conclude.

IV

Autobiographies have been written over a long period of time and all of them have in common the author's need to give to the world his version of the truth of the events and personalities involved in his life. Prison autobiographies, however, have in common a feature which is generally absent from most others: they are centred on a debate that the prisoner has with the world and himself on the nature of his 'crimes' and the meaning that prison has given to his life. From the earliest prison autobiographies (the Book of Jonah), through the more notable early Christian and medieval ones (Boethius, Cellini) to the most recent (Wilde, Burney, Breytenbach) the autobiography is at least in part confessional, and, as chapter 3 on 'The Consolations of Philosophy' has tried to show, this confessional includes an attempt to rethink the author's 'crimes' in relation to his own cosmology. The 'confessional' autobiography in its contemporary form, however, has three immediate antecedents: the narrative of slave revolt; the self-projecting account of the bandit/criminal; and the moralizing appropriation of 'criminal' stories to the value of a law-and-order perspective. The problem of literacy in prison narratives is therefore of a different order to that of the blues singer or the balladeer. The autobiographer wants his story published and, from the eighteenth century to the present, telling and distributing the story have gone hand-in-hand. Distribution involves a perception of who will read the story, a perception formed by the author, the publisher and the editors or transcriber of the story. Thus the formulation of the text out of experience is predicated on the text that is already in place in the mind of the publishers and their perception of who the readers are. The bandit/criminal hero story perhaps has pride of place because it places the criminal as hero not only in his own terms, but also in the terms of a society which depends for its sense of itself not on any group action, but on personal heroism, individual autonomy. It is therefore not strictly a 'confession' but rather an individualistic assertion of the boldness of the individual in fighting against banks, policemen, bureaucrats, bungling politicians, landowners. Even if the 'editor' compelled the author to insert sections on prison as the necessary consequence for a life of crime, we read the story for the sense of bravado exercised by the writer or because of the salacious details of life in an underworld. Daniel Defoe's novel *Moll Flanders* (1722) is perhaps the first fictionalized work in this group from outside the United States. But the development of the frontier sense in American culture and politics led to the growth of many 'autobiographies' of which Henry Tufts's *A Narration of the Life, Advantages, Travels and Sufferings of Henry Tufts* (1807) and *Sketches of the Life of William Stuart, the First and Most Celebrated Counterfeiter of Connecticut* (1854) are two of the most celebrated. In both of those the heroes, while perfunctorily apologizing for their crimes, regale their readers with glowing details of how they were committed.[30] The stories are, of course, by white criminals on the run, the forerunners of such later figures as Jesse James, Buffalo Bill, Bonnie and Clyde, and Al Capone (though, as time goes on, the criminal hero gains a wider set of accomplices).

The 'moralizing' appropriation is present in most bandit/criminal stories (even if only in parentheses) but it also has a more direct lineage. The Bible provides the earliest examples: various of the Psalms (though these are mainly about people running away from God's appointed tasks), the Books of Jonah and Job; but the purest are in eighteenth- and nineteenth-century England and America where a Protestant conversion in prison compels the prisoner to read all of his activities as a saga en route to God and a better life in the next world. Criminal life was a flight from God, who finally caught up with the sinner in prison. (James Thompson's *Hound of Heaven* (1883), though not specifically about prison, provided a poetic version of the thematic of these confessions. It was written just a few years before Oscar Wilde's *De Profundis*.) *The Dying Lamentation and Advice of Philip Kenniston, who was executed at Cambridge in New England (for burglary) on Friday the 15th day of September 1738* is one example, and James A. Clay's *A Voice from Prison: or Truths for the Multitudes and Pearls for the Truthful* (Boston, 1856) is another. In England, Mrs Lachlan's *Narrative of the Conversion (by the Instrumentality of Two Ladies) of James Cook, the Murderer of Mr Paas* (1832) is a superb example of special pleading, as is Henry Nowlake's *The Convict Converted* (1858). Arthur Orton's *Entire Life and Full Confession* (1895) is perhaps the classic case of a false 'confession' made after release in order to gain money from the press.

The 'confessional,' however, exists more as an ideal type than as reality and has hardly survived into the twentieth century.[31] In some cases these 'confessions' are obvious forgeries, the most notorious of such being the *Confessions of Nat Turner*, which overlaps with our third category, the slave narrative. Turner was the leader of a slave rebellion in the early nineteenth century, finally arrested by the slave owners who tried and executed him as a criminal. Before his execution, however, they forced him to present his life story, using the 'confessional' as a framework. The transcriber/publisher, Thomas R. Gray, constructed the narrative, in Bruce Franklin's words, 'to fit into a widely read popular genre, the lives of bloodthirsty outlaws and bandits. A political prisoner is thus transmuted into a conventional criminal.'[32] Turner's own account of the uprising, while forming the core of the book, is twisted by his transcriber into providing exactly the opposite message to the one that Turner presumably intended: that law and order must be preserved, that slave uprisings were basically led by criminal bandits and that, after reflection, the criminal now 'frankly acknowledges his full participation in all the guilt'.[33]

Autobiographies by escaped slaves and political prisoners opposed to slavery, far from providing 'confessions' or self-serving moralizing heroics, were accounts of social systems (slavery and prisons) that tried to expose working and prison conditions in order to change them. The authors did not see themselves as criminals, but as reformers, if not revolutionaries, and their accounts reflect this. Early versions include George Thompson's *Prison Life and Reflections* (1847) and Lewis W. Paine's *Six Years in a Georgia Prison* (1851). In some cases these are direct attacks on the penitentiary system itself, as in *An Autobiography of Gerald Toole, the State's Prison Convict, who murdered Daniel Webster, Warden of the Connecticut State Prison on the 27th of March, 1862 (written by himself)*. Thompson, Paine and Toole wrote their own accounts, and thus are not put in the context of having to use transcribers (or translators) to get their message across.

The essential aspect of those early narratives was that there were competing modes which framed the ways that stories might be told. The bandit-hero,[34] who acted purely for himself, ccould write his story appealing to the bandit in each of us. His story, however, was framed by the confessional on the one hand (moral justice of the society deemed that he was guilty and be punished, otherwise we would all live in the 'law of the jungle') and the idea that he represented a social movement on the other. Of course neither of them was viable: he represented nothing more than his own experiences, and these imposed frames constrained him to provide a story which both exaggerated and diminished his own struggles. If he was illiterate he was at the mercy of his scribe as well as his publisher; even if he was not, the exigencies of publishing might compel him to tell a story that would result in sales to a public who expected a particular kind of narrative.

Black prison writing in particular was subject to these kinds of pressures in that throughout the nineteenth century there were no black publishing houses and anything that was published had to be negotiated either through anti-slavery societies (who were not necessarily sympathetic to prison reform) or through independent liberal publishers in the South who might be hostile to Northern penitentiaries but were unsure how to deal with slavery. It was not until the twentieth century that accounts began to emerge from black prisoners which displayed a distinctive style. Malcolm Braly, Chester Himes in the 1930s and 1940s, and George Jackson, Eldridge Cleaver and Malcolm X in the 1960s showed that black prison narratives could be written by seeing through the forms that would otherwise frame them.

V

This might sound like a suggestion that the anti-texts did not exist until the twentieth century, and therefore that articulation was absent. Nothing could be further from the intention of this chapter or indeed this book as a whole. The mark of prison writing is the fragmentary scratchings on the walls of a cell, the articulation of hope against the imposed textuality of incarceration. *The Book*, any book, therefore stands in judgement against the inmate, whose only response is a hermeneutical one, in order to find the meaning of the book not in its own terms, but in the inmate's. The prisoner's work is therefore never done, and accordingly he or she can never have a Book in any definitive, authorial sense but only the beginnings of a song, a poem, a play or a story. With whatever equipment is available, the prisoner establishes the grounds for difference, placing it in a counter-ritual, which is the basis for any textuality.

NOTES

1   See, in particular, Jack Goody, *The Logic of Writing and the Organization of Society* (Cambridge: Cambridge University Press, 1986) and *The Interface between the Writing and the Oral* (Cambridge: Cambridge University Press, 1987).

2 'I would wish . . . to suggest that the alleged derivativeness of writing, however real and massive, was possible only on one condition: that the "original", "natural", etc. language had never existed, never been intact and untouched by writing, that it had always been a writing' (Jacques Derrida, *Of Grammatology* (Baltimore: Johns Hopkins University Press, 1976), p. 56.

3 For a discussion of the linguistic, mythological, metaphysical and typographical implications of this as it relates to the Bible, see Northrop Frye, *The Great Code* (New York: Harcourt Brace Jovanovich, 1982).

4 The debate on whether carnival is essentially radical or conservative has a long history. However, the most thoughtful assessment of the current state of the debate is probably that by Allon White in 'The Struggle over Bakhtin: Fraternal Reply to Robert Young', *Cultural Critique*, 8 (Winter 1987–8), pp. 217–41: 'It is important to point out that both politics and carnival are changing historical practices and their interconnection cuts across racial, gender, class and national identities' (p. 240).

5 Mikhail Bakhtin, *The Dialogic Imagination* (Austin: University of Texas Press, 1981), p. 69.

6 Gertrude Katz, ed., *The Time Gatherers: Writings from Prison* (Montreal: Harvest House, 1970), p. 106.

7 Eldridge Cleaver, *Soul on Ice* (New York: McGraw Hill, 1968), pp. 30–1.

8 George Jackson, *Soledad Brother* (New York: Coward–McCann, 1972), p. 35.

9 Andreas Schroeder, *Shaking it Rough* (Halifax, Nova Scotia: Formac Publishing, 1983), p. 69.

10 For examples and analysis see A. J. Symons, *Bloody Murder* (Harmondsworth: Penguin, 1985) and Chris Steinbrunner and Otto Penzler, *Encyclopaedia of Mystery and Detection* (New York: St Martin's, 1976).

11 For the best account of this see Symons, *Bloody Murder*.

12 But, here's the thing on comedy. If I were to do a satire on the assassination of John Foster Dulles, it would shock people. They'd say, 'That's in heinous taste.' Why? because it's fresh. And that's what my contention is: that satire is tragedy plus time. You give it enough time, the public, the reviewers will allow you to satirize it. Which is rather ridiculous when you think about it. And I know, probably 500 years from today, someone will do a satire on Adolf Hitler, maybe even showing him as a hero, and everyone will laugh. There'll be good fellowship. Hitler'll be just a figure. And yet if you did it today it would be bad. Yet today I could satirize Napoleon Bonaparte. Because, you know, he's gone. (Lenny Bruce, *The Essential Lenny Bruce* (New York: Ballantine Books, 1967), p. 116)

Bruce did, of course, use Hitler in satire, but the ultimate joke was on Hollywood's Jewish directors. See Ioan Davics, 'Lenny Bruce: Hyperrealism and the Death of Tragic Jewish Humor', *Social Text*, 22 (Spring 1989), pp. 92–114.

13 See Eric J. Hobsbawn and Terence Ranger, *The Invention of Tradition* (Cambridge: Cambridge University Press, 1985). The examples of this syndrome are almost too numerous to list, but in a sense almost everything produced by Hollywood about Russia, Germany, Italy, Britain, France, China, Japan, Latin America, any part of South-East Asia or Central Europe

would qualify, not because the stories picked up were not intrinsically important in their countries of origin, but because, in the manner of their telling, they are projected as events that could not happen 'here' (i.e. in the USA), or else their heroic protagonists are viewed as those who would have been here if only circumstances had been different. The cold war, the Vietnam War and the Second World War in particular produced a spate of such films and also a range of television series, mini-series and instalments in series which saw *other people's* criminals as *our* heroes, other prisons as fundamentally worse than ours. The apogee of this activity is probably the children's cartoon film *An American Tail*, which displays a group of Jewish mice escaping from Russian incarceration to the welcoming arms of Lady Liberty. For a whimsical look at Hollywood's version of world history, see also George Macdonald Fraser, *The Hollywood History of the World* (London: Michael Joseph, 1988).

14 Schroeder, *Shaking it Rough*, p. 71.
15 Victor Serge, *Men in Prison* (London: Writers and Readers Publishing Cooperative, 1977), pp. 149–50.
16 Jackson, *Soledad Brother*, p. 35.
17 The zippiest English translation is by Robert Lowell, but Villon's original poem is printed first. Both should be compared with the anonymous gypsy's poem in the body of the text.

> *L'Epitaphe Villon*
> *Freres humains qui après nous vivez*
> *N'ayez les cuers contre nous endurcis*
> *Car se pitié de nous povres avex*
> *Dieu en aura plus tost de vous mercis.*
> *Vous nous voiez cy attaches cinq, six.*
> *Quant de la chair que trop avons nourrie,*
> *Elle est pieça devorée et pourrie.*
> *Et nous, les os, devenons cendre et pouldre.*
> *De nostre mal personne ne s'en rie*
> *Mais priez Dieu que tous nous vueille absouldre.*
>
> *Se freres vous clamons, pas n'en devez*
> *Avoir desdaing, quoy que fusmes occis*
> *Par justice. Toutesfois, vous sçavez*
> *Que tous hommes n'ont pas bon sens rassis.*
> *Excusez nous, puis que sommes transsis,*
> *Envers le fils de la Vierge Marie*
> *Que sa grace ne soit pour nous tarie*
> *Nous preservant de l'infernale fouldre.*
> *Nous sommes mors; ame ne nous harie*
> *Mais priez Dieu que tous nous vueille absouldre.*
>
> *La pluye nous a debeuez et lavez*
> *Et le soleil dessechiez et noircis.*
> *Pies, corbeaulx, nous ont les yeux cavez*
> *Et arrachié la barbe et les sourcis.*
> *Jamais nul temps nous ne sommes assis;*

Puis ça, puis la, comme le vent varie
A son plaisir sans cesser nous charie,
Plus becquetez d'oiseaulx que dez a couldre.
Ne soiez donc de nostre confrairie
Mais priez Dieu que tous nous vueille absouldre.

Pince Jhesus qui sur tous a maistrie
Garde qu'Enfer n'ait de nous seigneurie.
A luy n'ayons que faire ne que souldre.
Hommes, icy n'a point de mocquerie;
Mais priez Dieu que tous nous vueille absouldre.

(François Villon, *Selected Poems*
(Harmondsworth: Penguin, 1978)

Villon's Epitaph
Oh brothers, you live after us,
because we shared your revenue.
God may have mercy upon you,
if you have mercy upon us.
Five, six – you see us tied up here,
the flesh we overfed hangs here,
our carrion rots through skin and shirt,
and we, the bones, have changed to dirt.
Do not laugh at our misery:
pray God to save your souls and ours!

We hang in chains to satisfy
your justice and your violence,
brothers humans – surely, you see
that all men cannot have good sense!
Here no man may look down on us –
Oh Child of Mary, pity us,
forgive our crimes – if dying well
saved even the poor thief from hell,
the blood of Christ will not run dry:
pray God to save your souls and ours!

The rain has soaked and washed us bare,
the sun has burned us black. Magpies
and crows have chiselled out our eyes,
have jerked away our beards and hair.
Our bodies have no time to rest:
our chains clank north, south, east and west,
now here, now there, to the wind's dance –
more beaks of birds than knives in France!
Do not join our fraternity:
pray God to save your souls and ours!

Prince Jesus, king of earth and air,
preserve our bodies from hell's powers –
we have no debts or business there.
We were not hanged to make you laugh.

Villon, who wrote our epitaph,
prays God to save your souls and ours!

(George Steiner, ed., The Penguin Book of
Modern Verse in Translation (Harmondsworth:
Penguin, 1966))

18   János Kádár was the First Secretary of the Hungarian Communist Party from 1956 to 1988. Károly Grosz was his successor.

19   Peter Farrell, 'This Stors is writen by me *Peter Demitro*, (the master) of modern mystery (by hook or by crook) or by me' and 'An interview with Peter Farrell by Peter Murphy and Janet Urquhart', *Prison Journal*, 7 (1988), Burnaby: Simon Fraser University, Department of Continuing Education, pp. 6–7, 8–14.

20   Ibid., pp. 8–14.

21   For discussions of this process see Imamu Imiri Baraka (alias Leroy Jones), *Blues People: the Negro Experience in White America and the Music that Developed from it* (New York: William Morrow, 1963); Francis Newton (alias Eric J. Hobsbawm), *The Jazz Scene* (Harmondsworth: Penguin, 1959); and H. Bruce Franklin, *Prison Writing in America: the Victim as Criminal and Artist* (Westport, Conn.: Lawrence Hill, 1982).

22   Baraka, *Blues People*, p. 41.

23   Ibid., p. 47.

24   Ibid., pp. 44–5.

25   Franklin, *Prison Writing in America*, p. 118.

26   Ibid., pp. 120–2.

27   Newton, *The Jazz Scene*, pp. 32–3.

28   A recent important study of blues in relation to the black American oral tradition is Houston A. Baker, Jr, *Blues, Ideology and Afro-American Literature: a Vernacular Theory* (Chicago: University of Chicago Press, 1984).

29   Until the early 1970s virtually every black writer used the term 'negro' to describe movement, culture, race, etc. During the 1960s it became clear that while 'negro' history was an attempt to show white America that blacks could be good Americans like them and had already made an important contribution to America, 'negro' itself was a racist term (whites were not known as Caucasians by themselves or anyone else). Negro-ness was a false reading of history, white and black.

> Black history suggests that the American past upon which so much hope has been built never really existed, and probably never will. We who have been forced to be both black and white in America have seen the society from the dark side, and are therefore dangerous, just as on street brothers are dangerous when they refuse to be absorbed into the corruption they have seen around them since childhood.
> (Vincent Harding, 'Beyond Chaos: Black History and the Search for the New Land', *Amistad*, 1 (1970), p. 279)

30   For details, see Franklin, *Prison Writing in America*, pp. 124–30.

31   The Watergate conspirator, Charles Colson, may, however, claim to have put the clock back with his *Born Again* (New York: Bantam, 1976) and Eldridge Cleaver's bizarre last book, *Soul on Fire* (Waco, Texas: World

Books, 1978) may be another such version, but with a peculiar twist of its own.

32   Franklin, *Prison Writing in America*, p. 132.

33   Ibid.

34   As a genre, the self-proclaimed bandit-hero must be distinguished from the bandit as a centre-piece of guerilla warfare. See Eric J. Hobsbawm, *Bandits* (Harmondsworth: Penguin, 1972) for an attempt at illustrating the importance of banditry in popular culture.

6

Underground Man / Hollow Man / the Time of the Hero

I

The author who has established the tone for our literary understanding of male criminals is surely Dostoevsky who, initially in two novels, *Memoirs from the House of the Dead* and *Notes from the Underground*, and later, more fully, in *Crime and Punishment* and *The Brothers Karamazov*, developed the motif of 'underground man' and the employment of self-conscious discourse as a device for understanding the criminal as anti-hero. Dostoevsky's focused interest in crime was developed as a consequence of his four years in the prison fortress in Omsk, western Siberia, and five years of compulsory military service, both sentences served as a result of his involvement in an anti-Tsarist conspiracy. Even before his imprisonment he had written a short novel, *The Double*, whose theme (that of a man who is haunted by the idea that there is another man who is exactly like him in physical characteristics but the obverse in moral and psychological ones) was developed by Robert Louis Stevenson in *The Strange Case of Dr Jekyll and Mr Hyde* over forty years later. This theme is not only central to Dostoevsky's more mature work, but is also part of the self-image of many prisoners.[1] It is also, after Freud, part of the clinical text which is used to 'treat' prisoners.

The theme of much of Dostoevsky's work is the ludicrous command that outward appearances have on our everyday lives. In *The House of the Dead* and *Notes from the Underground* Dostoevsky develops characters who are dominated by the idea that they have to show the world how significant they are, both by what they did and by how they tell their stories. Everything that they did (or that they want the listeners to believe they did) is displayed with bravado. Although underground man projects the hero as storyteller, yet he cannot attain the status of a cockroach as a person. 'Not only couldn't I make myself malevolent, I couldn't make myself anything: neither good nor bad, neither a scoundrel nor an honest man, neither hero nor an insect.'² For if underground man tells one set of stories to others in order to be taken as hero, to his imaginary ('fantastic', in Dostoevsky's words) inner self he conducts a different dialogue, one which exposes his inherent hollowness.

Thus for Dostoevsky there are at least two prison stories to be told: the monologic, boasting story of surface achievements, and the dialogic, inner story. In the words of Bakhtin, 'the "truth" at which the hero must and indeed ultimately does arrive through clarifying the events to himself, can essentially be for Dostoevsky only *the truth of the hero's own consciousness*.'³ The surface, monologic, story is, in one sense, no story because it is Everyman's story appropriated by this particular prisoner as if he is the only worthy teller, or, alternatively, as if the story only makes sense if told about him. (As we shall see below, much prison writing is precisely of this nature.) What this does is to traduce Everyman's story, because it does not allow for diversity in either the experiencing or the telling of the story.

The only story worth listening to is therefore the one that reveals the 'man in man', that displays man on the threshold of realizing himself. The character cannot be known if *thingness* is imposed on him, if he is a stereotype or a caricature, nor if he accepts other people's words about himself as necessarily what he is about. Prison is essentially about playing out a script written by others: the prisoner can play it out by acting out the part assigned to him (as criminal hero, stool-pigeon, simpleton) or he can rethink the entire imposition of text on himself in order to establish his own authenticity. The task is to be the author of his own stories, and that can only be achieved through dialogue between the inner and outer selves.

How complex this process might be is suggested by one of Dostoevsky's best-known stories. In the legend of 'The Grand Inquisitor' in *The Brothers Karamazov*, the principle of the dialogue is clearly expressed by way of monologue. During the Spanish Inquisition, Christ appears in Seville. He is instantly recognized by the people. He blesses the poor, heals the sick. Noticing Him and what He is doing, the Grand Inquisitor confines Him to the dungeon and berates Him for coming back: 'Thou didst hand on the work to us. Thou hast promised, Thou hast established by Thy word, Thou hast given us the right to bind and unbind, and now, of course, Thou canst not think of taking it away. Why, then, hast Thou come to hinder us?'⁴ The message is that there is now a greater text than His, a text which is the opposite of the one that He intended (the Inquisitor tells Him that He made all the wrong choices when tempted by Satan in the wilderness). He will be burned at the stake with other heretics in the morning. Christ says nothing, gives him a Judas kiss, and leaves. The apparently symmetrical nature of this encounter is belied by the context within which the story is told. Ivan, the atheist, is telling the story to his brother, Alyosha, a priest, in a tavern. The story is repeatedly interrupted by Alyosha. There are other stories outside this one which, once interrelated, show that this story is not simply one of text/countertext or of clear dialectical symmetry, but, as Bakhtin wrote, 'an internal dialogic disintegration at its very ideological core'.[5] The purpose of the stories and the interruptions is to reveal the essence of Ivan, to expose his threshold. The use of a dialogic structure has more in common with the Book of Job than with Plato, with the search for the inner self having more prominence than an abstract conception of the Good. (An example of this is the use of parables within the text. The 'Legend of the Grand Inquisitor' is part of an interconnecttng series of dialogues, whereas the 'Parable of the Cave' in Plato's *Republic* is presented as an *illustration* for the main theme of the book.)

What Dostoevsky provides for us is a template for reading the pattern – and hence the purpose – of the storytelling, and his novels – from the few, deft strokes of *Notes from the Underground* to the much more complex polyphony of *The Brothers Karamazov* – work out the problem of being authentic at all. It is in *Notes from the Underground*, however, that Dostoevsky spells out the problems of any writing by the criminal. The first problem is the problem of the confession, and Dostoevsky, in a pre-Stalin era, explored the issue of false confessions, not as confessions which were forced out of anyone, let alone confessions that were forged, but as confessions that were freely given. He does this by using situational satire on the one hand (a graphic account of a man's expression of his toothache compared with telling the worst about himself) and a parody of what the criminal's imaginary literary production would look like.

> Everything always ended happily, however, with a lazy and entrancing transition to art; that is, to beautiful ready-made images of life, forcibly wrenched from poets and novelists and adapted to every possible kind of service and requirement. For example, I triumphed over everybody; everybody else was compelled to recognize my supremacy voluntarily, and I forgave them all. I, a famous poet and courtier, fell in love; I received

countless millions, and immediately bestowed them on the whole human race, at the same time confessing all my shameful deeds to all the world, deeds which of course were not simply shameful, but had in them an extremely large admixture of the best and highest' . . . Everybody wept and embraced me (how unfeeling they would have shown themselves otherwise), and I went out, barefoot and hungry, to preach new ideas and rout the forces of reaction.[6]

Between the satire and the parody, underground man struggles to be authentic, but he never quite gets there because always he leaves a loophole, or what Bakhtin calls a 'vicious circle of self-consciousness with a sideward glance. The loophole creates a special type of fictive ultimate world about oneself with an undisclosed tone to it, obtrusively peering into the other's eyes and demanding from the other a sincere refutation.'[7] In the *Notes*, underground man does receive a 'sincere refutation' but he cannot recognize it. Into his life comes a woman called Liza, whom he can only see through a bad, sexist, romantic poem by Nekrasov. He abuses her, physically and mentally. She leaves him and walks out into the snow. But underground man goes on with theorizing-with-a-sideward-glance. Another loophole. He says he must stop his account. But as Dostoevsky concludes: 'This is not the end, however, of the "Notes" of this paradoxical writer. He could not help going on. But to us too it seems that this will be a good place to stop.'[8]

Although Dostoevsky's approach is useful as an introduction to how to read prisoners' accounts of themselves, the problem with taking it much further is that it is clear that there can be no ultimate 'authentic' account because the search for the 'main-in-man' is an impossible one, just as Plato's search for the 'good' is. What is important in reading Dostoevsky is the method he uses to try to arrive at the distinction between the authentic and the inauthentic. Earlier I referred to Boethius's *The Consolation of Philosophy*, and of course in many respects Dostoevsky's search is for the person who truly has a philosophy as opposed to one who has not, though if it were put that simply distinction between Dostoevsky and Plato would disappear – the distinction being, surely, between the person who evolves the philosophy from within, and the one who seeks to grasp at a philosophy from above. A person who 'survives' prison through anger, self-indulgence or mere cunning cannot be said truly to have survived. A person who sees him- or herself as a victim cannot be said to have survived. Thus a person who thinks that the telling of his or her story is an act of salvation and survival may be on the way to survival, but may not necessarily have arrived at it. Nadezhda Mandelstam noted that most of the intellectuals who went to the Gulags died almost at once, because there was little point in living except to remember it all and tell the story as a warning to others.[9] Thus Osip Mandelstam, even though he died, survived. This presupposes both an external and an internal philosophy, and not simply the self-projection of the underground man.

There is another aspect of writing out of prison which pushes this issue further. Dostoevsky saw the criminal as an anti-hero, but an anti-hero who could not realize himself because he was dominated by surface appearances. But in what does heroism consist? Dostoevsky drew on the swashbuckling pirate/bandit as his image of how the criminal wished to be seen. For the time when he was writing, and to some extent even today, this is a valid enough parody of the criminal's literary dreams. And yet two aspects are missing from it. One is the conception of heroism as legend (Robin Hood is legend, Jesse James is legend) and the other is that of the hero in his own terms. The legendary hero is remembered by what he is reputed to have done (through others' accounts of those deeds), while the other kind of hero writes his own script. Dostoevsky plays with the thought that both these conceptions represent different forms of inauthenticity, because the second form, like the account of the toothache, necessarily conveys its own escape clause. What is missing from Dostoevsky is the idea that the personal account may necessarily (as in Camus's *The Rebel* or Freud's *Moses and Monotheism*) represent a struggle to replace the father, that on aspect of the authentic is a conflict over paternity. The choice to write a personal account may quite specifically be an attempt to write in order to overturn the father's biographical inscription against the son. In doing so, the prison writer might therefore write himself into legend, which becomes, as it were, the legitimation of his claim against the father who incarcerated him. It is true that Dostoevsky considered this problem in his novel *The Devils*, but largely only to discredit it. (In 'The Legend of the Grand Inquisitor', however, he deals with the problem in reverse, with the Inquisition contesting the paternity of Christ.) As Earl Shorris has written, 'To be a hero in our time it is necessary to write a book. Autobiography therefore abounds. And to hell with literature, the purpose of autobiography is to prove that the writer is a hero.'[10] Faced with so many autobiographies that are not about heroes, it is necessary, in the light of what we have discussed, to ask why they exist, and why we should read them.

II

An autobiography, or a fictionalized version of oneself, is always an attempt to assert the self against the others who might either ignore the subject or tell the story in a quite different way. Most prison writing is autobiographical, and yet, like all autobiographies, it is inserted into other situations, other dialogues. The account can never stand by itself, however it is written. Sometimes the author will try to make the connections, anticipating the reader's own curiosity or scepticism, as Jack Henry Abbott does when he says that 'there are not many books of philosophical importance I have not read', and then goes on to tell us which of these make sense to him, and then, by way of that, how we should make sense of his own life.[11] This does not, of course, necessarily convince us: we are more likely to read Abbott as a footnote to Mailer's *The Executioner's Song* than as a continuation of an American tradition of black prison writing. For what Abbott has written, in spite of its form as letters to Mailer, is a monologue that he wants Mailer to overhear. And it is a monologue that reveals the hollow man beneath the revolutionary rhetoric:

> I want consolation more than anything in this world. I cannot help it if I have not been consoled by God, by a vision of the true glory of God ... *God, I need a fix now.* It is the only respite possible after so many years. Next month I begin working on my seventeenth year behind bars.
>
> To feel the glow that begins like a fire in my belly and rises up through my nerves and organs, up to my temples, is something nothing else can give me. It gives me what I need to live with all this.[12]

Abbott is neither a hero nor an anti-hero; rather, he is a typical phenomenon, a product of a cultural industry where very real desolation has become part of the business of writing mega-novels. The occasional phrases that come through this production and make sense, do so in spite of the production. If only the author had allowed himself to probe deeper, rather than become an instant, and forgettable, media hero . . .

The problem, of course, is partly related to the imagined or real audience for such autobiographies. The commonsensical reader of prison autobiographies will say that most accounts by prisoners are in the form of excuses for their 'misbehaviour', and that accounts by people like Abbott are the less convincing because they try to cover up their obvious misdemeanours or felonies by making them appear to have been part of a political crusade. (In terms of Dostoevsky's work, the underground man does not become more convincing because he casts himself as a character in *The Devils*.) But the commonsensical view must be replaced by a more thoughtful examination. Two books – both Canadian – may help us understand the problems of creating an 'authentic' account.

The first is by the novelist Daivd Helwig. His account, *A Book about Billie*, has been referred to briefly earlier. The problem he presents to us is that of the petty criminal who wants to tell his story without writing it himself, who wants the book that Helwig is to write for him 'to be more than a book. It was to be his justification, his revenge; it was to balance the scales for everything that had ever gone wrong. And I was to relive his life with him, to experience what he had known and somehow set him free from himself.'[13] Helwig outlines the emotional negotiations he had with Billie, the disappointment that Billie shows in Helwig, his 'use of a strange mixture of anger, depression, attack and emotional blackmail' and Helwig's meditations on why he should write the book at all.

> After he left, I found myself wondering what I had taken on. In ways I didn't want to write the book; I had other things planned and wanted to work on those, but I'd always thought someone should write about the kind of man who had been in trouble since childhood, had gone from training school to reformatory to penitentiary, that the experience of such a man could tell a lot about our society. I knew Billie had that kind of record. I thought he probably had a book in him that should be written.[14]

The material for the book was collected over a summer while Billie was on parole. Based on taped conversations with Billie, Helwig worked with 'the narrative he left behind, attempting to edit this without changing his words, keeping his voice and accent, putting the bits and pieces together without falsifying or judging.'[15] The book consists of Billie's account, chronologically arranged as biography, but punctuated throughout by Helwig's accounts of what was happening to Billie (and himself and his wife, Nancy) throughout that summer. In one chapter Helwig punctuates Billie's account with newspaper reports when these refer to events in which Billie claims to have been involved. In this way three voices are preserved: Billie's, Helwig's and that of the press. Towards the end of the book, after

Billie has disappeared to New York, Helwig meets one of Billie's friends who writes down an encounter with him there. Thus a fourth voice is added.

Most of Helwig's account is matter-of-fact. It deals with Billie's life as it unfolds over the summer: his drunken bouts, his use of drugs, his girlfriends, his attempts to hold on to jobs, his relations with parole officers. The interruptions into the flow of Billie's narrative act as something of a Greek chorus: Billie's story and Helwig's play point/counterpoint. The apparently heroic acts as Billie tells them are put in perspective when Helwig shows us what Billie is doing now. The narrative includes accounts of growing up at home and in institutions, of a series of petty robberies and acts of fraud, of a prison riot, of many encounters with the police and undercover agents, of several attempts at going straight, of being a junkie and being a pusher. In Billie's story there is also a series of relationships, sexual and non-sexual, almost all of them displaying a lack of fidelity due, in general, to the influence of drugs and alcohol. What is important about Billie's story, however, is the tone, the style of the telling. The accounts of prison life are no different to the accounts of life on the street, as if they were all part of the same adventure. The whole world, with the exception of Billie and one or two friends (and he has doubts about them, too) is stupid, or dishonest, or vicious. Even though Billie is let down, beaten up, imprisoned, he maintains a sense of his paramount importance. It comes through in many ways. 'I remember one time I went to Montreal. There was a panic on in Toronto, there was no heroin, and I was about the only one who could score . . .' 'They got three years. I could probably have got them off with a year or something . . .' 'And he had this beautiful big pine tree. I don't know how many feet it went up, but this pine tree was fantastic in the sunset . . . I got an axe, and I had to go down along a creek bed and up this hill. I went up onto the hill and chopped the tree down.'[16] Super-pusher, super-attorney, super-vandal: Billie is your man, cutting a swathe through the under- and over-ground.

Helwig's interjection into this self-aggrandizing narrative is not so much to expose it for what it is, but rather to build in the reflexive sense that is absent from Billie's own account. Helwig's account and that of the friend from New York show another Billie, cunning rather than clever, uncourageous, bombastic and shallow and in need of love. The stories that Billie tells about himself have been drawn from a wide range of other prison stories. Billie would like to believe that they were all about him, that his book would prove to the world that he was the hero of the underground. Of course Helwig would never tell *that* story. Instead he helps to convey a sense of the real story that is waiting to be told.

Billie's real story has a tragic conclusion. The man who is called 'Billie' in the book was a Canadian prisoner whose real name was Richard Armer. He died in the United States of a drug overdose some years after the book was published. In his collected poems Helwig published a 'Footnote to a Book about Billie', dedicating it to Richard Armer:

> You knew two ways, and neither one made sense.
> You offered weaknesses as if they were gifts,
> cried for yourself and hated those you loved.
> Wherever you went, you were part of the wrong story.
>
> I am wary of you, even when you are dead.
> I can't believe that you won't arrive at the door
> demanding love, demanding justice, your brain
> fuddled, irrelevant, sunk in gibberish.
>
> [. . .]
>
> Alone in a strange city you were still a child,
> stupid with fear, brilliant with maudlin cunning.
> The hole inside you grew until you were gone.
> Nobody knows the name for the piece that was missing.[17]

Helwig provides the groundwork for understanding the hollow man without necessarily giving us much hope for him, without giving us much sense of how we might connect with him:

> You elected me your magical perfect brother.
> You wanted someone to live your life and save it.
> I was accused by your weaknesses, unfairly
> perhaps, but then you never practiced fairness.[18]

The problem with the hollow man is that he lives in the surface-world of his stories. If there is a real world beneath, as in the man-in-man of Dostoevsky, there is no way that we can have any rapport with it, except, perhaps, to confront the storyteller himself. But the storyteller lives in the limbo-world of the collective stories he would like us to believe in (even if he personalizes them) and the hyperreal stories that we have constructed about him. We, too, are caught up in the same limbo.

The usefulness of Helwig's book is that he brings to the exercise a critical, informed and sensitive mind, unlike Mailer's editing of Abbott which is romantically befuddled and opportunistic. Both 'Billie' and Jack Henry Abbott are hollow men, but Helwig does not for one minute want us to accept the surface nature of Billie's story. He wants us to probe deeper, to be involved, with him, in the search for the story behind the story, the man behind the man. Whether there is any such man there is open to debate, but at least we know what the issues are. With Mailer, Abbott is what he seems, and the rhetoric that Mailer would like us to believe in is validated in the text. The Mailer/Abbott book is a promotional blurb for Mailer's own curious romanticism, while the Helwig/Armer book is a discourse between Helwig and Armer.

Richard Armer (like any politician or film star) wanted his story to be written in order to justify himself, and David Helwig to be his scribe. But Armer's story would have been his own fiction. A wider fiction, encompassing the other issues relevant to understanding Armer and his social and personal predicaments, could not be written by him. The novel that might have been inside Armer was suffocated by his need to be loved.

III

The format for the prisoner's novel is circumscribed by the autobiographical possibilities. Prisoners' novels may be about everything else *but* prison, except for prison as interlude, as something to be avoided. They would therefore have to be about the fun, the heroism of being bandits. In Leonard Cohen's words, they would have to be about beautiful losers, about the 'bandit in all of us'. This type of novel would have to be the reverse of the crime thriller, the detective story. It would have to be the story of how the criminal *wins* against the machinations of the police and 'civilian' society. In this the prisoner on the run has much in common with the spy, the detective, the political fugitive. His novel is a battle of wits, as is theirs, only he wins. He may even, if he wants to be ambitious, see himself as the underworld version of all of these together, which in many respects Jean Genet does, though Genet holds the whole work together by a reverse sexuality as well. Such a novel embodies the recognition that there is another story to be told, but one that can only be told by appropriating the existing genre which is concerned with entrapment and, as it were, flipping it over. Such a novelist takes the parodic function of the prisoner-novel as central to writing about himself.[19] Whether he is successful or not is discussed below.

The novel that concerns itself with the experience of imprisonment, dealt with in earlier chapters, is basically framed by the prison itself. The narrative moves around and out from the cell, and essentially is claustrophobic; but, in its treatment of interpersonal relations, it recognizes that prison is a place where the world is locked out (in contrast to Solzhenitsyn, who argued that prison is a place where people are locked in). It is the absence of others that frames the discourse of the inmates. The books that bring this alive (Solzhenitsyn's, *One Day in the Life*, in spite of his theory, Serge's, *Men in Prison*, Wole Soyinka's, *The Man Died* and Dostoevsky's *House of the Dead*) are striking examples, perhaps because they ask the nagging questions as to the grounds of the philosophy that keep anyone alive. Even in notoriously poor novels, like notoriously poor autobiographies (Roger Caron's *Bingo!* and *Go Boy!*, or Gregory Bell's *Birdsong*),[20] the thing that maintains our interest, if a philosophy is absent, is the strategy of survival.

But the problems of writing a heroic novel out of a criminal subculture are immense. The obvious advantages of the criminal story, for those of us who read it, are those of the lottery on the one side and the rebel on the other. Most of us indulge in gambling in one way or another; stories of successful gamblers and stories of successful bank-robbers are cut of the same cloth. We would like to know that we can win, and it is possible (unless we depend entirely on horoscopes or pin-pricks in the Bible or stock-exchange quotations for our predictions) that we may have to engage in some hanky-panky to pull if off. The cards are stacked against us. But, as Dostoevsky warned us in *The Gambler*, the chances of success are minimal, whether we trust our horoscopes or our sense of cunning, or try to pull off a revolution. We are trapped because we want to pull it off, but also want to be able to enjoy the fruits of our luck or cunning in the here and now. For this reason we read detective stories in order to know that there is a law and order which will preserve our world, once we have inherited the millions or won them in the lottery – but we also want to know that there is a chance for us in this cruellest of cruel worlds. Underground man gives us hope that we can pull it off.

The prison novel and autobiography would work if they showed us that that were possible. In fact, they show the opposite. They show, if anything, the perils of holding the system up to ransom, the dangers of living on the ultimate gamble. Several novels have been written by prisoners which try to display the possibilities of *jouissance* on the rampage, which attempt to give us the frenetic fun of being the populist bandit-hero. Of these, I have selected one, because it is well-written, determined, engaging, literate and only minimally dominated by pusillanimous chest-beating, as a symptom of the problem.

Jack-rabbit Parole, by the Canadian author Stephen Reid, is a story about robbing banks and trying to get away with it. It is a story which is devoid of the whimpering attempt at self-flagellation that is typical of the confessional account, but also it has nothing to do with the writing that claims that this life is important because it happened to *me*. In terms of much of conventional morality the story is amoral. The central character does what he does because he enjoys it. He knows what the risks are in going on, but he persists because he enjoys it. 'Some days I hated what I did, and it troubled me. But mostly I loved what I did, and that troubled me more.'[21] But his morals are no different from anyone else's. He quivers at the possibility of hurting a child or her mother in a bank robbery, he is loyal to his woman as long as she seems to be loyal to him, he sees through the duplicity of others who double-cross. Essentially he is at least as moral as anyone else in interpersonal relations. He is as tough as The Equalizer and as morally concerned as Kojak, but he is neither tough for the sake of it (like the cops) nor soppily moralistic for the sake of it (like the clergy or the social workers). Ethically he knows where he stands, and this has nothing to do with the world's ethics. He is Nelson Algren's man on the wild side, grounded in the sense of what he is, the man who constructs his ethics from the existential present.[22] So why does the novel not work? Why has Stephen Reid created a novel which takes us part of the way, but not far enough?

The answer, in part, goes back to Dostoevsky. Reid is astute enough to know that the discourse has to be with those of us who have shared the genre out of which he feels compelled to write. He knows that we have read the detective stories and watched the cops-and-robbers shows, even that the television news is part of our 'text' in understanding the criminal on the run. He punctuates his novel with references to all of these, and his writing is literate, perceptive and colloquial. He also knows that he cannot validate his claim to authenticity by being seen as a 'political' prisoner, as a prisoner of conscience or as the representative of a major ethnic group which inevitably finds its members locked up. He disowns religion as a solution, and he is not a woman. Thus all of the moral alibis are out. *Jack-rabbit Parole* is about the rest of us and our fantasies of bucking the system. Its failure is part of our failure in reality to resist the system, take our ill-gotten gains, and create our world without being sucked back into the system from which we tried to escape. The obverse of *Jack-rabbit Parole* would be the account of a major capitalist who made a lot of money out of the system and managed to get away scot-free, living happily in Florida or the south of France to his dying day. But that story is not worth telling again. If we seek its monument, we need only look around us. It was because of *that* story that Stephen Reid wrote his story in the first place.

Thus *Jack-rabbit Parole* forces us back, like the untold but often seen story of the successful corrupt businessman, to ask for the man-in-man, the reality behind the surface story. It won't come, of course, unless we take the two stories together, because they are cut of the same cloth. Both stories are born out of the hyperreality of the present world that we live in, and our urge to grasp the superficial as our own.

Dostoevsky's answer would have been to create a dialogue between the two stories, as well as our interest in listening to them, so that there might be a discursive field within which we might all make sense to each other. Reid's sense is to assume that the other stories that we are obliged to listen to provide the real grounds for hearing his story, which is the punctuation of ours. But for Dostoevsky our story is the most significant. The failure of the hollow man, the underground man, is the failure to engage with that.

IV

There is another kind of prison fiction and that is one which not only sees the prison experience as part of a criminal subculture, but which sees that subculture as part of an entire dispossessed culture. Thus the underground man is underground not simply because he is a criminal, but because he comes from an entire society which is underground.[23] This is no imaginary camaraderie of bandits, but a life where prison experience and everyday life intersect. The argument was made in chapter 5 that American black culture was essentially a prison culture, born of slavery and refined in the penitentiary. There are other such cultures (the South African blacks, the North American Indians, gypsies everywhere, Palestinians in Israel, even perhaps the French Canadians, the Basques and the Irish) and no society is entirely free of the presence in its midst of a group of people who have been defined as second-rate, not just because of their pigmentation, religious beliefs or language, but because of the economic power that defines some groups of people as subservient to others.[24]

But the United States contains within itself the most systematic culture of dispossession. Any writing that comes out of such a culture cannot be slotted into our voyeuristic sense of life as a roulette game. It must be pushed back into a sensibility that recognizes both our complicity in forming that culture and also that the only honest thing we can do is to listen to what that culture is saying. The novels will not be our novels. They will overturn our sense of what novels are all about. The writing of Chester Himes (at least as dramatically as that of Jean Genet) provides such an occasion.

What Himes did was to try to overturn all the genres that we have come to associate with prison, from autobiography to detective story to cop-and-robbers show to political manifesto. Himes started with underground man as his point of departure:

> If this plumbing for the truth reveals within the Negro personality [he said to a white audience at the University of Chicago in 1948] homicidal mania, lust for white women, a pathetic sense of inferiority, paradoxical anti-Semitism, arrogance, Uncle Tomism, hate and fear and self-hate, this then is the effect of oppression on the human personality. These are the daily horrors, the daily realities, the daily experiences of an oppressed minority.[25]

Himes's writing was therefore about a season in hell, without any recourse to the white man's sense of escape. Reid's publisher, for example, wanting to validate the author as a 'good guy', notes that 'the first and only time Reid fired a gun during a robbery, he shot himself by mistake.'[26] With Himes there are no such escape clauses. When the trigger is pulled there is no mistaking whom it will hit. Himes published his first novel nine years after being released from Ohio State Penitentiary in 1936, to which he had been sentenced for armed robbery. (He served seven-and-a-half years of a twenty-year sentence.) But while in prison he wrote, and published short stories, and worked on his autobiographical novel, *Cast the First Stone*, which was finally published in 1952. The reception of his early work was largely hostile, on grounds of implicit homosexuality and explicit violence. Five novels, all based on autobiographical material in and out of prison, were published between 1945 and 1955. Mainly because of the vindictive attitude to his work, Himes (like Richard

Wright and James Baldwin) left the USA for France. He lived and wrote in Paris until his death in 1984, and all of his subsequent books were first published in French. His French publisher, Marcel Duhamel, suggested that he write some detective fiction and, from 1957 to 1969, eight detective stories appeared, all set in Harlem, New York, and all starring two black detectives, Coffin Ed Johnson and Grave Digger Jones. The books are explicit parodies of the crime novel genre. As Julian Symons wrote of them:

> Coffin Ed has been quick on the trigger ever since a hoodlum threw a glass of acid on his face, and when we first meet Grave Digger he has been off duty for six months after being shot up, although 'other than for the bullet scars hidden beneath his clothes and the finger-scar obliterating the hairline at the base of his skull where the first bullet burned off the hair, he looked much the same'. The humans among whom the detectives move in the eight novels are credulous, lecherous, treacherous, greedy and savage. Coffin Ed and Grave Digger are savage too, although they are not monsters masquerading as heroes, like Mickey Spillane's Mike Hammer.[27]

Himes's writing is thus in two periods: the social realism of the pre-1955 fictionalized autobiographies, and the parodic invention of a black criminal novel in his Paris years. But the two periods closely interconnect. In both, violence is taken as a fact of life, as part of the everyday routine. For example, in *Cast the First Stone* he writes:

> Something clamped over my head, hot and tight, blinding me. Turning, I went back and hit him over the ear. He fell half from his seat and clambered to his feet on the other side. I leaned across the desk and hit him twice in the face. When I hit him the third time my feet slipped and fell across the desk. While lying there I hit him again in the stomach. He began screaming but he didn't hit back.[28]

And in *The Big Gold Dream*, one of the Harlem novels:

> As he reached the door, he heard feet clatter down the stairs. His body collided with another. In the dark neither could see. He stabbed out with his chisel and heard a sharp cry of pain. At the same time he felt the cool, quick, almost painless slash of a knife across his cheek. Theirs was a brief but furious

struggle. He stabbed out crazily, pumping the chisel with an insensate fury. He could feel the difference when it chopped into the wall and when he made contact with cloth and flesh. He couldn't see the knife, but he knew it stabbed the air about him. He felt it enter his flesh several times. He felt no pain, but he was crazed with terror.[29]

In both cases, impersonal bodies collide in personal violence. The act of survival, on both sides, is necessarily an act of violence. But is an act of survival which questions every aspect of identity. If Himes is concerned with the survival of blacks, (but it is black *man* above all that interests him), the stories that he creates to demonstrate this are fables based on dead ends, on a lifestyle and a genre which is in the process of deconstructing itself. In an interview quoted by Pfeil, Himes said: 'I would like to see produced a novel that just drains a person's subconscious of all his attitudes and reactions to everything . . . Since [the black writer's] reactions and thoughts will obviously be different from that of the white community, thhis should create an entirely different structure of the novel.'[30] Himes's novels must be seen as the commencement of a project that would achieve just that.

Detective stories rest on the premise that there is a truth to be known, that there is a justice to be done. The detective (police or private) has a duty to preserve the good that is in society against the evil that might tear it apart. Yet from the origins of the genre with Edgar Alan Poe and Conan Doyle there has always been an ambiguity in the pursuit of justice. Sherlock Holmes has a 'Bohemian soul', is addicted to cocaine and morphine, and believes that there is a justice behind justice. As the genre evolves through the 1920s and 1930s the self-appointed detective/police hero who is beyond the law takes over, unashamed and uninhibited. With Raymond Chandler, Dashiel Hammett and Mickey Spillane he is violent for the sake of it, but also for the sake of those private organizations, like Pinkertons, that have a vested interest in the manufacture of crime. Chester Himes brings this development to its ultimate conclusion. Coffin Ed and Grave Digger are black agents of a white system. Their task is to bring to ground an entire population which is venal, gullible and vulnerable, a population whose identity crises are the products of having been labelled as a criminal subculture. Clearly with such a scenario there cannot be good guys and bad guys, there can be no 'solutions' to crimes (though in the earlier novels Himes does at some point tell us who dunnit) and the violence on both sides must be seen as an ingredient of the entire system. The novels are sexist because the whole system is sexist. People are conned because they are gullible and cunning and passionate all at the same time. Sexism, gullibility, cunning, passion are all seen together in this extract from the conclusion of *The Big Gold Dream*. Alberta is recovering in a police station after attempting to kill a charlatan religious figure called Sweet Prophet after she had given him a large sum of money which she had won while gambling. She is interviewed by Homicide Sergeant Ratigan.

'Why did you do it, Alberta?' Ratigan asked in what he mistakenly thought was a kindly tone of voice.

'He stole my money,' Alberta replied in the whining Southern voice she employed when talking to white people.

Ratigan's eyes popped in amazement, but he controlled his voice.

'How did he steal your money?' he asked, as though reasoning with a child.

'I gave it to him,' she said.

'Oh,' Ratigan said. 'But that doesn't mean he stole it.'

'Nawsuh, but he didn't give it back.'

'All right, let's get this straight,' Ratigan said. 'You gave him the money, and he didn't give it back. Did you ask him for it?'

'Nawsuh. I forgot I gave it to him.'

Slowly, and at first unnoticeably, she began to cry.

'All right,' Ratigan said, 'Don't get upset. Take your time and tell me just what happened.'

She swallowed. 'I went to him Sunday morning to pay for to get baptized,' she said, 'and I told him I needed to get religion because I had won all that money on the numbers.'

'It was thirty-thousand, wasn't it?' Ratigan asked.

'Yassuh, but I didn't have but twenty-nine thousand, four hundred left,' she said.

'Yes, go on,' Ratigan prompted.

Everyone in the room was staring at her unblinkingly, their mouths half open as though their breathing was suspended.

'He told me to look him straight in the eye,' she said. 'I kept looking him in the eyes until my head seemed to get empty of everything but just his eyes. Then he said "You will do exactly as I say". And I said, "Yes, Sweet Prophet." He said "Go back to your house and get all the money from where it is hidden and bring it to me." I said, "Yes Sweet Prophet."

'And the next thing I knew I was sitting there talking to him about getting baptized, and I had forgotten everything else. I had no idea where my money had gone until I came in to the hospital after I got knocked on the head. Then I remembered everything. He knowed I was looking for my money, and he wouldn't give it back.'

She started crying out loud. Her big-boned body was racked by uncontrollable paroxysms. The hard-boiled cops stared at her in awe.

'He thought I didn't know everything about hypnotism,' she wailed. 'He thought I was just a big fool. He didn't have to go and hypnotize me and take my money and then keep it,' she blubbered. 'I would have given it all to him if he had just come right out and asked for it.'

Ratigan stared at her in speechless amazement. 'You mean you would have given that charlatan all of that huge sum of money that you won if he had asked for it? Good God, woman, why?'

'Because I believed in him,' she said, crying almost hysterically now. 'That's why. If you is a black woman like me you got to believe in something.'[31]

With Himes all the belief systems have crumbled and the only ones that make any sense are those of self-interest. When Alberta is told that her boyfriend is also trying to steal her money she comments, 'Oh I ain't mad at him for doing that . . . He was just doing what comes natural.'[32] But if in all of this Himes seems to be the nihilist who wants to destroy everything in the name of self-interest, it is worth considering that Himes's work is supremely parodic and that parody in this sense involves a satire of a social system that created nihilism. Drawn from social relations in prison and in the ghetto which display that nihilism, Himes's fictive realism begs us to consider what a non-nihilistic world would be like. Dostoevsky's search for the man-in-man would have to recognize, at least in part, the need for collective transformations, without the possibility of which even the most personal of survivals would not be possible.

Our perception of criminals' accounts of themselves is affected partly by ourselves, what we are looking for in listening to their talk, hoping that they will confirm something that we know already, and partly by the insistent voices that tell us that there is a world that is totally different if only we will hear. Prisoners, like all of us, write both kinds of story. It is easy to reject the first kind of story, precisely because it confirms what we thought we knew about ourselves (that we are handling the roulette wheel of life better than others), but the other story we put aside, saying, with one of Chester Himes's early reviewers, 'Such men are glib, reasonably literate, authoritative in a superficial way, full of self-pity and whining mannerisms; they are the propounders of highly complicated systems of thought based on irrational, deeply neurotic premises.'[33] All gaolers say the same. Himes, more than Genet, is talking about collective incarceration and collective alternatives. It is a voice to which, together with those of the political prisoners, we should listen carefully, particularly if we want to know the basis on which we can understand the creative impulse emanating from prison and how the alternatives to prison can be constructed.[34]

NOTES

1   A recent example of this may be found in a song composed by an inmate of
    the Edmonton Institution in Alberta, Canada:

    > It's so warm being Jekyll
    > It's so cold being Hyde
    > I can save all the people
    > I can kill when I die
    > To the fate of this bottle
    > That has twisted me inside
    > To a cold, brutal monster
    > Who is living a lie.

    (Bob Johnston, 'Dr Jekyll Mr Hyde', from *Inside Out* (Scarborough,
    Ont.: Salt Records, 1981)

2   Fyodor Dostoevsky, *Notes from the Underground and The Double* (Har-
    mondsworth: Penguin, 1972), p. 16.
3   Mikhail Bakhtin, *Problems of Dostoevsky's Poetics* (Minneapolis: University
    of Minnesota Press, 1984), p. 55.
4   Fyodor Dostoevsky, *The Brothers Karamazov* (London: Dent, 1927), p. 257.
5   Bakhtin, *Problems of Dostoevsky's Poetics*, p. 278.
6   Dostoevsky, *Notes from the Underground*, p. 60.
7   Bakhtin, *Problems of Dostoevsky's Poetics*, p. 234.
8   Dostoevsky, *Notes from the Underground*, p. 123.
9   Nadezhda Mandelstam, *Hope against Hope* (New York: Atheneum, 1970),
    passim.
10 Earl Shorris, 'To Be a Hero in our Time it is Necessary to Write a Book',
    The Nation, 10 May 1986, p. 641. Earl Shorris's piece appears in *The
    Nation* ostensibly as a review of Vallardares's *Against all Hope* and
    Cabezas's *Fire from the Mountain*. It is, however, much more than that and
    is arguably one of the most succinct critiques of writing out of prison

anywhere. The perceptive observer will note my debt to him throughout this chapter, and sporadically throughout this book.

11   Jack Henry Abbott, *In the Belly of the Beast: Letters from Prison* (New York: Random House, 1982), p. 22.
12   Ibid., p. 105.
13   David Helwig, *A Book about Billie* (Toronto: Oberon Press, 1972), p. 7.
14   Ibid., p. 8.
15   Ibid., p. 5.
16   Ibid., p. 65.
17   David Helwig, *The Rain Falls like Rain* (Toronto: Oberon Press, 1982).
18   Ibid.,
19   Throughout this chapter, I refer to authors as 'he'. This is quite deliberate. The style of writing that I am discussing here is exclusively male. With the possible expection of Albertine Sarrazine's novels, I have not come across any writing by women in prison which approximates to the theme of this chapter. But see Elissa Gelfland, *Imagination in Confinement* (Ithaca, NY: Cornell University Press, 1983) and Teresa de Lauretis, *Technologies of Gender: Essays on Theory, Film and Fiction* (Bloomington and Indianapolis: Indiana University Press, 1987) on why this may be so. The work of women prison writers is discussed in other chapters of this book.
20   The unsatisfactory nature of these books may be seen in comparing them with Helwig's *A Book about Billie*. Caron's books are bristling with inauthenticities, particularly *Go Boy!* which reads like the book that Richard Armer might have written if Helwig had not decided to provide the Brechtian alienation effect. We never know whether Caron performed all the acts he claimed to have done. Ultimately our only interest is in why and how he started to write. Caron, like most prison writers, has no self-criticism built into his work. He has neither the reflection of a Boethius nor the parodic sense of a Genet. See Roger Caron, *Bingo!* (Toronto: McGraw-Hill Ryerson, 1985) and *Go Boy!* (Toronto: McGraw-Hill Ryerson, 1978); also Gregory Bell, *Birdsong* (London: Arrow Books, 1986).
21   Stephen Reid, *Jack-rabbit Parole* (Toronto: Seal Books, 1988), p. 85.
22   Nelson Algren, *A Walk on the Wild Side* (New York: Farrar, Straus and Cuhady, 1956).
23   One of the masters of exploring the situations of the dispossessed and their strategies within the language of popular culture is surely Dick Hebdige. His *Subculture: the Meaning of Style* (London: Routledge, 1979) both attempted a semiotic interpretation of the styles adopted by British punks, and also established a trajectory of where they came from. In *Cut 'n' Mix* (London: Routledge, 1987) he explored the evolution of Jamaican and Trinidadian music from slavery to its transmission to Britain and the United States, while in *Hiding in the Light* (London: Routledge, 1989) he examined tattooing, rock music, reading material and fashion among working-class youth in Britain, as well as considering the theories loosely associated with post-modernism.
24   The world is filled with curiosities which overturn the dichotomies of white/black, Catholic/Protestant, guards/prisoners. In Guyana a black minority controls a predominantly Indian one, in Israel a group of Jewish settlers dispossess the original inhabitants, in Iran Shiite Muslims control, in Saudi Arabia Sunni Muslims control. After twenty years of prosperity and civil

peace, Northern Ireland from 1970 to the present has become a terrain for conflict between Protestant and Catholic. (Over the same period, Newfoundland, with the same distribution of Catholic and Protestant populations, has suffered no visibly violent discord.) It all depends on who the power brokers are.

25   Fred Pfeil, 'Policiers Noirs', *The Nation*, 15 November 1986, p. 523.

26   Reid, *Jack-rabbit Parole*, p. 261.

27   A. J. Symons, *Bloddy Murder* (Harmondsworth: Penguin, 1985), pp. 196–7.

28   Chester Himes, *Cast the First Stone* (New York: Signet Books, 1972), p. 105.

29   Chester Himes, *The Big Gold Dream* (London: Allison and Busby, 1988), pp. 32–3.

30   Pfeil, 'Policiers Noirs', p. 525.

31   Himes, *The Big Gold Dream*, pp. 154–6.

32   Ibid., p. 156.

33   H. Bruce Franklin, *Prison Writing in America: the Victim as Criminal and Artist* (Westport, Conn.: Lawrence Hill, 1982), p. 208.

34   There are many books by black prisoners in the United States that have said this explicitly. George Jackson's *Soledad Brother* (New York: Coward–McCann, 1970), Eldridge Cleaver's *Soul on Ice* (New York: McGraw–Hill, 1968), Angela Davis's *If They Come in the Morning: Voices of Resistance* (New York: New American Library, 1971) and *The Autobiography of Malcolm X* (with the assistance of Alex Haley) (New York: Grove Press, 1965) are among them, and in his study *Prison Writing in America* Franklin gives them great prominence, as he does to Himes and Malcolm Braly. And there is no doubt that these are among the classics of contemporary American prison literature. But it seems to me that Himes, more than any of them, lays the issue out clearly, because he knows how to talk in the language of the oppressors, cut their rhetoric cold, and ask us what *we* do next. The others anticipate our answers and tell us what *they* will do next. Himes, as Pfeil argues, is 'something like submitting to a special kind of Rorscharch test: your reactions to the lurid images, actions and characters they hurl forth reveal at least as much about you as about Harlem or Himes' (Pfeil, 'Policiers Noirs', p. 523).

7

Riven Situations

The tightness and the nilness round that space
when the car stops in the road, the troops inspect
its make and number and, as one bends his face

towards your window, you catch sight of more
on a hill beyond, eyeing with intent
down cradled guns that hold you under cover

and everything is pure interrogation
until a rifle motions and you move
with guarded unconcerned acceleration –

a little emptier, a little spent
as always by that quiver in the self,
subjugated, yes, and obedient.

So you drive on to the frontier of writing
where it happens again. The guns on tripods;
the sergeant with his on-off mike repeating

data about you, waiting for the squawk
of clearance; the marksman training down
out of the sun upon you like a hawk.

And suddenly you're through, arraigned yet freed,
as if you'd passed from behind a waterfall
on the black current of tarmac road

past armour-plated vehicles, out between
the posted soldiers flowing and receding
like tree shadows into the polished windscreen.

Seamus Heaney, 'From the Frontier of Writing',
in *The Haw Lantern*

I

At the time of writing, most of the nations of the world live under conditions of military control or armed police surveillance. In such situations political opposition takes the form of violence. The causes of the violence are multiple – ethnic, religious, linguistic, ideological, colonial – but what is clear in most cases is that violence has become institutionalized as a means of control, of opposition, and therefore often of expression in everyday life. In such situations the writer may find himself in gaol, under house arrest or in exile, and the practice of writing may be seen by himself and many others as a highly political act. It is these circumstances that Seamus Heaney, himself an exile from Northern Ireland now living in Dublin, has called 'riven situations.'[1]

Recent examples are numerous, but some strategic ones are worth citing: South Africa from 1948 to the present, the Soviet Union from the early 1930s to the early 1980s, Israel since the late 1970s, Central Europe (Hungary, Czechoslovakia, Poland, Romania, Bulgaria) periodically from 1948 until the late 1980s, Ireland as a whole from the late nineteenth century to the 1920s, Northern Ireland in the 1970s and 1980s, Chile and Argentina in the 1970s and early 1980s, Germany and Italy in the 1930s and 1940s, East Germany since 1945, the Greece of the Colonels, Spain under Franco and Portugal under Salazar. (This book does not, of course, deal with the many cases in Asia and Africa; for Latin America, Chile and Argentina are significant because they represent interruptions in what had almost become a tradition of freedom of expression.)

Historically, any society in a state of civil war or revolution has provided examples of writers being incarcerated or 'banished', the most dramatic cases being the English Civil War of the seventeenth century, the French Revolution of the late eighteenth century, and the American Civil War of the nineteenth century, all of which also laid the groundwork for subsequent discussions on what freedom of expression entailed in a political and cultural sense. They also mark boundaries into what Camus called the Age of Rebellion. All of the riven situations fall firmly within that age and play out the tensions between rebellion and control.

It would be presumptuous to attempt in a single chapter to document the vast amount of literature that has emerged out of these situations, and no attempt is made to do that here. What I do attempt, however, is to provide a thematic way of looking at narratives so that the material, in more detailed readings, can begin to speak for itself. With some trepidation, I therefore offer a 'translation' of the translations, treading gingerly on dangerous ground covered with the shattered glass of other broken formulations.

II

Politico-economic definitions of what constitute military, fascist, communist, democratic, racist or oligarchic states may not help us much in considering the writer as prisoner. The riven situations may be all or none of these in a pure form, just as the writers themselves do not constitute any cohesive group except in being victims of a society that wanted to silence them. That they were not silenced – for a time at least – is why they are examined in this chapter. (Another chapter, primarily on the European Holocaust, tries to write the unspeakable about those who were silenced.) It is necessary, however, to indicate a few common characteristics of riven situations. They are situations in which a ruling (often secretive) elite wishes to prevent another group (whether a minority or a majority) from gaining power. They are situations in which freedom of speech and expression are severely curtailed as possible threats to the status quo. They are therefore situations in which, as the Czech writer Václav Havel put it, the population is forced into a situation of 'living a lie'.[2] And, finally, they are situations where violence by government and sometimes by the opposition becomes a fruitless way of conducting political dialogue. By these criteria it is possible to make the definition more flexible than Heaney seems to do. If I understand Heaney correctly, his definition refers to a people split apart, by which he seems to mean a cultural group split up by political divisions (as in Ireland, or in Poland between Poles in Poland and Poles in Russia and Germany, or Hungarians between those in Hungary and those in Romania, or, indeed, Germans in Germany's two contemporary halves). This, if taken alone, would lead us into another investigation, not the one which I think Heaney intends, which is about people being kept violently apart. (Otherwise we would have to consider other situations of diversion where writers are not locked up for what they say, as in Quebec, or Belgium, or in the Basque divide between Spain and France, however tenuous these accommodations remain.)

The writer who is exiled, gaoled or put under house arrest may therefore be a major political figure, or a writer whose work offends the regime, or someone who is simply caught up in a series of raids on opposition groups, or a suspected 'terrorist' who happens to be a writer, or someone who escapes abroad because he or she does not want to be part of the internal uncertainties or believes he or she can be more useful to the opposition outside the country than in it. A few – though in these situations it is unlikely – may become writers while in prison. The occasion of arrest or exile in general affects the nature of the writing as much as any specific local conditions of writing or politics.

The magazine *Index on Censorship* has been in the forefront of a campaign to expose censorship in all its forms throughout the world. Its late editor, George Theiner, himself an exile from Czechoslovakia, wrote that '"Unwholesome" books, unwelcome criticism, unsuitable authors – unsuitable because they are of the wrong colour or race, because they do not toe the party line, because they try to write the truth as they see it – all these will sooner or later find their way to the pages of *Index on Censorship*.'[3] In many ways the *Index*, magazines such as *Granta*, book clubs like *The Reader's Selection* and organizations like PEN and Amnesty International are the international consciences of the liberal world, in the tradition of Milton's *Areopagitica*, though without the politics. The apolitical stance is, of course, one of the strong advantages of these organizations in that it allows them to print material and campaign on behalf of individuals irrespective of their ideologies. As the Secretary-General of Amnesty International said at a conference in Toronto in 1981:

> We work for three things. First, we seek the immediate and unconditional release of all prisoners of conscience. Second, we try to ensure fair and prompt trials for all political prisoners. Third, we oppose torture and executions in all cases . . . Many of the prisoners of conscience for whom Amnesty International works are writers, journalists, or artists. Some of them are imprisoned because they tried to publish their works independently, defying state censorship. Some are in jail for manuscripts that were confiscated and that remain unpublished. Some have become victims because they tried to tell others of their prison experiences.[4]

PEN and Amnesty International have organized numerous conferences and published the transcripts of several symposia on such topics as 'The Writer and Human Rights' or 'Censorship in the World Today', and in all of them an uneasy tension exists over the definition of what politics is about, as the International conference of PEN held in New

York in 1987 indicated, where Norman Mailer's definition of 'great' writing was juxtaposed with a strong feminist critique, as well as some opposition from Third World writers.[5] In one respect the tension is based on disagreements over what constitutes 'writing', and in another on what constitutes 'politics', and it is these tensions that are at the heart of any examination of writing in riven situations.

The search for 'great' literature is, of course, a feature of our modern world, with a whole array of awards made for 'great' writing – Nobel Prizes, Booker Awards, Wang Awards, Pulitzer Prizes, Prix Concourt, Lenin Orders of Merit, to name the most obvious. And it is not surprising that the riven situations should be viewed as places to look for as the producers of such writing. But, as Joseph Skvorecky has noted,

> Sometimes one hears Western writers expressing envy for the writers who have come out of the cold or even for those who still pine away in the cold, for they – say the Western writers – have ready-made, dramatic subject matter. Writers in our tolerantly repressive society seem to be suffering from writer's block half the time. Some people, including some of the people expressing such opinions, think this is meant only as a joke, not to be taken seriously. But I wonder. Hemingway believed war to be the best school for a writer, and I think he was absolutely right – of course, on the condition that the writer survives the war, which cannot be guaranteed. Life in the cold certainly contributed greatly to the making of a Dostoevsky, a Solzhenitsyn, a Kundera, a Malparte, or a Gunther Grass – but it also killed Mandelstam, Babel, Pilnyak, von Ossietzky, Gramsci, Vladislav Vancura, Zavis Kalandra, and obviously hundreds, if not thousands of nameless artists.[6]

It is therefore important to distinguish between the motives that Westerners have for looking at these societies and their writers – even if some of the effects might seem to be beneficial – and the situations as they appear from inside. In his study *Orientalism*, the Palestinian/American critic Edward Said tried to document the ways that Western scholarship and politics created an 'Orient' and in doing so appropriated elements of 'Oriental' culture for its own ends.[7] There is little doubt that much of the work of PEN is of the same order, even if the purpose appears to be more open-endedly supportive, while that of *Index on Censorship* and Amnesty International is more rigidly impartial.

There is no initial reason why writing from prisons in South Africa or Poland should be treated any differently from writing from prisons in England or Canada, except that there is probably less of it and that what there is is of a relatively high literary standard. If the literacy rate among most of those who are imprisoned is relatively low, and if the literate have a good chance of being incarcerated, then the profile of 'good' writing will appear to be significant. In most of these societies the gap between the privileged (privilege including literacy) and the underpriviliged is particularly marked. Prison is frequently the place where the privileged writer makes his or her first (and often, only) contact with the illiterate underprivileged of his or her country. But even this is not a situation unique to prisons outside the West. Oscar Wilde, Victor Serge, Constance Lytton, Emma Goldman – all in various ways display the shock of recognition of, and the necessity for identification with, the underprivileged groups who populate the prisons. As Constance Lytton, the early twentieth-century suffragette, wrote of her companions in the exercise yard at Holloway Prison in London:

> I thought of them as beads in a necklace, detached, helpless, and useless, and wondered how long it would be before they were threaded together by means of the women's movement into a great organized band, self-expressive yet co-ordinated, and ruled by the bond of mutual service. The test of a chain's strength is in its weakest link. Where is our chain weakest? Not in the wretched victims who daily paced this yard, not in the debtor, the drunkard, the thief, the hooligan, the prostitute, the child murderer. These miseries were mostly the outcome of harmful and unjust laws . . . No, the weakest link in the chain of womanhood is the woman of the leisured class. Isolated and detached, she has but little sense of kinship with other women. For her there is no bond of labour, no ties of mutual service; her whole life is spent in the preservation of appearances.[8]

Thus the first, and perhaps the most significant, element of the writer in prison is the contact made with social criminality as an aspect of a nascent movement. The writer–prisoner is compelled to come to terms with other prisoners and assess his or her political attitudes as they relate to the conditions that place other prisoners in gaol. Because the writer was sent to prison for political reasons, it is by political identification that he or she is able to recognize the other prisoners, even if this identification is tinged with a certain elitism.

(As Lytton wrote of the 'leisured class': 'only when their eyes have been opened will their "influence" and "example" bear out a reasonable meaning of those words and their position of privilege make them worthy to lead.'[9])

The political prisoner, not surprisingly, behaves politically, wherever he or she is imprisoned, and unless there is systematic brainwashing involved, imprisonment becomes an occasion for clarifying and heightening the political philosophy, now with an exposure to people in their most extreme situations. Eighty years after Constance Lytton's imprisonment, we find Václav Havel writing about his experiences in Czech prisons:

> Almost every prisoner had a life story that was unique and moving. As I listened to these different accounts, I suddenly found myself in something like a 'pre-totalitarian' world, or simply in the world of literature. Whatever else I may have thought of my fellow-prisoners' colourful narratives, there is one thing they were not: they were not documents of totalitarian nihilisation. On the contrary, they testify to the rebelliousness with which human uniqueness resists its own nihilisation, and the stubbornness with which it holds to its own and is willing to ignore this negating pressure . . . prison tends to be a gathering place for people who stand out in one way or another, the unclassifiable misfits, highly individual people with all sorts of obsessions, people who are scarcely able to adapt . . .
>
> The wider the scope of those instruments by which the system manipulates, de-individualises and circumscribes life, and the more powerful its embrace, the more thoroughly everything truly unique is pushed to the periphery of 'normal' life and ultimately beyond it – into prison. The repressive apparatus that sends people to jail is merely an organic part and, in fact, a culmination of the general pressure totalitarianism exerts against life.[10]

Both Lytton and Havel make a connection between the people they met in gaol and the prospect of a better society outside it. In fact, the prisoners themselves are the people who contain the germs of the new society, though while Lytton sees this coming about through a parliamentary revolution led by an enlightened leisured class using working-class organization as its model, for Havel the possibilities are much less clear: 'I am merely trying to draw attention to the inconspicuous, unspectacular and undramatic war that life wages every day against nothingness.'[11] The reasons for this difference are not hard to find. They relate in part to the politics that were brought into the prison, in part to the authors' sense of what writing is for, and in part to a time-gap of eighty years which, in Europe at least, has affected the way that revolution is conceptualized. Lytton wanted to be 'a missionary to preach war in [this] peace-bedeadened country',[12] while Havel is 'merely attempting to say that the struggle of the story and of history to resist their own nihilisation is itself a story and as such belongs to history. It is our special metahistory.'[13] If Lytton, and many other political writers with her, wanted to change the conditions that gave rise to the writing of this story, Havel (and many anti-political writers like him)[14] is not so sure that this is possible. It is better to tell the story, the meta-story too, and leave the rest to history and the emergence of an opposition based on a critical 'civil society' unencumbered by the political apparatus. Havel elsewhere defined the 'civil society' as a 'parallel polis', which 'points beyond itself and only makes sense as an act of deepening one's responsibility to and for the whole, as a way of discerning the most appropriate locus for this responsibility'.[15]

Of all the writers in prison from situations of violent repression, these two represent contrasting ideal types, though there are infinite gradations between them. Personal survival is clearly an issue and how one survives is partly related to the strength of one's identification with movement, with writing and with self. Constance Lytton's identification with movement was near total: she assumed another name so that she would be taken as working-class, she went on hunger strike, she refused special medical treatment even though she had a serious heart condition; she did not write in prison because of her activities there, but composed the memoirs afterwards with her left hand because a stroke had paralysed her right side. Ultimately Lytton died because of that stroke: she is perhaps the clearest case of the will-to-martyrdom. Her writing is therefore part manifesto, part autobiography, part critique of prison conditions, demonstrating the transformation of English 'gentlewoman' (her father had been Viceroy of India) into militant activist.

The few political autobiographies that exist demonstrate similar features, where they are written *as* autobiographies, though, interestingly enough, not many are.[16] Most political writing from prison takes two forms: letters or diaries, and works of political philosophy, and it is essential to take the forms together in order to understand what political writing in prison means. I have discussed earlier aspects of Victor Serge and Rosa Luxemburg; here it might be useful to discuss another prominent case from Europe, that of Antonio Gramsci, imprisoned by Mussolini's Fascists in November 1926 until just before his death of tuberculosis in April 1937. For Gramsci's case is much more that of the political *intellectual* in prison than, as with Lytton, that of the political activist who happens to become a writer.

The documentation on Gramsci is extensive, and the debate around his political theory even more so. For the purpose of this account I rely on *Selections from the Prison Notebooks*, Paolo Spriano's *Antonio Gramsci and the Party: the Prison Years*, Guiseppe Fiori's *Antonio Gramsci: Life of a Revolutionary* and Teresa de Lauretis's *Technologies of Gender*.[17] From these sources it emerges that certain themes set Gramsci apart from many other incarcerated political writers of this century. Unlike most political prisoners, Gramsci was not able to make common cause with other prisoners; though he did try to set up a political education class, this resulted in such disagreement that he noted in a letter to his brother, Carlo: 'In order to stick rigidly to my absolutely correct behaviour in accordance with the necessities of prison life, I've come into conflict with some other prisoners and been forced to break off personal relationships.'[18]

In fact, Gramsci's writing in prison sometimes appears to have consisted of a series of hermetically sealed compartments. The prime work was his thirty-three prison notebooks, concerned largely with rethinking Italian politics on the basis of the Southern Question (i.e. the unification of northern Italy with the Kingdom of the Two Sicilies) and using Beneditto Croce, the major Italian phenomenological philosopher, as well as Machiavelli, to help define a Marxist theory of practice. His enormous contribution to political theory was bought at great cost. Not long after his imprisonment, Gramsci's wife, Julca (Julia) Schucht, moved to Moscow with their two children, to stay with her younger sister, Eugenia. The family was never reunited. Her letters to him were very infrequent and in 1930 she suffered a serious nervous breakdown. The correspondence between Gramsci and Julca was desultory and filled with the pathos of loneliness. On 13 January 1931 he wrote:

> Once, we promised each other we would always be frank and truthful in our relationship – do you remember? Why haven't we kept our promise? . . . Naturally I am always very happy to have a letter from you, it helps occupy my empty, meaningless hours, and breaks my isolation from life and the world. But I think you should write for your own sake too, as I feel that you too must be rather isolated.[19]

At the end of November 1931, he wrote to her:

> You have aggravated my isolation and made me feel it even
> more painfully. You often insist in your letters that 'we are
> closer together, stronger,' but it seems to me that this is less and
> less true, and that you know it very well, and are fighting off
> the knowledge even as you write the words.[20]

Much more powerful was his relationship with Julca's elder sister,
Tatiana (Tania), who regularly visited Gramsci while he was imprisoned at Turi, and moved close to the prison clinic at Formia in 1933.
Throughout his imprisonment, Tania provided constant encouragement and care, and Gramsci's most vital correspondence was with
her. It was with Tania that he shared problems about his health, his
writing, general prison conditions, and his personal relationship with
his family and the Party. (Formal contacts with the outside world –
petitions for release, relations with the Party, requests for books and
paper were handled mainly by the prominent economist, Piero
Sraffa.) It was Tania, not Julca, who was beside his bed when he died
on 27 April 1937.

Tania was the only person who was privy to *all* Gramsci's
correspondence and provided a substitute for all the fragmented
communications with the outside world; and yet even here Gramsci
was not sure. In June 1930 he wrote to Tania:

> But there's always you, you are bound to say. It is true. You
> are very good, and I love you greatly. Only there are some things
> for which one person can simply never take another's place.[21]

And a year later:

> Don't think that the feeling of being personally isolated is
> making me desperate, or inducing in me any other such tragic
> state of mind. The fact is that I have never felt the need of moral
> support from outside to live my own life, even in the worst of
> conditions; I require it even less today, when my will-power has
> become even stronger and more highly developed. The difference
> is, that whereas I used to feel almost proud of my isolation,
> now I feel all the meanness, all the aridity and narrowness of a
> life based exclusively on such efforts of will.[22]

In 1932 he put it bluntly:

Julia believes you are staying on in Rome and can't decide to go back to your parents because you can't decide to break off your (relatively) close relationship with me. I don't know if this is right, or if this is the only reason, or the one that is keeping you here. If it is, you ought to come to a decision, and leave right away.[23]

Thus even the relationship with Tania was potentially fractured. Gramsci's personal conflict was between being a self-disciplined hermit and being the 'Socratic' political figure sketched by Nicola Potenza in an article in a Paris-based Communist weekly in 1934:

If one was discussing a definite body of fact, Gramsci examined its various aspects, its various phases, its various relations with other facts, and its developments, until he saw it, and made others see it, in broad daylight . . . If a discussion had no set theme, he willingly let himself be carried along by our questions . . . and in the course of the argument he himself raised new problems.[24]

Just after his arrest in 1927, he had written to Tania about writing a project 'for ever' that would 'give focus to his inner life' but three years later he wrote to her that 'thinking "disinterestedly" or study for its own sake are difficult for me . . . I do not like throwing stones in the dark; I like to have a concrete interlocutor or adversary.'[25] His project was nothing less than rethinking the whole of Italian history and philosophy from the Roman Empire to the present, a project which also involved rethinking Marxist theory. The obstacles to doing this in prison were formidable. His health (he was effectively living on borrowed time throughout his imprisonment), the difficulties in obtaining basic research materials, the conditions within the prison and, later, the clinic at Formia all conspired to turn the grand project into a series of meticulous fragments:

To amuse myself, I imagine a racy beginning and ending, and a chain of irresistible arguments in between, like so many straight lefts in my opponent's eye. But I don't write down such irresponsible outbursts, of course. I confine myself to putting down weighty philological and philosophical discourses, the sort of thing of which Heine wrote: they were so boring that I fell alseep, but that proved so boring that I just had to wake up again.[26]

Of conditions in prison he wrote:

> You are not faced abruptly with an instant's choice on which
> to gamble, a choice in which you have to evaluate the alternatives
> in a flash and cannot postpone your decision. Here postponement
> is continual, and your decision has to be continually renewed.
> This is why you can say that something has changed. There is
> not even the choice between living for a day as a lion, or a
> hundred years as a sheep. You don't even live as a lion for a
> minute, far from it: you live like something far lower than that.
> Image of Prometheuss who, instead of being attacked by the
> eagle, is devoured by parasites. The Hebrews produced the
> image of Job. Only the Greeks could have imagined Prometheus,
> but the Hebrews were more realistic, more pitiless, and their
> hero more true to life.[27]

How does this directly affect what Gramsci actually wrote in the
Prison Notebooks? His appropriation of Job (rather than Prometheus
who was generally taken on the left, as by Shelley, to be the epitome
of the revolutionary's state) for the metaphor for his condition is
instructive. Job, it will be remembered, is tested by God through his
friends, through a plague of boils, through the loss of his family. The
false friends are used alternatively to test Job's belief in God and to
show that they have a higher sense of righteousness than he does.
His pride and his sense of righteousness break down so that in the
end God blesses Job and punishes his friends. It does not take much
imagination to read the Italian Communist Party Central Committee
as the three friends (one of the touch-and-go elements for Gramsci
while he was in prison was whether he should be expelled as a
'Trotskyist'), Julca and the children as Job's deserting family ('My
kinsmen have failed, and my familiar friends have abandoned me,'
wrote Job), and the *Prison Notebooks* as well as the various letters
as Job's rethinking of himself and his beliefs. ('The starting point of
critical elaboration,' Gramsci wrote in 'The Study of Philosophy', 'is
the consciousness of what one really is, and is "knowing thyself" as
a product of the historical process to date which has deposited in you
an infinity of traces, without leaving an inventory'.[28] The *Notebooks*
would be Gramsci's justification, and so they were. As Gramsci was
buried, Tania collected the thirty-three notebooks and took them to
Moscow, but it took a post-Stalinist Marxism to release the documents
so that they could begin the task for which Gramsci intended them.
One way of liberating Gramsci's work is to liberate it from a purely

male hagiography. The Gramsci industry has been almost entirely male-dominated: the publications of his *Notebooks*, his letters, the biographies by Fiori, Spriano, Cammett and Merrington, and most of the theorizing has been male-directed. Consequently, the discussion of the evolution of Gramsci's thought of its socio-political context has been seriously inhibited. Of Adele Cambria's *Amore come rivoluzione*, published in 1976, Teresa de Lauretis writes:

> Cambria's project was a political one: to rewrite history, inscribing in it the missing voices of women, and therefore to examine the relationships between the private and the public, love and revolution, personal/sexual/emotional needs and political militancy – relations which she sees as the moving forces of all revolutionary struggle.[29]

She adds that 'in restoring to Gramsci's epistolary monologue its real nature as dialogue, Cambria adds depth to the cultural image of a person whose complex humanity has been expediently stereotyped.'[30]

Cambria's book includes selections of letters from Julca, Tania and Eugenia to Gramsci, selections from Gramsci's own letters and other writing, quotations and statements from others involved in the events, and her own comments linking and interpreting these documents. In addition there is a play based on the documentation, with direction notes and a discussion of the production. In her account of Cambria's book, Teresa de Lauretis argues that the relationships among the three sisters, first with their father, Apollo Schucht, and then, later, with Gramsci, must be read as an interconnected whole.

> The early writings of Giulia and Eugenia reveal how deeply they had absorbed their father's late romantic–humanitarian values: a sense of duty toward the poor and dispossessed; contact with nature as a source of happiness, goodness and personal fulfillment; the love of children idealized as a pure unspoiled manifestation of Good Nature; a sentimental attachment to family as nest and shelter from the disorder and potential danger of the outside world.[31]

In their relationship with Gramsci they acted out these stereotypes. Eugenia 'played the male role as head of the household. While praising and mythicizing Gramsci as a revolutionary leader (she translated his writings for the Soviet workers), Eugenia increased the human distance between him and Giulia.' Tania, 'in defining herself as Giulia's representative, . . . slowly made herself indispensable to the man she loved . . . and gradually acquired a wife's right to husbandly gratitude, a wifely possessiveness, and the subtle power gained by female self-denial.'[32]

Giulia was dispossessed by her two sisters. De Lauretis's account of her is worth quoting at length.

> She is still alive, as far as we know, in some psychiatric hospital, where she has spent most of her life, imprisoned in her 'mental illness' as Antonio was in his cell. He burned in the hell of pain, captivity, and death, but he won – he is a protagonist of history. Giulia is still burning, quietly, bothering no-one, unnoticed, useless . . . [Cambria] sees Giulia as a sensitive, intelligent, gifted woman in which the traditional female socialization, with its emphasis on dependence, frailty, and childlike trust, found a most receptive terrain. Giulia did not relate intellectually to others or to her own experience. Women of her time were not supposed to. She needed direct sensuous contact with reality, her children, her man. She gave up her violin for her children and the Party.[33]

Deprived of her man, usurped by her sisters, she retreated inwards, 'in total passivity. That is precisely what is often diagnosed as madness in a woman.'[34]

Cambria's account, based on the letters by the three women and Gramsci, does not in any way denigrate what Gramsci said or wrote; rather, it retrieves it from a posture that would define theory as something that has no connection with practice. Gramsci himself had written in 1924 in a letter to Giulia, before his imprisonment:

> How many times have I asked myself whether it was possible to tie oneself to a mass without ever having loved anyone . . . whether one could love a collectivity if one hadn't deeply loved some single human beings . . . Wouldn't that have made barren my qualities as a revolutionary, wouldn't it have reduced them to pure intellectual fact, a pure mathematical calculation?[35]

De Lauretis and Cambria suggest not only the problems in answering Gramsci's own question, but also why the question has a persisting importance if the production and message of the text is to be understood.[36] We do not live in two separate and incompatible worlds, one for men and one for women. Rather, we live in one world which is shared. How it is shared is surely the issue.

III

Both Lytton and Gramsci were in prison for political acts and their commitment to political ideas was paramount, overwhelming their personal relationships and their interpretation of the prison condition. (Havel was a writer who became – necessarily – political because of his incarceration.) Before returning to the committed political activist as prisoner/writer, it is important to examine symptomatic cases of the creative writer who has been imprisoned for political reasons, because it is only by doing so that we can begin to rethink why we should in any case even bother to consider the riven situations, what is their significance.[37]

I have borrowed Seamus Heaney's terminology to head this chapter, partly because I share his sentiment that the 'note sounded by translated poetry from that world beyond – pitched intently and in spite of occupation, holocaust, concentration camps and the whole apparatus of totalitarianism – is so credible, desolating, and resuscitative'.[38] Here it is important to explore what that means in the light of the writing that has emerged out of Eastern and Central Europe and from South Africa.

The problem is: why bother to write, especially poetry or song, when being imprisoned or deported to outer Siberia? In many ways we can understand the political writer, because politics is his or her business, has become part of the everyday world. Politics is about the transformation of this world into something presumably better, or at least different. But poetry? I don't think we can answer this *purely* out of the poetry, because the poetry is the inscription on the wall, the voice of the hopeless, the graffiti of the angry, the echo that catches the sensibility from outside. Is it true that all we can do with poetry is to let it speak to us out of the cavernous recesses as long as we do not want to know more? (Witness hearing countercultural songs from the 1960s being used as advertising jingles in the 1980s.)

In order to listen to a voice we have to know which occasion brought us to the listening. There is little doubt in my case that Seamus Heaney provided the occasion (even though he accepts Nadezhda's story as the absolute version). I had read Osip Mandelstam before, much as one reads an obligatory author, out of general duty to a sense of culture, dipping into him from time to time and not getting very far. Reading Heaney on him is a bit like hearing Keats singing on discovering Chapman's Homer. Heaney speaks no Russian and discovers Mandelstam, like all of us must, out of translations and his own poetic sensibility.

Heaney's Mandelstam is two people, husband and wife, Osip and Nadezhda. He works with 'moving lips', she with a pen. Throughout his life he composed his poems verbally and committed them to memory. Nadezhda memorized them and wrote them down.[39] But it was Natalya, the lame schoolteacher who was the 'Mandelstams' companion in the last years of exile, who carried the 'Voronezh Poems' (those written between 1934 and 1937) into exile in Russia in 1942 after the German invasion, and who brought them back to life to be published in 1956. Her role in Mandelstam's work is similar, in many ways, to Tania Schultz's in the production of Gramsci's *Prison Notebooks*, though Natalya becomes the focus of Mandelstam's later poems as well as the courier of his final work; such may be the difference in the fates that affect women associated with poets and those associated with political activists. (In Gramsci's case, however, his wife was in Moscow throughout his incarceration; thus Tania *became* his 'wife', and therefore, in a sense, taken for granted. In Mandelstam's case, Nadezhda was with him all the time, and her *Memoirs* refeer to Natalya sporadically, as if to a casual acquaintance. Nadezhda, however, celebrated her life with Osip in two books, which stand on their own literary merit: Natalya is remembered for what she did and what she became in Mandelstam's later poetry.)

But Mandelstam is not merely the poet of exile and prison, and if there are two Osip Mandelstams (before exile and after) they are Mandelstams who interconnect (in spite of periods when there was no speaking/writing) in the imagery of the apprehension and the realization that

> Everything cracks and shakes.
> The air trembles with smiles.
> No one word's better than another;
> the earth moans with metaphors.[40]

That poem was written in 1923, but even earlier, in 1911, he wrote:

> And over the evening forest
> the bronze moon climbs to its place.

> Why has the music stopped?
> Why is there such silence?[41]

The early, pre-incarcerated Mandelstam, prefigures the pending holocaust, but in the juxtaposition of spoken/sung words and archaeological/architectural excavation. The poems on 'Haggia Sophia', 'Notre Dame' and 'The Lutheran' form a triptych which connects the archaeology of knowledge and the architecture of belief, and questions the permanence of both.

> All ages take example from Justinian's
> when from her shrine in Ephesus Diana
> allowed the plunder of one hundred seven
> green marble pillars for the gods of others.[42]

In 'Notre Dame' ('In the place where a Roman judge judged an alien people there stands a basilica'), he contemplates the edifice:

> The more attentively, O stronghold Notre Dame, I studied thy monstrous ribs, the more frequently I thought: some day I too will create beauty from thy cruel weight.[43]

But to create the new requires a recognition that human energy is already weakened by previous burdens of building:

> To liberate the captive age,
> to make a start at the new world
> the passages of knotted days must be connected by a flute.
> That's the age that rocks the wave
> with human melancholy
> and in the grass the adder breathes
> to the age's golden measure.
>
> And the buds will go on swelling
> and the sprint of green will burst,
> but your backbone has been shattered,
> my beautiful, pitiful age.
> Cruel and weak, you'll look back
> smiling senselessly
> like an animal that used to be supple
> on the tracks of your own paws.[44]

This poem ('The Age'), written in 1923, more or less concludes the period of prefigurement/apprehension (also, as Nadezhda argued in *Hope Abandoned*, a period of consolidation). A long silence follows, to be broken in the early 1930s by the sound of

> a prisoner intoning a rough song, at the hour
> when dawn draws the first thread, outside the jail.[45]

The singer composes a 'Stalin Epigram':

> Our lives no longer feel ground under them.
> At ten paces you can't hear our words.
>
> But whenever there's a snatch of talk
> it turns to the Kremlin mountaineer,
>
> the ten thick worms of his fingers,
> his words like measures of weight,
>
> the huge laughing cockroaches on his top lip,
> the glitter of his boot-rims.[46]

The singer is arrested, of course, but if the early work prefigured of what would happen, the happening itself shattered the early architectural/geological images. With Stalin climbing the Kremlin, Mandelstam's sense of architecture leads him to build roads. ('I want this thinking body . . . to be changed into a thoroughfare, a country;' 'What street is this? / Mandelstam Street. / What the hell kind of name is that? / No matter which way you turn it / it comes out crooked.'[47] To understand the architecture, one has to have hope in the soil and the water beneath it, remembering the natural origins of the matter of architectural monuments. ('The cities kneel by the river on oaken knees'.) Mandelstam's reaffirmation of himself (in spite of or because of his exile) is unmetaphysical, material, but a materiality which recognizes the architecture of nature that has to be reclaimed, if only we can do so:

> So in cathedrals of crystals not found on earth
> the prudent spider of light
> draws the ribs apart and gathers them again
> into one bundle.
>
> And gathered together by one thin beam
> the bundles of pure lines give thanks.

One day they will meet, they will assemble
like guests with visors up.

and here on earth, not in heaven,
as in a house filled with music,
if only we don't offend them, or frighten them away.
How good to live to see it!⁴⁸

Hence the roads, the plough-furrows on the black earth, the lost ways in the sky, and the girl (Natalya) 'limping like a clock on her left leg . . . What's holding her back/drives her on./What she must know is coming/drags at her foot.'⁴⁹

In her account of their lives together, Nadezhda writes where Osip works 'from the voice'. As he wrote in his autobiographical essay, *Fourth Prose*:

I have no manuscripts, no notebooks, no archives. I have no handwriting because I never write. I alone in Russia work from the voice while all around the bitch-pack writes. What the hell kind of writer am I!? Get out you fools!⁵⁰

Not only does Nadezhda transcribe the voice into notebooks, she composes the lives into memoirs where everything that she can remember, to the minutest detail, is recorded. As Heaney writes,

As a writer, Nadezhda possesses a quality of tenaciousness, a ledger-maker's appetite for entering everything, making a record as unremitting as it is unadorned. The details remain literal and clear as rivets brightened by the punch: the uneaten egg that had been borrowed as a treat for Akhmatova only to sit on the table all night during a search of the apartment; the marks that Stalin's greasy fingers left on books he was lent . . .⁵¹

Although Nadezhda might seem, as the blurb on the jacket of my copy of *Hope against Hope* says, merely 'his devoted wife', it is clear from reading the book that, although she was loving and devoted to her husband, her account is as much her account of herself as it is hers about him. The difference between her writing and his is not simply the difference between poetry and prose, or between the voice and the pen, it is the difference of two different lives, different sensibilities, perhaps, even, different genders, but differences caught up in the same moments of space and time. In spite of his tough, materialist imagery, Osip used that imagery to project possibilities of alternative worlds, using comparisons from classical literature, philosophy, cinema, religion, architecture. Throughout her memoirs, Nadezhda is more immediate, down-to-earth, and (dare one say it?) practical. With Osip it is all in the head; but it is Natalya, not Nadezhda, who provides the imagery which the head carries with it as the body is escorted to the grave.

An example of Nadezhda's practicality is presented by her account of the last months in Voronezh when it was essential that they both find some alternative means of livelihood. (Osip had been making some money from translations but this source had dried up.)

> My plan was summed up by the word 'cow' . . . Thanks to the vagaries of our economic system, a family could support itself for many years by keeping a cow. Millions lived in wretched huts, feeding themselves from the products of their tiny plots of land (on which they grew potatoes, cabbage, cucumbers, beets, turnips and onions) and their cow . . . A cow would have saved us, and I was sure I would be able to learn how to milk it. We would have merged with the background somewhere, living very obscurely and never leaving our house . . . M.'s plan was the reverse of mine – instead of merging with the background, he wanted to attract attention to himself. He believed that if only he could induce the Union of Writers to arrange a public reading of his poetry, then it would be impossible to refuse him work.[52]

Both plans failed, for different reasons which need not concern us here. What is important are the quite different strategies, practically and in composition. Nadezhda's commonsensical account must be set against Osip's poetry which must have been ringing in her head as she made her practical suggestion:

> How good the fat earth feels on the plowshare.
> How still the steppe, turned up to April.
> Salutations, black earth. Courage. Keep the eye wide.
> Be the dark speech of silence laboring.[53]

And yet, after both lives are over, voices sound as one.[54]

These two (connected) voices provide the necessary link between that of the committed political prisoner and the reflective voice of the writer struggling to know why he or she should be committed to a particular course of action at all. It is difficult, in any sense, to find a *politics* in the Mandelstams, apart from the everyday politics of wanting to be left alone to do their thing. But they were dragged into politics, by the Revolution, by industrialization, by their Jewishness, and ultimately by Stalin. Their story is that of the politicization of the writer under conditions of extreme pressure. In semiological terms they initially thought of themselves as being the signifiers, only to discover after the Revolution that they had become signified (hence Osip's confusion over making money by asking the Writers' Union to set up a poetry reading). What the Mandelstam story tells us is that a politics of the everyday becomes necessary after politics has taken over. The poet becomes the unacknowledged legislator – not of the world, but of his imagination and of his immediate habitable community.

This is a far cry from Constance Lytton and Antonio Gramsci, but shows an alternative side of the prisoners who use their time in gaol to create philosophies for the transformation of the world. What none of these have is the combination of a sense of political commitment, a reflexive sense of prison life in general, and a commitment to being a creative writer. The ambiguity that follows from that dilemma is most clearly seen in the work of the South African writer Breyten Breytenbach.

IV

On the face of it, South Africa presents the clearest case of a morally clean cause. A minority of whites hold all the instruments of power which deny the blacks and other races their part in managing the country. The apparatus of power is such that violence is institutionalized to *prevent* the blacks from gaining any measure of control. Thus any kind of resistance to the government and its clique would seem to be justified, and, indeed, in the work of most opposition writers in South Africa it is so justified. Most prison autobiographies from South Africa read like prisoner-of-war accounts or spy stories, where the incarcerated are engaged in a battle of wits with their captors. The most notable of these are probably *The Prison Diary of Albie Sachs*, D. M. Zwelonke's novel *Robben Island* and Ruth First's *117 Days*. In First's book (written in 1965 after she had been 'detained' under the 90-day Act) all of the ingredients of interrogation, torture, attempted brainwashing (suggestive of Orwell's *1984* or Koestler's *Darkness at Noon*) are present, except that unlike Winston Smith or

Rubashov, First is unflinching in her dedication to her cause. (She remained unflinching: in 1982 she was assassinated in Mozambique by a letter-bomb planted by the South African secret police.)

> I could now see unravelled the campaign of attack against me. Solitary confinement for an undetermined period was the basic requirement. Nel would pay routine but uninterested visits, except he would vary his introduction to each interview with a slice of good or bad news ('You have not been charged in the Rivonia trial! or 'Your children are leaving the country!') to measure my reaction. From neglect by him I would then be introduced to the more concentrated attention of Viktor, when three months was almost up and I must be feeling the accumulated effects of so many weeks in isolation. But before he appeared with his apparent concern to spare me the worst of eventualities, I had to be subjected to carefully planted hints about a prosecution for possession of a copy of a banned magazine, which would be an enormous relief compared with the ordeal of the Rivonia trial or another spell of detention . . . He had come to make a deal but withdrew, disappointed, when I turned the proposition down, disappointed at my stubborn refusal to save myself. Enter the villains to make the phony release and the rearrest, but not before a visit from the children, eager and expectant for my release, had given me another emotional jar.[55]

First's account is clear, and is written as a document of (necessary) personal hardship on the route to collective victory. ('Every new stretch of prison for a group of political prisoners gave birth to a new batch of freedom songs. Gaol spells had not broken us; they had helped to make us.')[56] Much of First's book is taken up with the strategies of the captors and their effectiveness on the prisoners:

> The key judgement was when to apply really stiff pressure, at what moment the victim was emotionally most fragile. People's 'cracking-points' did vary; some were demoralized quite early in their detention; others took longer; many lasted out altogether. It was so difficult to know beforehand who would fare well or badly. Men holding key positions in the political movement, who had years of hard political experience and sacrifice behind them, cracked like egg-shell. Others, with quiet, reticent, self-effacing natures, who had been woolly in making decisions and

slow to carry them out, emerged from long spells of isolation shaken but unbroken.[57]

All of this is part of a longer tradition of (mainly psychological) literature, concerned with brainwashing and individual survival, the philosophical version of which is displayed in Maurice Merleau-Ponty's classical study of Koestler, Bukharin and Trotsky, *Humanism and Terror*, while the more detailed case-studies are explored in the work of Robert Jay Lifton, notably in *Thought Reform and the Psychology of Totalism* and *The Future of Immortality*.[58] The connecting thread linking these approaches is both the psychology of survival in political prisons *and* the moral grounds on which opposition to state terror must itself be terrorist. The *moral* grounds on which revolutionary violence is tolerable are expressed thus by Merleau-Ponty:

> He who condemns all violence puts himself outside the domain to which justice and injustice belong. He puts a curse upon the world and humanity – a hypocritical curse, since he who utters it has already accepted the rules of the game from the moment that he has begun to live. Between men considered as pure consciousness there would indeed be no reason to choose. But between men considered as the incumbents of situations which together compose a single *common situation* it is inevitable that one has to choose – it is allowable to sacrifice those who according to the logic of their situation are a threat and to promote those who offer a promise of humanity.[59]

This argument is double-edged, of course, and in messy situations like South Africa, Israel/Palestine, or the Six Counties of Ireland, the self-generating violence on both sides may seem less of a 'promise of humanity' and more like a series of persistent vendettas and counter-vendettas, with each party generating its own narratives of survival and transcendence. In the face of this our language begins to dissolve its sense of certitude, without necessarily offering solutions to the persisting moral dilemmas. The issues themselves remain, and no post-modernist apocalyptic dismissal helps much in resolving them.[60] But the sense of thoughtful frustration has become as much a part of our literature of political incarceration as the staccato remembrances of past certainties; so much so that it is wise to end this chapter with a consideration of the most celebrated post-modern prison writer of all. As the committed political writer *manqué*, Breyten Breytenbach is the one writer (or perhaps with Milan Kundera and Václav Havel in Czechoslovakia) who confronts writing, political action and incarceration head-on.

Breytenbach's writing since his imprisonment in 1975 (for trying to recruit two trade unionists inside South Africa for work with the opposition-in-exile) is masterfully parodic. This is true of his 'mirrornotes of a novel', *Mouroir*, of his 'autobiography', *True Confessions of an Albino Terrorist*, of his various collections of poems and short stories, and even of his 'travel book', *A Season in Paradise*, an account of an earlier visit to South Africa.[61] By saying that the work is 'masterfully parodic', I am, of course, suggesting that the works are more than parody and that Breytenbach, who is familiar with a very extensive literature on incarceration, is able to blend this acquaintanceship with his own experiences and into his own art. In reading Breytenbach one is frequently not aware of the extent to which his work is either mimetic or parodic, because the composite effect is that of self-reflective autobiography. In some cases the parody is fairly explicit, as when in *Mouroir* he reveals 'certain papers left in my possession' which relate to a proposal for 'digging – erecting? – creating – the grave of the Unknown Poet (UP) in Rotterdam'.[62] The pseudonymous author goes on in a tragi-comic explanation:

> *Why for a poet?* We all know of examples in the world of the grave for the unknown soldier. Apart from perhaps wishing to piously respect the unknown, these graves speak to us of patriotism, of nationalism, even of praising the military virtues. Are they not also intended to increase the cohesiveness of the nation state? Are they not used sometimes to whitewash the past? The tombstones of history . . . For all soldiers are anonymous. (I am not speaking of the generals: have you ever come across the grave of the unknown general or the unknown dictator?) Indeed, it is not the soldiers who build cenotaphs or monuments to the unknown number, but the politicians who ever survive indestructibly. At the other end of the scale, but it is really the same end, I've heard of the statue commemorating the anonymous political prisoner. He doesn't need that, and the least we can do for him is to give him the face he struggled for. (Is the anonymous torturer ever celebrated other than by the poisonous stone in his chest?) And Paul has written of a pedestal to the unknown and absent god . . .
>
> For us it is different. Poets aren't gods, neither are they absent. Poets aren't incarcerated or tortured for their poetry – at least

not very often: the powers that be, have been, shall be, prefer to lobotomize their poetry, and it is a more refined form of torture. Poets aren't a nation. Poets aren't a class. Workers do it/students do it/the bourgeois do it/even kings and beggars do it/so let's do it . . . Let's talk tough! And yet we are everywhere, taking our maggots for a walk . . .

We are conceiving of a living grave for the poet, be he dead or alive or in limbo.[63]

The piece bristles with parody, with direct literary allusions, and even with autobiographical ones. The parody, however, is what is strikingly present.

In most of Breytenbach's work the parodic takes more the form of the consciousness of other works and its appropriation into his context. His great work directly related to his prison experiences is undoubtedly *True Confessions of an Albino Terrorist*, where the title itself is parodic (but so is *Mouroir*, of Michel Butor, and *Season in Paradise*, of Rimbaud), and it may be useful to examine some of the major elements of this novel because it reflects in large measure the problems of literature coming to terms with political commitment, imprisonment and its own purpose.

The structure of the novel takes the form of a report by Breytenbach to the Investigator, whom we discover during the course of the book is someone appointed by a revolutionary black South African movement to examine his case. ('I must warn you that the system by which we are trying to replace the present one will grind us down, *me and you*, as inexorably.') Thus the parodic nature of the text is established at the beginning. Breytenbach is in the role of a Trotsky or Bukharin explaining his case to, say, a Gorbachev, or, perhaps, given the second half of the title, a (white) Marcuse explaining his case to a government of Black Panthers. More than this, however, Breytenbach is a composite of all prisoners, from Nat Turner to Václav Havel, who were concerned that their prison experiences and their political commitment should not be distorted. Above all (as the excerpt from *Mouroir* already quoted makes clear), he is concerned with the ambiguity of his profession as a writer.[64] In *A Season in Paradise* he invokes Kafka's short story, 'A Report to an Academy': 'I am not appealing for any man's verdict,' wrote Kafka, 'I am only imparting knowledge, I am only making a report.'[65] In his own version, he wonders whether perhaps he ought to stop writing, 'because I have become attached to an absence; because I occupy a false and loose position within the Afrikaans community and the Afrikaans literature.'[66]

Such a complex sense of who is writing the book, and for whom, necessarily affects the entire pattern of writing. Like a spy (we are all 'God's spies', says King Lear to Cordelia), the author has many names ('a name is exactly the absence of definition');[67] he writes in several languages (Afrikaans, English, French) and speaks more. The book itself, although a 'written' text, was in fact dictated to Breytenbach's Vietnamese wife, Hoang Lien (Yolande).

> The document itself took shape from the obsessive urge I experienced during the first weeks and months of my release to talk talk talk, to tell my story and all the other stories . . . My wife typed the tapes. I used her transcripts as 'rough copy'. These I would blacken, add to, delete from, change about – and she would retype a clean version for me to go over again if needed. Therefore I was in the first instance, in all intimacy, talking to her . . .[68]

Thus even 'Mr Investigator' had his origins in a Vietnamese woman, just as this autobiographical *briccolage* had its origins in an attempt to produce a 'political' text: 'It was my intention to produce a political text – if it turned out to be more literary than expected it can only be because I couldn't help it. It is the lability of the job, it is the seductiveness and the *life* of the world.'[69]

As a former prisoner, Breytenbach is very conscious of the importance of oral storytelling which lies at the heart of prison narrative and pushes expression back to the 'frontier of writing', in Heaney's words. Prison requires that we rethink *all* of our experiences and *all* of the language that we are accustomed to use to give meaning to them. His book, therefore, comes at the issues from several angles, and is in many respects consistent with Bakhtin's sense of the Mennipean discourse. This involves examining the nature of writing itself (pp. 154–78), the stories that other prisoners tell (pp. 164–71), a perception of himself as a counter-spy and hence the spy story as a genre and indication of a way of life (pp. 40–5 and 91–119), the perception of power and freedom (pp. 308–9 and *passim*), various sets of relationships between prisoners and guards, prison and the outer world, blacks and Afrikaaners, and ultimately all victims and all police/spy/secret society organizations (especially pp. 339–40). In appendices to the book he also includes poetry, a manifesto, accounts of torture and of South African prisons, a statement on being

Afrikaans, another one on the African National Congress's struggle, and an indication of how the book was put together. Thus, in most respects, Breytenbach has covered the possible angles and has deliberately tried to provide us with the material we need to engage with his story. In this respect the book is quite unique among prison accounts (though traces of its style are found in Mandelstam's *Journey to Armenia* and some anthologies put together by prisoners suggest a similar route).[70] The important issue is: what do we learn from Breytenbach's book which is different from what we learn from all of the other political and prison accounts?

At the beginning of this section I suggested that Breytenbach was a 'post-modern' writer. In one respect, all prison writing is post-modern, or post-classical or post-Renaissance. (Post-gothic it is not: if there is one period style which forever captures the texture of prison experience and writing anywhere it is surely 'gothic'; which is perhaps why Piranesci's etchings – and their contemporary versions by M. C. Escher – have become the epitome of the architectural sense of incarceral loops).[71] Every prison writer writes against the grain of the dominant language that provided the rules of enclosure. The issue with Breytenbach is surely whether he writes effectively against the grain, or whether his writing is a confirmation of the spirit of the age that brought about his incarceration.

This question is not as tautological as it sounds. At one level everyone writes out of the climate of their own age: without those intellectual, social and economic conditions there would be no writing. In that sense Breytenbach's writing is 'post-modernistic'. It reflects on those aspects of culture that display a loss of values, particularly those values associated with the era of the 'modern' – rationality, science and causality, faith in human emancipation, progress and the class struggle. It displays a distrust in any institutions that have been established to embody those values. And it concludes that the great 'meta-narratives' of the modern world hold no faith for the future.[72] The only realistic strategy of the present is a decentered politics, based in large measure on Michel Foucault's conception that to have knowledge is to have power, and therefore that the apprehension of knowledge and making connections between different knowledge sites is the basis of any viable politics. What 'knowledge' means, and how the connections might be made in order to create any strategy for action, is the salient point of any political philosophy.

The agendas adopted in face of this analysis are varied, ranging from a conservative/neo-Fascist complacency in believing that market forces contain within themselves the only acceptable logic (the only 'meta-narrative' that continues to command institutionalized support), through to an attempt to rethink the essential pedagogical tools to maintaining a modern culture (the work of Alan Bloom and E. D. Hirsch stands as a popular academic American version of this reaction), to an apocalyptic sense that all is lost because the mass media, having now gained the ascendancy in controlling the manufacture and distribution of knowledge, have turned reality into its facsimile.

Breyten Breytenbach's writing stands in sharp contrast to these positions. In many respects, precisely because he speaks from prison experience and out of a personal sense of the 'riven situations', Breytenbach cannot adopt the conservative/apocalyptic complacency of many of the post-modernist writers. If writers like Ruth First and D. M. Zwelonke from South Africa are modernists, employing a righteous/rationalist stand against the distortions of institutionalized madness, Breytenbach, the Afrikaans who dares to be counted among the blacks, is a post-modernist with a difference. His price for being a political activist is a recognition by the political movement that his own life is bound up with being a writer and an artist (Breytenbach was a well-known painter long before he was recognized as a writer). This recognition entails a dialogue between the movement and his own creative post-modernistic uncertainty, a recognition by the movement that the creation of an alternative society is one that must be predicated on openness and tolerance. In 'A Note for Azania' (Azania is the name he uses for a future South Africa) he writes:

> Strive for the growing realization, through heritage and through struggle, of one South African cultural identity composed of an incredibly rich variety of sources and expressions . . . Realize that ruptures can be flashes of comprehension. Do yourself a selfish favour: if you want to remain whole, recognize the humanity of your enemy. But recognize also that there are irreconcilable interests. Don't make yourself a fool by killing him. No cause can justify the destruction of life.[73]

The echo of Central Europe is clear. Adam Michnik wrote this from the Gdansk prison in 1985:

> Sooner or later, but I think sooner, we shall leave the prisons and come out of the underground onto the bright square of freedom. But what will we be like then?
> I am afraid not of what they will do to us, but of what they

can make us into. For people who are outlaws for a long time may feed on their own traumas and emotions which, in turn, strangle their reason and their ability to see reality. Even the best people can be demoralized by years of persecution and the shock of regaining their lost stature. I pray that we do not return like ghosts who hate the world, cannot understand it, are unable to live in it. I pray that we do not change from prisoners into prison guards.[74]

The messages from the political prisons of Central and Eastern Europe, Ireland, Fascist Italy and South Africa all have an urgent concern with the creation of a humane society, and that the struggle against terrorism and incarceration should not lead to the prisoners, on release, introducing yet another form of terror. These prisoners are conscious of other situations where, after their release, ex-prisoners went on a rampage, killing off their guards and their erstwhile comrades alike. They are conscious of Stalin's 'purges' and Gulags, of Hitler's Holocaust, of Mussolini's use of *ad hoc* measures to silence opposition, of the Boers (for whom the concentration camps were created by the British), of an Ireland which James Joyce described as 'an old sow devouring its own farrow', of an Ezra Pound who, after his incarceration was over, could go back and *still* give the Fascist salute. They are conscious of earlier sagas of prisoners becoming judges: the English, American, Haitian, French, Russian Revolutions. Their memories run deep, but they struggle to find a reason why this time might be different.

Utopia has returned to the prison cell from which it emerged, but now with a consciousness that it was the writer who transmitted the message. Today the writer, shorn of the ambition to command but conscious that there is a duty to transmit, knows that there is a task to return to the roots of writing in the lives of those who are also incarcerated. The modern utopias were monologic, hence could be taken over by any mechanistically minded wind-bag who wanted to impose his will on 'the people'. The machine was all. The new writing – and our reading of that writing – is conscious of the processes that called it into being.

There is a section in *True Confessions*, called 'The Writer Destroys Time', in which Breytenbach recounts the writing he was obliged to do while in prison. This included acting as a clerk for the prison authorities, writing letters on behalf of other prisoners, being a scribe for guards, writing *Mouroir*. He finds, as he says, 'his own function in terms of his usefulness to the inmate community . . . I was the scribe'.[75] And he comments, later: 'I realized how many unnecessary words one produces in the course of a day. Not even counting those scurrying around inside, unuttered, like ants . . .'[76] It is a retrieval of Kafka, the actuary, for our sense of politics. It is a savage reminder of Mandelstam, who refused to write. It is a confirmation that *The Trial* was written in the margin of an accountant's Book of Death.

Meanwhile, the manifesto at the end of the book against, and on behalf of which, Breytenbach writes his texts.

NOTES

1 This term evolves in Heaney's collection of essays, *The Government of the Tongue* (London: Faber, 1988) and is a recurrent theme of his poems; see especially *North* (London: Faber, 1975) and *The Haw Lantern* (London: Faber, 1987).
2 This argument is developed by Havel in the collection of essays *The Power of the Powerless* (Boston: E. J. Sharp, 1985); see especially pp. 22–96.
3 George Theiner, ed., *They Shoot Writers, Don't They?* (London: Faber, 1984), pp. 14–15.
4 Toronto Arts Group for Human Rights, ed., *The Writer and Human Rights* (Toronto: Lester and Orpen Dennys, 1983), pp. 3–5.
5 Precisely because the theme of the 1987 conference was 'The Writer and Power', with George Bush as the guest of honour, the divisions were bound to be evident. Mailer organized the conference as a demonstration of Western male writerly power, making it look more like the old Congress for Cultural Freedom than an impartial 'liberal' forum.
6 Toronto Arts Group, *The Writer and Human Rights*, p. 134. Although Skvorecky is right *in principle*, there is a different way of looking at these comparisons which has less to do with seeing the incarcerated writer as living in an enviable situation than in seeing writers who live in the West as living in a very special one. Talking about current influences of Eastern European writing on English writing, Seamus Heaney has this to say:

> Many contemporaries writing in English have been displaced from an old at-homeness in their mother tongue and its hitherto world-defining poetic heritage . . . I am reminded of Stephen Dedalus's enigmatic declaration that the shortest way to Tara was via Holyhead, implying that departure from Ireland and inspection of the country from the outside was the surest way of getting to the core of an Irish experience. Might we not nowadays affirm, analogously, that the shortest way to Whitby, the monastery where Caedmon sang the first Anglo-Saxon verses, is via Warsaw and Prague? To put it more directly, contemporary English poetry has become aware of the insular and eccentric nature of English experience in all the literal and extended meaning of those adjectives. England's island status, its off-centre European positioning, its history of non-defeat and non-invasion since 1066,

these enviable and (as far as the English are concerned) normative conditions have ensured a protracted life within the English psyche for the assumption that a possible and desirable congruence exists between domestic and imagined reality. (Heaney, *The Government of the Tongue*, pp. 40–1)

7   Edward W. Said, *Orientalism* (New York: Random House, 1978).
8   Lady Constance Lytton, *Prison and Prisoners* (London: Women's Press, 1988), pp. 134–5.
9   Ibid., p. 135.
10 Václav Havel, 'Stories and Totalitarianism', *Index on Censorship*, 17, 3 (1988), p. 18.
11 Ibid., p. 21. This should be contrasted with Milovan Djilas's observations:

The reader should not be amazed that the solidarity I found in prison was made easier by my being isolated with murderers and, more particularly, with old ones. Unlike pickpockets and all kinds of petty thieves who are, almost without exception, cowards, stoolpigeons, and malingerers, and unlike embezzlers – all of whom put on an independent front while in fact being servilely 'cooperative' with the prison administration, and unlike burglars – the knights of the prison, who are on the whole merely rebellious and not informers – murderers are the most tolerable, the most patient, and most honourable part of the prison population. (Milovan Djilas, *Of Prisons and Ideas* (New York: Harcourt Brace Jovanovich, 1986), p. 81)

12 Lytton, *Prison and Prisoners*, p. 137.
13 Havel, 'Stories and Totalitarianism', p. 21.
14 The term 'anti-politics' was coined by the Hungarian writer György Konrad in his book of the same name, occupying a space somewhere the political and the apolitical:

A society does not become politically conscious when it shares some political philosophy, but rather when it refuses to be fooled by any of them. The apolitical person is only the dupe of the professional political, whose real adversary is the antipolitician. It is the antipolitician who wants to keep the scope of government policy (especially that of its military apparatus) under the control of civil society. (György Konrad, *Anti-Politics* (New York: Harcourt Brace Jovanovich, 1984), p. 227)

It is the debate over what exactly civil society is that is at the core of this definition. See John Keane, *Democracy and Civil Society* (London: Verso, 1988).
15 Václav Havel, *The Power of the Powerless* (Boston, E. J. Sharp, 1985), p. 81.
16 Some of the most notable are Victor Serge, *Memoirs of a Revolutionary* (Oxford: Oxford University Press, 1963); Leon Trotsky, *My Life* (New York: Russell and Russell, 1963); Emma Goldman, *Living My Life*, 2 volumes (New York: Dover, 1934); Elizabeth Gurley Flynn, *The Alderston Story: My Life as a Political Prisoner* (New York: International Publishers, 1963); Angela Davis, ed., *If They Come in the Morning: Voices of Resistance* (New York: New American Library, 1971); Milovan Djilas, *Memoir of a*

Revolutionary and *Land without Justice* (though *Of Prisons and Ideas* is much more specific). The most notorious prison autobiography-as-manifesto is, of course, Adolf Hitler's *Mein Kampf* (New York: Houghton Mifflin, 1973), which bears no traces of a will-to-martyrdom, but which rather uses personal biography in the service of a will-to-power. Also, Hitler did not come from a well-off family and most of his 'autobiographical evidence' is fictitious.

17 Antonio Gramsci, *Selections from the Prison Notebooks* (London: Lawrence and Wishart, 1971); Paolo Spriano, *Antonio Gramsci and the Party: the Prison Years* (London: Lawrence and Wishart, 1979); Guiseppe Fiori, *Antonio Gramsci: Life of a Revolutionary* (London: New Left Books, 1970); Teresa de Lauretis, *Technologies of Gender: Essays on Theory, Film, and Fiction* (Bloomington and Indianapolis: Indiana University Press, 1987).
18 Fiori, *Antonio Gramsci*, p. 258.
19 Ibid., p. 259.
20 Ibid., p. 260.
21 Ibid., p. 248.
22 Ibid., p. 265.
23 Ibid., p. 268.
24 Spirano, *Antonio Gramsci and the Party*, pp. 100–1.
25 Gramsci, *From the Prison Notebooks*, p. x.
26 Fiori, *Antonio Gramsci*, p. 266.
27 Gramsci, *From the Prison Notebooks*, p. xciii.
28 Ibid., p. 324.
29 de Lauretis, *Technologies of Gender*, pp. 86–7.
30 Ibid., p. 87.
31 Ibid.
32 Ibid., p. 88.
33 Ibid., p. 89.
34 Ibid.
35 Ibid., p. 87.
36 The major problem is conceiving of a feminist as opposed to a masculinist approach is well expressed by de Lauretis when she argues for a cultural and contextual approach to writing as opposed to, for example, Gelfland, who argues for a specifically womanly one:

> We can perhaps develop a *feminist theory of textual production* which is neither a *theory of women's writing* nor just a theory of textuality. In other words, it is not a matter of finding common elements among the texts written or produced by women and defining them in terms of a presumed femaleness or femininity, which to my mind, is highly suspect of sexual metaphysics; rather, it is our task to envision a feminist theory of textual production and consumption, which is of course inseparable from a theory of culture. (de Lauretis, *Technologies of Gender*, p. 92, emphasis in original)

37 Ezra Pound, who is often taken as the classic case here, is, of course, in a category of his own. He is one of the few poets anywhere in the twentieth century who saw himself in any way as a political activist, if we except people like Mayakovski, d'Anuntzio and Brecht who at least worked primarily in their own countries. The interest taken by biographers and

literary critics in his work and life is partly related to his apparent literary influence: but ultimately it must be related directly to the fact that he was, and continues to be, the odd example of the right-wing poet who took his ideas seriously enough to get involved for them by taking the 'other' side. Pound is of the generation before Hemingway, Malraux, Orwell, Auden, Spender – all of whom served briefly in the Spanish Civil War. His case is not unlike that of Heidegger, whose apparent brilliance seems to conflict with his Nazi sympathies. However, Pound *is* different. Much of his poetry is gibberish, and he never ceased to proclaim his Fascist ideas, up to the time of his death. His *major* contribution is probably not in any of his best-known work but in the 'Pisan Cantos' (Cantos 74–84), written while he was imprisoned at the Disciplinary Training Centre near Pisa, in cages which were otherwise death cells for people suspected of treason, rape or murder, and later in a tent in the medical compound. In this he reviews themes from the earlier Cantos in the light of his incarceration, and debates the loss of his powers, his world, his hope. Humphrey Carpenter quotes from a letter from Robert Lowell to Pound in 1952: 'long stretches . . . have a loveliness and humour that's hard to find anywhere else. But damn it – I wish you'd read them over, they're too long, the drift must be *cut* somewhere. I think I can get, or can suppose, most of the connections; yet there's something that blankets me . . .' (Humphrey Carpenter, *A Serious Character: the Life of Ezra Pound* (London: Faber, 1988), p. 680).

38 Heaney, *The Government of the Tongue*, pp. 43–4.
39 Osip Mandelstam, *Selected Poems* (Harmondsworth: Penguin, 1977), p. 133.
40 Ibid., p. 71.
41 Ibid., p. 24.
42 'Haggia Sophia', in Clarence Brown, *Mandelstam* (Cambridge: Cambridge University Press, 1973), p. 186.
43 Brown, *Mandelstam*, p. 197.
44 Ibid., p. 296.
45 Mandelstam, *Selected Poems*, p. 88.
46 Ibid., p. 98.
47 Ibid., pp. 112, 106.
48 Ibid., p. 128.
49 Ibid., p. 133.
50 Brown, *Mandelstam*, p. 2.
51 Heaney, *The Government of the Tongue*, p. 88.
52 Mandelstam, *Selected Poems*, pp. 300–2.
53 Ibid., p. 105.
54 Much of what I have written about the Mandelstams is a deliberate slurring of Roland Barthes's distinction between the speakerly and the writerly texts, between the written and the oral, just as I have hinted at, in order to gloss over, the methodological caveats contained in his semiology in abusing terms like 'meaning' when what I really want to say is that such-and-such only makes sense when I recognize that it stands in a particular relationship to so-and-so or such-another-such. The ramifications of 'reading' the Mandelstams are, of course, quite comprehensive, both in time and space. (Gorbachev, George Faludy, the Canadian Jewish Congress and Ronald Reagan have all made readings quite different to mine, and so they should.) But Osip and Nadezhda should not be raised on a flagstaff. I have tried to

read them from inside, though with a Heaneyist perspective that asks: why read them at all? But see Roland Barthes, *The Grain of the Voice: Interviews 1962–1980* (New York: Hill and Wang, 1985), and especially Susan Sontag's Introduction, for suggestive ideas on the voice and the text. Above all, see de Lauretis, *Technologies of Gender* for why gender matters.

55   Ruth First, *117 Days* (Harmondsworth: Penguin, 1982), p. 136. The Rivonia trial was held between 1963 and 1964 and involved charging several opposition leaders under the Suppression of Communism Acts. Among those incarcerated as a consequence were Nelson Mandela, Alfred Sisulu, Govan Mbeki and Dennis Goldberg. The substance of the charges was that they had organized sabotage and armed resistance against the South African government. The trial followed the banning of several hundred South Africans from any political activity and the prohibition of any publication of anything they said or wrote.

56   Ibid., p. 134.

57   Ibid., pp. 134–5.

58   Maurice Merleau-Ponty, *Humanism and Terror: an Essay on the Communist Problem* (Boston: Beacon Press, 1969); Robert Jay Lifton, *Thought Reform and the Psychology of Totalism: a Study of Brainwashing in China* (New York: Basic Books, 1960); Lifton, *The Future of Immortality and other Essays for a Nuclear Age* (New York: Basic Books, 1987).

59   Merleau-Ponty, *Humanism and Terror*, p. 110.

60   There is, of course, a growing literature on post-modernism as both a literary and a sociological phenomenon, and while it is not the purpose of this book to enter into the nuances of the debate, it is essential to give some sense of what I mean by the term. The most succinct summary of the issues, so far as I know, is by the Hungarian/Canadian scholar John Fekete, who argues, in his 'Vampire Culture' in *Life after Postmodernism: Essays on Value and Culture* (Montreal: New World Perspectives, 1987), pp. 70–1 that contemporary ('post-modern') culture has three aspects. The first is a society where the relationship between knowledge and power is such that the genesis, administration and transmission of knowledge operate on the circuit towards a 'dead' power which justifies its existence purely in the name of survival. Any opposition to such power/knowledge must therefore operate on the basis of the dysfunctionality of the power/knowledge nexus. The second is a tendency for values to be centralized in the name of political domination in order to establish a juridical definition of everyday life, but at the same time allowing a 'relaxation of norms and normative guidance in many areas, and a spreading of disorientation and irrationality through all strata of Western societies'. The third is the existence of a communications system where symbols, significations and signs relate not to concrete social relations or everyday utility, but to each other 'as autonomous and mobile values'. For other explorations in the culture of the post-modern, see Hal Foster, ed., *Postmodern Culture* (London: Pluto Press, 1985) and, for the political implications, Ernesto Laclau and Chantal Mouffe, *Hegemony and Socialist Strategy* (London: Verso, 1986).

61   Breyton Breytenbach, *A Season in Paradise* (New York: Persea Books, 1980).

62   Breyten Breytenbach, *Mouroir: Mirrornotes of a Novel* (London: Faber, 1985), p. 190.

63   Ibid., p. 191.

64 This should be contrasted with Wole Soyinka's account of his incarceration
    in 1967 for denouncing the Nigerian military dictatorship and writing in
    support of the Biafra secession. Soyinka's story is primarily political and
    only secondarily about writing. See Wole Soyinka, *The Man Died* (New
    York: Farrar, Straus and Giroux, 1988).
65 Franz Kafka, *The Complete Stories and Parables* (New York: Quality
    Paperback Book Club, 1983), p. 259.
66 Breytenbach, *Mouroir*, p. 173. This might be contrasted with other prison
    literature from South Africa. D. M. Zwelonke's *Robben Island* (London:
    Heinemann, 1973), for example, is quite clear as to the message and point
    of writing:

> I am proud of the man on Robben Island. He rejected a slave-life. He
> chose to fight. My concept of fighting is not limited only to action on
> a battle-field. Fighting means making no surrender to irrationality,
> not abdicating from one's convictions even when chained to a tree, at
> the point of a gun. And the warders knew it. There is only one thing
> to fight in this world: it is irrationality. (p. 2)

67 Breytenbach, *Mouroir*, p. 178.
68 Ibid., pp. 337–8.
69 Ibid., p. 339.
70 An example of this is found in Larry Krotz, ed., *Waiting for the Ice-cream
    Man: a Prison Journal* (Winnipeg, Manitoba: Converse, 1978). This includes
    articles, stories and poems by prisoners (Canadian and non-Canadian),
    photographs, extracts from government reports and legislation, a plea for
    action, and an article arguing for the abolition of the penal system. See
    chapter 10 below.
71 For perceptive observations of the basis of Escher's work, see Douglas R.
    Hofstadter, *Godel, Escher, Bach* (New York: Basic Books, 1980); in particular
    chapter 20 on 'Strange Loops, or Tangled Hierarchies'. For Piranesi, see his
    Carceri d'Invensione (1761) and contrast them with his earlier *Invensioni Capric
    di Carcere* (1745–50).
72 The high priest of this philosophy is Jean-François Lyotard, whose book *The
    Post-modern Condition: a Report on Knowledge* (Minneapolis: University
    of Minnesota Press, 1984) heralded the death of political commitment,
    Enlightenment-style. The challenge has been taken up on the left by several
    authors, notably by Laclau and Mouffe in *Hegemony and Socialist Strategy*
    and, in briefer and more lucid form, by Dick Hebdige in 'After the Masses',
    Marxist Today, January 1989, pp. 48–53.
73 Breytenbach, 'A Note for Azania,' *The True Confessions of an Albino
    Terrorist* (London: Faber, 1984), p. 360.
74 Adam Michnik, *Letters from Prison and other Essays* (Berkeley, Cal.:
    University of California Press, 1985), p. 99.
75 Breytenbach, *True Confessions*, p. 163.
76 Ibid., p. 177.

8

Death Row

I

George Orwell, in one of his periodical columns for *Tribune*, observed that although most people argued in favour of capital punishment, no one, when confronted with it, had a good word to say about executions themselves.[1] The evidence that he had for such a statement was based on literature: he refers to Thackeray, Dickens, Horace Walpole, Arnold Bennett, Zola, Byron, Plato, Kipling. And of course, in that sense he is right. Much of the 'evidence' of literature is clearly not a celebration of executions. Two well-known examples should indicate the general tone:

> 'What are the bugles blowing for?' said Files-on-Parade.
> 'To turn you out, to turn you out,' the Colour-Sergeant
>   said.
> 'What makes you look so white, so white?' said Files-on-
>   Parade.
> 'I'm dreading what I've got to watch,' the Colour-Sergeant
>   said.
>> For they're hangin' Danny Deever, you can hear the
>>   Dead March play,
>> The Regiment's in 'ollow square – they're hangin'
>>   him today;
>> They've taken of his buttons off an' cut his stripes
>>   away,
>> An' they're hangin' Danny Deever in the mornin'.[2]

As Orwell noted, Kipling's ballad is probably influenced by the old hanging ballads, which go back at least to the eighteenth century. Even further back, Villon's poetry has acted as the focal influence for much poetry on capital punishment, and his 'Epitaph' in particular has been translated many times into most major languages, perhaps because Villon himself seemed to the Romantic poets in particular as the epitome of the intellectual at war with society. But this tradition introduces another aspect of capital punishment which Orwell seems to have missed, and that is the execution where the criminal feels that it was an honour to have died. A. L. Lloyd quotes two verses of the eighteenth-century ballad 'The Unfortunate Rake', where the criminal demands to go down 'with more than military honours':

> Get six of my comrades to carry my coffin,
> Six girls of the city to bear me on,
> And each of them carry a bunch of red roses,
> So they don't smell me as they walk along.
>
> And muffle your drums, and play your fifes lowly,
> Play the dead march as you carry me on,
> And fire your bright muskets all over my coffin,
> Saying: 'There goes an unfortunate rake to his doom.'[3]

We will return to this theme shortly, but it is worth emphasizing the validity of Orwell's observation by examining that old standby of abolitionists, Oscar Wilde's 'Ballad of Reading Gaol'. Though it, too, is influenced by the hanging ballads, it is a transformation which is mediated by the voice of the Romantic poets. The direct antecedent of the Ballad is Coleridge's 'Rime of the Ancient Mariner', though it is as if Wilde were stuck with two stanzas from Coleridge which give him not only the metric pattern of his entire poem, but also the observation with which he has to wrestle.

> And I had done a hellish thing,
> And it would work them woe:
> For all averred, I had killed the bird
> That made the breeze to blow.
> Ah wretch! said they, the bird to slay,
> That made the breeze to blow!
>
> Nor dim nor red, like God's own head,
> The glorious Sun uprist:
> Then all averred, I had killed the bird
> That brought the fog and mist.
> 'Twas right, said they, such birds to slay,
> That bring the fog and mist.[4]

In Wilde's 'Ballad' the relationship of the other prisoners to the man who is to be executed is expressed thus:

> But there were those amongst us all
>   Who walked with downcast head,
> And knew that, had each got his due,
>   They should have died instead:
> He had but killed a thing that lived,
>   While they had killed the dead.
>
> For he who sins a second time
>   Wakes a dead soul to pain,
> And draws it from its spotted shroud,
>   And makes it bleed again,
> And makes it bleed great gouts of blood,
>   And makes it bleed in vain!⁵

The major difference between Coleridge's 'Rime' and Wilde's 'Ballad' is that Wilde writes as an observer of the execution while Coleridge writes on behalf of the man who is to be executed. Coleridge's Mariner believes himself guilty of the death of hundreds of other seamen; his fellows ultimately accept that he is indeed guilty, and hang the albatross around his neck. It is, however, they who die, not he. He is haunted by their dead bodies, their spirits, and the slimy creatures of the deep:

> The many men, so beautiful!
> And they all dead did lie:
> And a thousand slimy things
> Lived on; and so did I.
>
> I looked upon the rotting sea,
> And drew my eyes away;
> I looked upon the rotting deck,
> And there the dead men lay.⁶

The death sentence for the Mariner is to have to live in the gazes of the dead men:

> The cold sweat melted from their limbs,
> Nor rot nor reek did they:

The look with which they looked on me
Had never passed away.

An orphan's curse would drag to hell
A spirit from on high;
But oh! more terrible than that
Is the curse in a dead man's eye!
Seven days, seven nights, I saw that curse,
And yet I could not die.[7]

Wilde also uses the spirits of the dead as well as their bodies to create the atmosphere of terror, though the spirits do not belong to the same bodies, as they do with Coleridge. During the night before the execution

crooked shapes of Terror crouched,
In the corners where we lay:
And each evil sprite that walks by night
Before us seemed to play.[8]

As for the felon himself:

They hanged him as a beast is hanged:
They did not even toll
A requiem that might have brought
Rest to his startled soul,
But hurriedly they took him out,
And hid him in a hole.[9]

Ultimately with Wilde all the prisoners are as guilty as the rest of us – 'for each man kills the thing he loves' – and thus the act of execution is arbitrary, and the ghosts that haunt the prisoners on the night before the execution are not those of other criminals but of dead executioners. With Coleridge, of course, the Mariner is guilty, and he can only expiate his guilt by telling his tale whenever his 'agony' returns. He is haunted by the ghosts of his victims.

Through these examples we can begin to rethink Orwell's apparently commonsensical appraisal of the literature of capital punishment. It depends, in part, on who is telling the story, but it also depends on whether the perspective adopted is that of commenting on the whole human condition through this particular and grotesque aspect of it, or that of a sense of personal guilt and finitude. Take, for example, Victor Serge's account in *Men in Prison*, perhaps echoing Dickens in a *Tale of Two Cities*, where he describes the crowd at an execution in Paris:

I have seen a Paris crowd gather around an intoxicating and revolting execution. The hum of the night streets had grown more and more quiet, more and more uneasy in the dismal boulevards surrounding the prison, till, in the darkness, it collided, like a front consisting of thousands of livid faces, with the lines of troops. Bizarre revelers arrived by automobile. Under the street lamps, urchins with queer, mocking grins traced the gesture of decapitation in the air. Bewildered crowds of workers and young intellectuals were jostled, divided, dispersed, forced back in disorder by the black wedges of cavalry or police charges as they nursed their important anger in bitter idleness. Many couples exchanged vague caresses ... You could see them arriving in groups and bunches from the poor working-class suburbs and from the depths of the slums – la Bastille, la Chapelle, Charonne, Montmartre and Montparnasse – pimps and hookers, a world of victims liberated only by the knowledge that sometimes victims take revenge.

Dawn broke amid violent disorders, amid the cadenced cries 'Murderers! Murderers!' doubtless echoes – but with a profound feeling of being the righteous ones at last – by murderers standing in the darkness of their cells behind the bars of the Santé Prison. ... Dawn came up. We saw nothing, except for a whitish tinge which appeared indistinctly at the end of the boulevard above the waves of heads in the jagged foliage of the treetops. We did not hear the rumble of the car from which the condemned man emerged, half-naked, shivering, furious, desperate, alive, horribly alive in every ganglia of his brain, in every fiber of his nervous system. He shouted out his innocence, a macabre joke which no one understood among the guilty men lined up around the scaffold who represented the social mechanism behind Dr Guillotin's philanthropic machine. He appeared like a phantom among the concerns of pathetic, respectable people – appeared and disappeared, in a rapid movement of the seesaw plank, ending in the double fall: the still-thinking head with wide-open eyes falling into the basket, and the thick stream of warm blood falling onto the pavement of the boulevard, where someone had sprinkled a little sand as a precaution. None of us – the crowd – saw it with our own eyes; but at the exact moment we had, more or less clearly, the same inner vision. I remember the pallor which suddenly spread over everybody's face, the lips turning blue, the clamor which suddenly spread its huge dark wings over us and over the city, the fury in our chests – the collective feeling of the blade's fall.[10]

It is important to note that this account is not about Death Row; it is an account of an execution based on an observation of crowd behaviour. It is ultimately a *moral* statement about the fickleness of crowds and their interest in spectacle for whatever reason, about the human injustice of execution, and about the crowd's collective sense of death. It perfectly fits Orwell's case, and also reflects a large number of other accounts of executions. But there are two cases that do not quite fit. The first I take from the New Testament, the second from Jean Genet.

21   The governor answered and said unto them, Whether of the twain will ye that I release unto you? They said, Barabbas.
22   Pilate saith unto them, What shall I do then with Jesus which is called Christ? They all say unto him, Let him be crucified.
23   And the governor said, Why, what evil hath he done? But they cried out the more, saying, Let him be crucified.
24   When Pilate saw that he could prevail nothing, but that a tumult was made, he took water, and washed his hands before the multitude, saying, I am innocent of the blood of this just person: see ye to it.
25   Then answered all the people, and said, His blood be on us, and on our children. . . .
35   And they crucified him, and parted his garments, casting lots: that it might be fulfilled which was spoken by the prophet, They parted my garments among them and upon my vestments they cast lots.
36   And sitting down they watched him there;
37   And set up over his head his accusation written, THIS IS THE KING OF THE JEWS.
38   Then there were two thieves crucified with him, one on the right hand, the other on the left.[11]

The strategic significance of this execution is clear enough in the tradition of Western culture, but it is also relevant to stress its importance in studying prison accounts of death sentences. For what the Christian tradition did was to highlight a political execution against those of 'common malefactors': Barabbas (who 'was a robber') is freed, presumably because the 'crowd' preferred robbers to would-be messiahs, but, in spite of that, the tradition claims the erzatz messiah as more significant. The 'messiah', or his scribes, have validated his claim by a whole genealogy which reaches back to Adam. What do Barabbas or the two thieves on the either side of the 'King of the Jews' do to validate their own experiences? Every criminal has a genealogy, too, and that genealogy begins to provide another interpretation of execution.

If the Christian story is about miracles (the miracle of the risen Christ and the miracle of the sacred heart which pulses beyond its execution, but ultimately the miracle of historical validity), the 'felon's' story must, if it is to have any significance, also be about creative miracles, about turning the dross of the world into alchemic gold. Genet's account of capital punishment is just such a story. It is impossible with Genet to view an execution simply as a spectacle: it is as profound a part of our living as of our dying. Just as the dying Christ reached back into the hidden genealogies of his world to reclaim the living in his death, so must the damned reach back into their pasts to display the triumph of their execution: 'The melodious child dead in me long before the axe chops off its head.'[12] In *The Miracle of the Rose* Genet transforms the execution of Harcamone into a creative, sacred victory, a victory which is the triumph of the body as it becomes both city and countryside. As they come to take him away to be guillotined, four men in black explore his body.

> The judge and the lawyer wormed their way into the ear and the chaplain and executioner dared enter his mouth. They moved forward a little along the edge of the lower lip and fell into the gulf. And then, almost as soon as they passed the gullet, they came to a lane of trees that descended in a gentle, almost voluptuous slope. All the foliage was very high and formed the sky of the landscape . . .[13]

> The men were approaching the inhuman regions of Harcamone . . . [they] wandered at first through an extraordinary maze of narrow alleys where they suspected the houses (windows and doors were shut) of sheltering dangerous lovemaking punishable by law. The alleys were unpaved, for the sound of men's shoes was inaudible; they seemed to be walking on elastic ground, where they lightly rebounded. They were skipping. The meander-

ing alleys suggested a kind of Toulon, as if meant to contain the lurching walk of sailors . . .[14]

But the real problem is to know whether this piece of wild landscape, this cartography of interconnecting alleyways, actually contained a heart.

Finally, the four dark men came to a mirror on which was drawn (obviously carved with the diamond of a ring) a heart pierced by an arrow. No doubt it was the portal of the heart. . . . And that chamber was only the first. The mystery of the hidden chamber remained to be discovered. But no sooner did one of the four realize that they were not in the heart of the heart than a door opened by itself and we saw before us a red rose of monstrous size and beauty.

'The Mystic Rose,' murmured the chaplain.[15]

This is not merely a satire on the Catholic interpretation of the meaning of the crucifixion (though it is certainly that), but also a statement on behalf of Barabbas who in real life is more often executed than the Christly figures, the latter now being more likely to sit in judgement like the biblical Pharisees. The sensual topology of Harcamone's body is itself autobiographical, being part of Genet's own sense of remembrance and creativity. ('An odd fact: I had an erection all night long, despite my mental activity which kept me remote from sexual desire'. And again, 'Harcamone is dead, Bulkaen is dead . . . These papers are their graves. But I shall transmit their names far down the ages.') If Christ died to save the world from its sins and give it life everlasting, Genet's genius lay in recreating himself in the deaths of others, so that people might live now.[16] He gave hope to the 'melodious child' that it might continue to sing long before the axe fell.

II

And this *does* lead us to Death Row and beyond the spectacle of execution. Sooner or later the axe will fall for all of us, but how we build what D. H. Lawrence called the 'ship of death' is at least as important as knowing how to witness the exit. The accounts of Death Row from within prison are as much accounts of how people got there as of what happened to them in prison before and after they were sentenced. The statistics on who commits first-degree murder are much the same everywhere, if we exclude countries or regions where there is active political violence. The Jamaican writer, Mario Hector, who was himself on Death Row and gunned down almost immediately after his release, may speak for all those convicted as well as for official statistics. In discussing capital punishment he wrote:

> It could be shown and argued that capital punishment does deter people from premeditating murder, but such a line falls flat in the face of overwhelming evidence that those who behave brutally are not deterred by capital punishment and that the majority of murders were not premeditated. Of all the people I met on the Row, I knew of only two who planned to take a life. The act is, in the majority of cases, a spontaneous expression of anger of a moment, unpredictable and unplanned. Even if capital punishment did deter 5% of would-be murderers, what about the 95% undeterred?[17]

The issue here is not whether the men on Death Row were innocent or guilty of their crimes, but in what ways the writing machine was a factor in their execution. As Wilde guessed and Coleridge knew, most murderers either kill the objects of their affection or, by killing, displace the only home they know. Yet each murderer is not condemned to death. At worst he has to live with a slow, internal death. Judicial death is a textual murder, and, therefore, not surprisingly, many people on Death Row respond with their own version of textuality.

Writing against the judicial text is, of course, no guarantee either of peace of mind, or of a life-resolution, or, particularly, that the accused will be acquitted. After eleven years on Death Row, Mario Hector was acquitted only to be shot in the street shortly afterwards. After achieving fame for writing *In the Belly of the Beast*, Jack Henry Abbott was released from prison, only to find himself in a drunken brawl in which he killed yet another man, and then confined to a hospital for the criminally insane. And Caryl Chessman (to whose story we will return shortly) spent twelve years constructing a whole series of countertexts, only to find himself executed because he could not pierce through a series of drunken texts which presumed his guilt and foretold his death. Not all of the vast amount of literature created by and around the Rosenbergs prevented their execution. The same

goes for Bukharin, and Trotsky, and Rosa Luxemburg, and Ruth
Ellis, and Roger Casement, and Sacco and Vanzetti, and Michael X.[18]
In many cases the texts provided by the accused were used in court
to confirm guilt rather than mitigate it. (In one of the more spectacular
cases in Britain in the 1920s, Edith Thompson and her lover Frederick
Bywaters were hanged for the murder of Thompson's husband. The
evidence of guilt was based largely on correspondence between the
lovers in which they discussed novels that included plots with domestic
murders.[19])

Even if it could be shown that writing by prisoners and others has
contributed to executions being cancelled, the overwhelming evidence
is to the contrary. Writing on Death Row must therefore be seen in
other terms.

In the collection of documents edited by Michel Foucault and
entitled *I, Pierre Riviere, having slaughtered my mother, my sister,
and my brother* . . . an argument is advanced for reading a murderer's
text as part of a wider field of discourse. There are two basic acts
involved in committing murder and writing about it. The issue is
whether, in Foucault's observation of the judgement of Riviere's
contemporaries, 'the murder and the narrative of the muder were
consubstantial'.[20] In most murder trials where a text by the accused
is involved, the consubstantiality of text and the act of death (death
caused by the accused as well as the legal death of the accused) is
integral to the judgement. But what if we can separate the two basic
acts? What if the act of writing and the act of killing have different
momenta? Foucault's case study, however improbable it may seem,
is intriguing in that the murderer intended text and action to be
woven together. As Foucault writes:

> If Riviere's text is to be believed, his first project was that the
> memoir was to surround the murder. Pierre Riviere intended to
> start by writing the memoir; the announcement of the crime
> would have come first; then the explanation of his father's and
> mother's life; and, at the end, the reasons for the deed. Once
> he had finished the draft, he would have committed the murder;
> then, after he had mailed the manuscript, Riviere would have
> killed himself.[21]

Foucault notes that there were two revisions to this plan: one in
which the murder became the end product of the text, placed outside
the text which would 'narrate his parents' life in a memoir which
everyone might read; then', says Foucault, Riviere would 'write a

secret text narrating the murder to come, what he called "the reasons of the end and the beginning"; and only then would he commit the crime.' The other revision, which caused by 'a fatal drowsiness' which prevented him from writing, led to the murder coming first, then the writing of his account, and then dying. It was this final version that was carried out, though with a gap of one month between committing the murders and writing the account which he had rehearsed in his mind beforehand.

The interest in the Pierre Riviere case is based on several factors (including assessments of his mental state, the nature of the parricide and the reasons given for the verdict), but for the purposes of this chapter it is the theoretical argument provided by Foucault and his colleagues about the interrelationship of writing, murder and execution that raises the most important issues. Riviere inserted himself into several discourses: between father and mother, children and parents, 'madness' and reason, religion and secularity, popular culture and the law, and law, medicine and different levels of government. In order to 'save' his father from the terrorizing mother, Riviere not only had to kill his mother and the children who supported her, but also have himself executed by the guillotine so that the father could dismiss him as a good-for-nothing.

The argument advanced by Foucault and his colleagues is that Riviere's murder, taken together with all the texts against which it was written, Riviere's writing itself, and the guillotine, were all cut of the same cloth. Riviere's entire trajectory was rationally worked out, and thus the 'kind of idiot' had established an alternative interconnected reading of the way he was to die. The major part of the book is concerned with documenting the ways in which the various representatives of the established texts coped with this phenomenon and what was the resulting intertextual reading; the highlight of this was that Riviere was sentenced to death, then to life imprisonment, to which he responded by committing suicide. Riviere therefore continued writing his text to the end.

The case is written up in classic French proto-structuralist style, so that text and anti-text, reason and unreason contend with each other. Death Row then becomes a space within which the reasonable specialists try to deny the unreasonable felon the completion of the logic of his anti-reason. The victory of anti-reason/anti-text is assured, not by allowing the irrational to complete his text and the rational the final logic of their rationality by executing him, but by frustrating their clumsy paternalist reasonings in improvising a new irrational conclusion.

This was the death of which a clumsy psychiatry had tried to cheat him. By having him reprieved they were refusing to hear him, they were declaring that, all things considered, the native's speech had no weight, was not even an effect of monstrosity; such criminals were only disturbed children who played with corpses as they played with words . . . The death which Pierre Riviere voluntarily gave himself when there was no longer anything to inflict it on him, compels the later reader to give its full weight to a text which quite obviously is neither that of a madman nor of a savage.[22]

This introduces a set of factors into the subject of Death Row which clearly are not present in the accounts by Orwell and the authors whom he quotes, nor in those of Serge, Wilde, though they are closer to Genet and perhaps even Coleridge. Apart from the employment of a text/anti-text strategy, Foucault and his colleagues introduce the important issues of the will-to-death, in which 'the melodious child long dead' writes his murders and his ultimate execution into his text. Thus Death Row becomes not a situation which we are invited to witness and in doing so to meditate on our complicity in its execution, but rather a self-generated process which exists independently of us, indeed counter to our experiences. We can only watch the spectacle of the competing scripts. The issue becomes not the abolition of the death penalty, but the completion of the murderer's own mission.

That Foucault's case-study is not fanciful is shown by other studies, and perhaps most notably by Norman Mailer in *The Executioner's Song*, his study of the life and death of Gary Gilmore, which consists of a long excavation by Mailer into the personality of a man who refused all legal help in order to allow himself to die (including attempts at suicide). Unlike Foucault, however, where the structural patterning is a method for reaching the core of the story – indeed where the structural patterning almost *is* the story – with Mailer the search is for the 'real' Gilmore, explored through relationships, interviews, newspaper reports and other forms of documentation. Mailer is concerned with dialogues, descriptions of places and situations (including the execution itself), intending not to offer analysis, except in so far as the narrative is the analysis. Consequently, the patterning (if Foucault's work could be imposed on it) is much more ambiguous, leaving a perplexity about the human condition and doubting whether anything can be simply dichotomized under the concept of rationality. One of the reasons for this is the existence of another tradition in the United States in confronting Death Row which shows the Riviere/Gilmore cases in a somewhat different light. This is perhaps best indicated in the case of Caryl Chessman.

III

> Nor can who has passed a month in the death cells
>   believe in capital punishment
> No man who has passed a month in the death cells
>   believes in cages for beasts.[23]

Genet, perhaps, apart, there is no non-political prisoner who so consciously tried to write himself out of prison as Chessman. But, where Genet succeeded, Chessman failed. Between 3 July 1948 when, aged twenty-seven, he entered San Quentin's Death Row, and 2 May 1960, when he was executed, Chessman wrote four books and amassed a large number of documents, papers and legal reports in his defence. A classic liberal appraisal of Chessman and his writing by Elizabeth Hardwick appeared after the execution:

> With extraordinary energy, Chessman made, on the very edge of extinction, one of those startling efforts of personal rehabilitation, salvation of the self . . . The vigor of his creation aroused fear, bewilderment, suspicion . . . People on the street, talking about the case, found Chessman's energy, his articulation of his own tragic trap, his stubborn efforts on his own behalf, truly alarming. These efforts were not mitigating; indeed they were condemning. He had trained himself to sleep only a few hours a night so that he could write his books, study law, work on his case. But suppose another condemned man wanted his sleep, couldn't bother to work on his own destiny, hadn't the strength or the talent to bring himself from darkness to light – what then? Lest his very gifts save him, some people wanted him executed in order to show the insignificance of personal vigor before the impersonal law.[24]

In this argument, the vast output by Chessman in his defence did not in any way help his case, but had rather the opposite effect: even though his writings in detail argued a case counter to the one made by the prosecution, the more he wrote the guiltier he became in the estimation of the public. There are several reasons for this, beyond the ones indicated above by Hardwick. The first is probably related to Chessman's apparent honesty in listing his crimes, in his graphic description of criminal life, in his verbal fluency. In his autobiography, *Cell 2455, Death Row*, Chessman provides a vivid account of his youth, his criminal apprenticeship, his major criminal activities, and his final trial and imprisonment on Death Row. For their detail of criminal life, Chessman's books are as important and convincing social documents as any:

> I was one of the trees in this dark and forbidding forest. I knew what it meant to live beyond the reach of other men or God. I had 'proved' everything I had felt the need to prove: that I couldn't be scared or broken or driven to my knees, that I didn't give a damn. But here is where the tragedy lies: this felt need is compulsive and negative only. It is a need to prove one can do without – without love, without faith, without belief, without warmth, without friends, without freedom . . . If not checked, the ultimate (conscious or unconscious) need is to prove that one can do without even life itself.[25]

By taking his readers into the pit and challenging them not to be complicit bystanders, Chessman compelled them to face themselves. For most this was an experience they felt they could do without.

The second was the apparent violence with which he pursued his writing: not simply the violent subject matter, but the sacrificial violence of a writer in full public view who displayed the self-flagellating dedication of a hermit or a Trappist monk. The manic, perhaps maniacal, dedication to 'truth' displayed the strong possibility that both violences were the same. Chessman himself said as much: 'I had made it crystal clear that I considered Chessman quite capable of looking out for himself. My briefs to the court were technically correct in every detail; they were exhaustively researched and were coldly logical presentations, but they were also written in acid.'[26]

The third reason – and this is one that ties the above two impressions together – is that the writing itself, truthful and violent, was evidence of a creative world that obeyed its own laws. Were not all creative writers and artists unnatural and apart from the rest of society? Therefore, what they had to say was its own justification and had nothing to do with social policy, even if the central subject *was* social policy. Twelve years was enough for Chessman to demonstrate his creative talents and writing development. Society had given him time to work, but now it was time to execute him for his crimes.

These are the frameworks used to understand public reaction to Chessman and his writing ('perhaps by creating his life, Chessman had to lose it,' wrote Hardwick), but they only superficially touch on the significance of the writing itself. Chessman was convicted of rape, kidnapping and robbery, and was identified by one of the rape victims as the 'Red Light Bandit' of Los Angeles. He was sentenced to death on two kidnapping counts. No murder was involved. His defence centred on the nature of the court transcripts, the physical misidentification of himself with the Red Light Bandit, his own criminal past which included no sexual crimes, and his innocence of these (though not of other) crimes. Ultimately the case rested on writing, his and others', and the enduring importance of Chessman's case relates to the interconnected and disconnected readings, of which the 'public', so readily invoked by Hardwick, was only one.

An important factor missed by Hardwick was the contextual significance of the Chessman case. On 19 July 1953, Julius and Ethel Rosenberg were executed in the USA, two years after they had been convicted of treason in spying for the USSR. Their case, at the height of the cold war, was pivotal for the future of the American political left and right, for the concept of Americanism, for the idea of what was an 'ordinary' American or Jew. As Andrew Ross has written:

> In the trial itself, judgements of great importance came to rest upon the most insignificant commodity items: the famous, torn Jello box and the inexpensive, mass-produced console table from Macy's. Every further revelation about humdrum, middle-class reality served not to dull but to heighten the already 'monstrous' status of the Rosenberg's alleged crime, and in the absence of any 'real' evidence, the defendants were made to assume the spy's shadowy inventory of effects precisely *because* they themselves were all too real – and thus boring.
>
> At dead center of this farrago of fictions something only slightly more palpable was at stake. The first question – What is a spy? – was one thing. More important was the question – What is a Communist? – or even – Are Communists real people? – a question that would haunt the representation of 'aliens' in the science-fiction films of Cold War Hollywood science fiction ... If the Rosenbergs were Communists, then Communists were barely distinguishable from any ordinary American couple.[27]

In their lust for Communist blood, the media, an enormous collection of regional and national politicians and a strange assortment of intellectuals demanded that even the most ordinary of people must die, if need be, for the safety of the Republic. Thus the Rosenbergs were executed to demonstrate the importance of an external definition of the USA: their ordinariness made them even more of a threat than if they were intellectuals or artists. Toughness to them was a message to the other 'ordinary people' to beware of foreign dealings. (The highly ambiguous relations of the Federal government with Ezra Pound who, all this time, was confined to St Elizabeth's Mental Hospital in Washington for being a pro-Fascist traitor, could be seen to indicate a political leniency not only towards Fascism, but also towards intellectuals.)[28] What the Rosenbergs said in their various pieces of correspondence and publications, mostly written before they were on Death Row, did not matter a whit. It was interpreted at the time as inauthentic and not true to their 'real' selves.[29]

Thus the trial of Chessman, his twelve years on Death Row and his writing take on an added significance. The writing is authentic enough, but perhaps the person is inauthentic. The arguments that called for the death of the Rosenbergs carried with them the possibility that there *may* be authentic voices coming out of prison, that the Americans, no less than the Russians with Dostoevsky or the French with Genet, might be able to produce a writer out of prison who was untainted by foreign flirtations. But what no one counted on was the audacity of the venture. For what Chessman proposed ran completely counter to the idea of what an authentic voice might sound like. Chessman's voice was not confessional, it made no appeals to sexuality, it was not romantic, it was not religious, it bore no marks of speaking on behalf of political causes or minorities. Chessman's voice got nobody off the hook: it spoke out of the ambiguities of the entire system of American values without offering any clear indication of what to do about them.

> In an age so fear-ridden, so full of doubt that it can feel secure only by creating awesome weapons too destructively stupefying to imagine, it is no surprise that such an age would create an equally awesome 'psychopathic' personality whose attributes should appear, as well as clinically tragic to a few of us, symbolically desirable to many of us. Tragedy and desirability are merely opposite sides of the same coin. It is with this coin that we buy our destinies.[30]

Chessman spoke as a radical criminologist or psychiatrist. *No* prisoner should be allowed to do that. Above all, Chessman was clearly a nasty man ... The difference between Chessman and the Rosenbergs was that the latters' writing had to be set aside from their criminal identities. Death Row was an occasion to show how little the ordinariness of their writing had to do with their crime. Their writing was, after all, mundane, everyday stuff: their crime, however, was monumental. The Rosenbergs wrote and behaved as if they were true patriots, in a tradition descended from Thomas Jefferson. Essentially they were told that they were wrong in such an interpretation. True patriots were not Communists because Communists were agents of a foreign power. They were executed for misreading the meaning of the constitution, and for supposing that their ordinariness as people could excuse the extraordinariness of their ideas and affiliations.

None of this was true of Chessman who argued, lived, wrote from inside the system. It is for this reason that his defence is a more strategically textual one. For what Chessman realized was that his defence *was* a purely textual one. If a defence based on textuality could not hold, then it was possible that no defence could hold, because no one could defy the text – except, possibly, on the grounds of emotion and the potentiality of political intervention. Politics and text were therefore closely interwoven.[31] Chessman's resistance to his pending execution was therefore not based (ultimately) on whether he did or did not commit the crimes for which he was accused, but that he had proved himself as at least as competent a craftsman in textuality as his accusers. Chessman wanted (like Genet) to be pardoned as a writer who had seen through the dissembling nature of the accusatory text. In this he failed, and with that failure the possibility of an alternative textual reading of American justice died. The execution of Chessman (as opposed to those of Sacco and Vanzetti or the Rosenbergs, who might be seen as political cases) killed off the possibility of the alternative word, the self-trained lawyer, the intellectual *marabout* being taken seriously. After Chessman, George Jackson.

IV

We live under the sentence of death of our writing. As Edward Fitzgerald wrote, paraphrasing Omar Khayyaam:

> The moving finger writes, and having writ, moves on
> Nor all thy piety nor wit shall move it back to cancel half
> a line
> Nor all thy tears wipe out a word of it.

Death Row, when written about, is an attempt both to cancel out
the lines of experience and to reclaim a life that is fast disappearing.
Beyond that, writing on Death Row is ineffectual. We neither win
our personal stay of execution nor probably the cause which made
the death a universal message.

But there are people who, writing, planned their death. Or mis-
planned it. Rilke, knowing that he was dying of leukaemia, calling it
a rose-prick; Dylan Thomas protesting at the dying of his father's
light, but going out whimpering himself. And Maurice Blanchot.
What are we to make of him? A planned exit for himself is seized on
by a friend as her own possible way out. He will not allow it.

As gently as possible, I asked her:
'Are you listening to me?'
'Yes.'
'Will you give up your plan or not?'
She looked at me with a look which I thought was almost
willing.
'Say yes,' and I took her by the hand to encourage her.
'Otherwise I might just lock you up in this room.'
'Where is that?'
'Why, here, in this house.'
She listened for a minute, then she asked, 'With you?' I
nodded. I was still holding her hand, that hand which was alive
gave me hope. Of her own accord she finally spoke:
'What was that word you said?'
I searched her face. My God, I said to myself absurdly, remind
me of that word.
[. . .]
At one moment I saw her lips move and was aware that she
was talking, but now I, in turn, no longer made an effort to
grasp those words: I looked at them. By chance, I heard the
word 'plan'
'That's the word,' she said.
The memory of what she had been searching for returned to
me then, but I must say that even though I was attentive again
I was no longer in the least bit interested: all that belonged to

another world, in any case it was too late. Only, as so often happens, my lack of interest must have brought her back to life and now, perhaps because she had broken through a barrier, it was she who took the initiative.

'It isn't a plan any longer,' she said timidly.[32]

And one thinks of the writer whose work is a predicated on martyrdom, whose systematic 'plan' is to turn the world upside down whatever the personal consequences, and one thinks of those who take the message very seriously.

What a limiting thing is a weapon, Salahuddin thought, feeling oddly detached from events. – Like Gabreel when the sickness came. – Yes, indeed; a most confusing manner of thing. For how few the choices were, now that Gabreel was the *armed* man and he the *unarmed*; how the universe had shrunk![33]

But it isn't a plan any longer, as Blanchot wrote. The sentence of death is not only against the author, who must retreat to an armed fortress in order to be able to live and write; the writing itself is a sentence of death against those who would resist the will to life and truth. Death Row becomes the land that we all inhabit as text becomes the missile of authenticity.

> nel mezzo del cammin di nostra vita
> mi ritrovai per una selva oscura
> che la diritta via era smarrita.[34]

[In the middle of the way through our life
Lost in an obscure forest
I found out for myself that the righteous path was missing.]

NOTES

1 The thing that I think very striking is that no one, or none I can remember, ever writes of an execution with approval. The dominant note is always of horror. Society, apparently, cannot get along without capital punishment – for there are some people whom it is simply not safe to leave alive – and yet there is no one, when the pinch comes, who feels it right to kill another human being in cold blood. I watched a man hang once. There was no doubt that everyone concerned knew this to be a dreadful, unnatural action.

I believe it is always the same – the whole gaol, warders and prisoners alike, is upset when there is an execution. It is probably the fact that capital punishment is accepted as necessary, and yet instinctively felt to be wrong, that gives so many descriptions of executions their tragic atmosphere. They are mostly written by people who have actually watched an execution and feel it to be a terrible and only partly comprehensible experience which they want to record; whereas battle literature is largely written by people who have never heard a gun go off and think of battle as a sort of football match in which nobody gets hurt. (George Orwell, *Collected Essays, Journalism and Letters*, vol. 3 (Harmondsworth: Penguin, 1970), pp. 306–7.

2   Rudyard Kipling, *A Choice of Kipling's Verse* (London: Faber, 1963), pp. 170–1.

3   A. L. Lloyd, *Folk Song in England* (London: Panther, 1969), p. 222.

4   Samuel Taylor Coleridge, *Selected Poetry and Prose* (New York: Random House, 1951), p. 9.

5   Oscar Wilde, *The Complete Works* (London: Collins, 1973), p. 244.

6   Coleridge, *Selected Poetry and Prose*, p. 13.

7   Ibid., p. 14.

8   Wilde, *Complete Works*, p. 240.

9   Ibid., pp. 247–8.

10 Victor Serge, *Men in Prison* (London: Writers and Readers Publishing Cooperative, 1977), pp. 80–2.

11 Matt. 27:21–38 (Authorized Version).

12 Jean Genet, *Querelle of Brest*, quoted by Jean-Paul Sartre, *Saint Genet* (London: W. H. Allen, 1964), p. 1.

13 Jean Genet, *The Miracle of the Rose* (New York: Grove Press, 1966), p. 283.

14 Ibid., p. 285.

15 Ibid., pp. 285–6.

16 In his major study of Genet, Sartre makes much of the transition from Child to Thief to Writer, and there is little doubt that his study is still the only major critical, theoretical interpretation of Genet's work. In this chapter I accept Sartre's general evaluation, but *in toto* one has to conclude that Sartre was a romantic when it came to the political significance of prison writing. He contributed to an obfuscation of the incarcerated imagination, not its liberation. But see Sartre, *Saint Genet*.

17 Mario Hector, *Death Row* (London: Zed, 1984), p. 50.

18 Nikolai Bukharin (1888–1938), former editor of *Pravda* and *Izvestia*, Russian author, tried for treason in the third Moscow trial of prominent Bolsheviks and executed on 13 or 14 March 1938; Leon Trotsky (1879–1940), People's Commissar for Foreign Affairs and for Military and Naval Affairs, author, leader of Fourth International, assassinated by Stalin's agent in Mexico; Rosa Luxemburg (1871–1919), see appendix; Ruth Ellis (executed 1958), last woman to be executed in Britain, subject of the film *Dance with a Stranger*; Roger Casement (1864–1916), former British consular officer, Irish patriot, hanged by the English for treason on 3 August 1916; Michael X, alias Michael de Freitas, former pimp turned revolutionary, executed in Trinidad in 1974.

19 Rene Weis, *Criminal Justice: the True Story of Edith Thompson* (London: Hamish Hamilton, 1988).

20 Michel Foucault, ed., *I, Pierre Riviere, having Slaughtered my Mother, my*

Sister, and my Brother . . .: a Case of Parricide in the 19th Century (New York: Pantheon, 1975), p. 200.

21 Ibid., p. 201.

22 J.-P. Peter and Jeanne Favret in Foucault, ed., *I, Pierre Riviere*, p. 198.

23 Ezra Pound, *The Cantos of Ezra Pound* (New York: New Directions, 1970), p. 530.

24 Elizabeth Hardwick, *A View of my Own* (New York: Farrar, Straus & Co., 1963), pp. 70–1.

25 Caryl Chessman, *Cell 3455, Death Row* (Montreal, Permabook, 1956), p. 317.

26 Ibid., p. 314.

27 Andrew Ross, 'Intellectuals and Ordinary People: Reading the Rosenberg Letters', *Cultural Critique*, 9 (Spring, 1988), pp. 61–2.

28 The case of Pound is not directly relevant to us here, except for its adjunctive significance, and certainly some of those who were arguing for Pound's release were also against the Rosenberg executions. But not many. The Pound case existed in a political limbo, while the Rosenberg case was at the centre of American politics. On Pound, see Humphrey Carpenter, *A Serious Character: the Life of Ezra Pound* (London: Faber 1988).

29 There is considerable evidence for this from other sources, but for a well argued case and documentation, see Ross, 'Intellectuals and Ordinary People'.

30 Caryl Chessman, *The Kid was a Killer* (Greenwich, Conn.: Fawcett Publications, 1960), p. 167.

31 In the Sacco and Vanzetti case, for example, the collective (European) idea that the world might be made collectively better and nobler was shot to nothing by the (American) text which said equally that what came from Europe could have no (positive) effect on what was happening here. The Sacco and Vanzetti case happened during Prohibition and the spectre of Italian Mafiosi corrupting the purity of the nation cannot have been far from the minds of jury and judges: nor, indeed, from those of Sacco and Vanzetti. What comes through repeatedly in this case is the dislike of immigrants, particularly Latin ones, and thus the misreading of anarchism is grafted on to this distrust of importees. The writings of both Sacco and Vanzetti, their defence procedures (including an Italian lawyer and what were considered to be left-wing supporters) and the international protests against the sentences had absolutely no effect. Judge Webster Thayer repeatedly said out of court that he intended to ensure that both of them were executed. The case therefore became the epitome of a political trial, political in the sense that Sacco and Vanzetti insisted on their anarchism throughout the various court hearings, political in the sense that the prosecution insisted on their alien ideas/personae, and political in the sense that the rest of the world responded in the only political way that they could. In many ways the case was re-enacted in the Rosenberg trials. The genius of all the United States' judicial systems has been not to know when a case is political. Sacco and Vanzetti, Chessman, Cleaver, George Jackson – all were political cases in their ramifications. Everything else is shunted off to shadowy side-shows of Congress (e.g. the McCarthy hearings) or to show trials like that of the Rosenbergs where international politics over-rode any sense of normal justice. For Sacco and Vanzetti, however, the transfiguration

of the everyday into one glorious political moment is assured. In the inimitable words of Bartolomeo Vanzetti:

> if it had not been for these thing, I might have live out my life talking at street corners to scorning men. I might have die, unmarked, unknown, a failure. Now we are not a failure. This is our career and our triumph. Never in our full life could we hope to do such work for tolerance, for joostice, for man's understanding of man as now we do by accident. Our words – our lives – our pains – nothing! The taking of our lives – lives of a good shoemaker and a fishpeddler – all! That last moment belongs to us – that agony is our triumph. (Nico Sacco and Barolomeo Vanzetti, *The Letters of Sacco and Vanzetti* (New York: E. P. Dutton, 1960), p. v)

32 Maurice Blanchot, *Death Sentence* (Barrytown, NY: Station Hill Press, 1978), pp. 76–7.
33 Salman Rushdie, *The Satanic Verses* (London: Penguin/Viking, 1988), p. 546.
34 Dante Alighieri, *Inferno*, I.i.

9

Final Solutions

We passed: and found, as further on we went,
A people fettered in the frost's rough grip,
Flat on their backs, instead of forward bent.
There the mere weeping will not let them weep,
For grief, which finds no outlet at the eyes,
Turns inward to make anguish drive more deep;
For their first tears freeze to a lump of ice
Which like a crystal mask fills all the space
Beneath the brows and plugs the orifice.

(Dante, *Inferno*, XXXIII. 91–9)

I

Kubla Khan's Pleasure Dome, Rameses II's pyramids, the cotton fields of the Southern USA, the salt mines of Siberia and the first sheep of Australia were the products of convict and slave labour. From before 300 BC until well into the second half of the twentieth century, the crowning narrative of forcible confinement has emerged from the penal colony and the plantation. It is a spectrum so wide as to defy the possibility of analysis, an ongoing occurrence in different places, times, regions, cultures, political systems, economies; an apparently universal response to differences and deviations that strikes at the heart of any concept of civilization, and probably at the heart of most comparative sociological or political models of social change.[1] But unlike most other writing from prison, that from the camps has written itself across time and into the texture of whole societies. To read the writing from the camps is to begin to understand man's struggle with himself, his religion and his politics, and the ambiguity of human survival and transcendence.

Of all the literature out of prison, camp literature comes closest to providing any clue to what a universalism might look like. And it is important to emphasize that any focus on camp literature must recognize the collective nature of the enterprise, that camps are necessarily established as forms of collective punishment and collective labour, and therefore any attempt at coming to terms with the writing must begin with the collective culture and the struggles within it. Further, that although the organizations that established the camps were rationalistic and mechanistic, the response to them was not, and the structure of the narratives in opposition is a built-in deconstruction of the apparent rationality of the builders.

This chapter is about those writings. It is not in any way interested in the 'reasons' for establishing the camps, for example whether trans-Atlantic slavery was a system that was 'inevitable' in the development of mercantile capitalism, or whether the development of Siberia under both the Tsars and Stalin was a rational or irrational extension of Russian expansionism and a manifestation of the tensions of a rapidly modernizing society. Furthermore, it is totally uninterested in the internal British problems of law and order that resulted in the exporting of 150,000 convicts to the Antipodes, or the inherent logic of Nazism which led to the construction of concentration camps and the mass extermination of over six million people between 1937 and 1945. However important these cultural–social structural processes are, they do not help much in understanding what the writing is about, for historical actors are not simply pawns in an ongoing, relentless, 'historical' process, nor are they willing victims in other people's grand designs. They may know little and care less about these other designs, and when they know, they may actively resist them. In part our task is not unlike that of E. P. Thompson, who tried, in *The Making of the English Working Class*, to recover the forgotten

blind alleys, the lost causes and the losers themselves . . . Their hostility to the new industrialism may have been backward-looking. Their communiratian ideals may have been fantasies. Their insurrectionary conspiracies may have been foolhardy. But they lived through these times of acute social disturbances, and we did not. Their aspirations were valid in terms of their own experience; and if they were casualties of history, they remained, condemned in their own lives as casualties.[2]

Those who lived through slavery and through the camps are part of a greater problem than the working class in the industrial revolution, for the institutions through which they lived are remembered now – if at all – not as stops on a progressive evolutionary conveyor belt, but as dark moments of the human soul when the unspeakable happened, when men and women were treated, not as human, but as social pariahs or as tradable commodities. In retrospect, remembrance is easily categorized by protecting 'significant' survivors and notable martyrs, or, if we come from societies outside those that created the unspeakable, as an indication of the deep-rooted barbarism of the Enemy. Thus Americans can point to the barbarism of Soviet Russia by underlining the Gulags, and the Russians can indicate American evil by underlining slavery, the black ghettos and the massacres of American Indians. But such easy remembrances, confirming us in our own apparently comfortable certainties, do not take us very far in understanding either ourselves or others. Other people's gulags provide a convenient means of being amnesic about our own. The big examples – Russia in the nineteenth and twentieth centuries, Germany in the 1930s and 1940s, Australia from 1788 to 1868, and slavery and convict labour in the United States until well into the twentieth century – sit side-by-side with the lesser gulags – the internment of aliens in Britain, Canada and the USA in the Second World War, the French penal colonies of Devil's Island and the New Hebrides in the nineteenth and twentieth centuries, the kikuyu prisons in Kenya in the 1950s, and the wholesale imprisonment of blacks and dissidents in South Africa and Argentina after the early 1960s.

The major internments have certain common characteristics – the stripping from all individuals of their unique possessions, including hair, herding them like cattle and forcing conformity, the reduction of the self to 'pure' natural man, the attempt to deny all history, all culture, the imposition of a universalism of impotent nakedness. In this the incarcerations of the past two hundred years are very different from those that preceded them, where whole peoples were taken into captivity and some framework of the pre-slave culture was transported and developed. The post-Enlightenment camps (with the exception, to some extent, of the plantations in Brazil) tried to eradicate the old cultures by denying communication among people of the same language and imposing an alien set of values.[3] The culture of resistance therefore had to be created out of the cultural fragments that remained and out of the solidarity that was forged in the camps themselves. The production of writings out of such situations therefore represents the tangible results of a culture making itself against attempts to eradicate all dissent and all differences. We will not understand this process of creating a culture of resistance and survival if we impose on it another universalism and another monologue on behalf of our favourite causes. For it is crucial in examining the writings of slaves and convicts to see two competing eschatologies – one of collective messianic transcendence and another of individual death and finality. Being stripped of identity until only the breathing body is left is the beginning of death. If this is accompanied by an imposed guilt about the nature of race or religion or original sin, it is a double death. The possibility of 'hope – but not for us'[4] relates entirely to the collective either in this world or the next, and all the biblical promises of salvation come into play either for Jew or Christian. The community of those-about-to-die is retrieved by the community-that-will-be. And yet the community-that-will-be cannot be created except by us, and just as death is individual, collective or both, so is salvation. The 'narrative' of the camps and the slave trade thus has its competing life-allegories, from the sense of immanent individual terminality to the prospects for a reformulation of community, and any attempt to read the writing must be conscious of the multiplicity of stories that are woven into those readings of the future.

The writing out of the camps is therefore a writing which is face to face with terminality: it is the writing of the *tabula rasa*, captured by the sense of an ending, but not necessarily of everything ending.[5] Thus it is a writing which is necessarily conscious of the monologic which created the camps, and yet of a monologic which emerges from a society where dialogue is apparently encouraged.

> We know of personnel in the bureaucracy of the torturers and of the ovens who cultivated a knowledge of Goethe, a lore of Rilke ... One of the principal works that we have in the philosophy of language, in the total reading of Hölderlin's poetry, was composed within earshot of a death camp. Heidegger's pen did not stop nor did his mind go mute.[6]

That the cultivation of humanism had no correlation with creating a universal humanistic culture is evident again and again. The Georgian coffee houses and the writers of the Enlightenment existed side-by-side with the deportation of convicts to Australia and a flourishing slave trade; while Chekhov wrote plays and Rimsky-Koraskov music to great acclaim in cultivated circles, the Tsars sent thousands of intellectuals to Siberia. Indeed, the observation that the internal culture was so schizophrenic that it actively courted its own destruction was present in the autocritique of Western culture from Neitzsche, Dostoevsky and Freud down to Sartre, who could write in the introduction to Fanon's *The Wretched of the Earth*:

Violence has changed its direction. When we were victorious we practised it without its seeming to alter us; it broke down the others, but for us men our humanism remained intact. United by their profits, the peoples of the mother countries baptised their commonwealth of crimes, calling them fraternity and love; today violence, blocked everywhere, comes back on us through our soldiers, comes inside and takes possession of us. Involution starts.[7]

The glee with which Sartre pens this imperial reversal may read like a death-wish ('you will have to fight, or rot in concentration camps'), but it also strikes at the heart of the contradictions embedded in Western culture, and perhaps now reads like the clarion-call of a post-modern world where the humanities, having been demonstrated to have been complicit in barbarism, are reduced, as with all other belief systems, to absolute relativism.

II

In his essays on 'post-culture', George Steiner takes this argument further.

To be argued seriously, the question of 'the guilt of civilization' must include not only colonialism and the rapacities of Empire, but the true nature of the relations of production of great art and thought on the one hand and of regimes of violent and repressive order on the other. In short, it is an argument that does not only involve the white man's rule in Africa or India, but, each time in its own way, the Medicean court, Racine at Versailles and the current genius of Russian literature. (In what sense is Stalinism the necessary condition for a Mandelstam, a Pasternak, a Solzenitsyn?)[8]

We must take the argument further again. If the creative act is produced out of violence, to what extent is the culture of violence itself creative? And further again, if the culture is based on violence, in what ways can we measure the violence necessary to create culture? Or to destroy culture? For, in one sense, the survival of the American blacks and the convicts in Australia provides paradigmatic cases of the making of culture out of the detritus of imperial violence, and in many ways connections can be made between imposed ideologies and transformative utopias. The songs, the writing and the cultural artefacts help us by providing material on which the prisoners' inscriptions can be read against those who incarcerated them. But there are situations where nothing exists, where there was no writing, where the destructive policies were totally carried out, and where a whole people died.

> Thus, by 1834, the last Aborigines of Van Diemen's land had followed their evangelical Pied Piper into a benign concentration camp, set up on Flinders Island in Bass Strait. There Robinson planned to Europeanize them . . . In 1855 the census of natives was three men, two boys and eleven women . . . The last man died in 1869 . . . Realizing that his remains might have some value as a scientific specimen, rival agents of the Royal College of Surgeons in London and the Royal Society in Tasmania fought over his bones.[9]

The only artefacts that remain are fragments of skeletons, and thus human garbage becomes the major inscription left by those incarcerated. It is a fate that attended thousands of Indians over the North American continent, in the jungles of Brazil and in the Caribbean.[10] The Boethics, the Caribs, the Tasmanian Aborigines, the Xokieng – all gone, remembered, like the Bog People of Denmark,[11] only by their bones. And, in Western cultural terms, the same is largely true of the victims of Hitler's Holocaust. In his monumental book of reconstruction, Martin Gilbert begins by saying:

> Jews perished in extermination camps, execution sites, ghettoes, slave labour camps, and on the death marches. The testimony of those who survived constitutes the main record of what was done to the Jews during those years. The murderers also kept records, often copious ones. But the victims, the six million who were done to death, could leave no record. A few fragments of diaries, letters, and scribbled messages do survive. But in the main, others must bear witness to what was done to the millions who could never tell their own story.[12]

As with the Aborigines and the Indians, the sentence of execution was passed long before it was carried out, though in the case of the Jews the slaughter was deliberate. Martin Luther in 1534 had urged that synagogues should be burned, Jewish houses broken down and destroyed, Jews themselves stripped of their belongings and then driven out of Germany for all time.[13] The Jew, throughout the Middle Ages and down to the Enlightenment, was everywhere a folk devil. The Enlightenment itself was realizable only through nationalism, and seemed to provide a stay of execution, an opportunity for Jews to be bourgeois and mobile through the nation state. But as Adorno and Horkheimer wrote in 1943:

> Today race has become the self-assertion of the bourgeois individual integrated within a barbaric collective. The harmony of society which the liberal Jews believed in turned against them in the form of the harmony of national community . . . However successfully it may at times be concealed, force is the essential nature of this order – and we are witnessing its naked truth today.[14]

The nation state, coupled with the dark, mechanistic side of the Enlightenment, carried out the sentence, first in pogroms in Eastern Europe periodically through the nineteenth century and ultimately in the Holocaust. There is no writing from the camps because Jews had been writing from ghettoes, prisons and shtetls long before they were gassed in the camps.[15] The 'emancipation' of Jews in the liberal nation states, including the enablement to acquire property, was coupled with a political powerlessness, a recognition by many that life was dangling on a thread. One of the consequences of this was the importance of both Marxism and Zionism among Jewish intellectuals. For the philosophy of the Jew in the camps we have to read the philosophy of Jews before they went into the camps.

The accounts from the camps, whether written down at the time or recalled later, are in the nature of a roll-call of the dead, and books like Martin Gilbert's *The Holocaust* and Lucy Davidowicz's *The War Against the Jews* and the film *Shoah* provide, as George Steiner has remarked, 'an archivist's *kaddish*, the never-to-be-silenced act of remembrance for the dead'. The concentration camps provided the closure of one Jewish narrative, and the writing, the remembrances, are no more than the punctuation marks of that closure. For, had there been no Jews outside Eastern Europe, Jewish culture would have died as surely as that of the Tasmanian Arborigines or the Newfoundland Boethics. As Marek Edelman, the last surviving leader of the 1944 Warsaw ghetto uprising and still living in Warsaw, has said:

Jewry was the basin between the Vistula and the Dnieper. That's all. What existed in America, in France, in England didn't create a Jewish culture ... Those 5 million Jews from Odessa to Warsaw had a single culture, even the same economic conditions. And that no longer exists. That great Jewish culture is dead and gone and will never return.[16]

If Edelman is right, there is little doubt why the writing from the camps is purely fragmentary or non-existent, and why the writing that exists is either in the form of mechanized accounting by the murderers or a numb hopeless remembrance by the survivors.

As Claude Lanzmann's *Shoah* demonstrates, however, a carefully assembled recollection is necessary in order to understand the technical and social aspects of Nazi extermination. For, as almost every witness to the Holocaust emphasizes, the camps were part of a comprehensive mechanization of death, from the assembly-points in Lublin or Corfu, through the carefully co-ordinated railway system, to the reception areas and ultimately to the gas chambers. At first clumsy – as in the starving of Jews in the Warsaw ghetto – the mechanization of labour, of transportation and of the camps themselves was brought to near-perfection in the main Auschwitz camp where the machinery of death itself took over from all other functions. But the camps were run on pure capitalist lines. They had to be self-sufficient at least and turn a profit if possible. And the workers at the camps, the able-bodied, the political and religious and skilled prisoners who were responsible for all jobs at the camps, from barbers to oven-stokers and in the burial parties, survived off the 'profits' of the camps. The profits came from the booty stolen from those who were railroaded to the gas chambers. As Richard Glazar, one of the inmates at Treblinka, recalled:

The trainloads came from an assembly camp in Salonika. They'd brought in Jews from Bulgaria, Macedonia. These were rich people; the passenger cars bulged with possessions. Then an awful feeling gripped us, all of us, my companions as well as myself, a feeling of helplessness, of shame. For we threw ourselves on their food. A detail brought a crate full of crackers, another full of jam. They deliberately dropped the crates, falling over each other, filling their mouths with crackers and jam. The trainloads from the Balkans brought us to a terrible realization: we were the workers in the Treblinka factory, and our lives depended on the whole manufacturing process, that is, the slaughtering process at Treblinka.[17]

The chances of survival depended, too, in part on the section of the camp one was in, but also on the degree of mechanization. Rudolph Vrba, a survivor from Auschwitz, described the procedure this way:

> Auschwitz–Birkenau was far from being only a mass murder center. It was a normal concentration camp too, which had its order, like Mauthausen, like Buchenwald, like Dachau, like Sachsenhausen. But whereas in Mauthausen the main product of prisoners' work was stone – there was a big stone quarry – the product in Auschwitz was death. Everything was geared to keep the crematorium running. This was the aim. This meant the prisoners would work on the road to the crematorium, would build the crematorium. They would build all barracks necessary for keeping up prisoners and of course, apart from that, there was an element of a normal German concentration camp – the Krupp and Siemens factories moved in and utilized slave labor. So the Krupp factory and the Siemens factory were built partly within the concentration camp Auschwitz–Brikenau.[18]

But in the tension between the needs of regular production and the production of death, death won out. Improving conditions in one part of the camp did not mean a reduction of death in the other. Vrba again:

> If the needs of the camp were, say, thirty thousand prisoners, and five thousand died, they were replaced by a new force from the Jewish transport which came in. But if only a thousand died, well, only a thousand were replaced and more went into the gas chamber. So the improvement of the conditions within the camp itself made a higher death rate in the gas chamber, straight into the gas chamber. It decreased the death rate among the prisoners in the concentration camp. So here it was clear to me that the improvement of the situation in the concentration camp does not impede the process of mass executions of those people who are brought into the camp. Consequently, my idea then of the Resistance movement, of the sense of the Resistance movement, was that the improvement of the conditions within the camp is only a first step, that the main thing is to stop the process of mass execution, the machinery of the killing, and that therefore it is a time of preparation, of gathering forces for attacking the

SS from inside – even if it is a suicide mission – but destroying the machinery.[19]

The Resistance movement was therefore caught in an impossible dilemma:

> But it was clear in my mind that the only objective of any resistance within the concentration camp of the type of Auschwitz has to be different from that in Mauthausen or Dachau. Because whereas in Mauthausen or Dachau this policy of resistance improved the survival rate of political prisoners, the same very noble policy improved and oiled the machinery of mass annihilation as practiced by the Nazis within the Auschwitz camp.[20]

A number of things stand out from these accounts. The booty capitalism that buttressed the whole system was reinforced in the first place by the use of Jewish and other prison convict labour and by a mechanization of production and destruction, the productive side being necessary for building and maintaining the camps and their services. In Nazi logic, the Jews had to finance their own liquidation – including paying for the 'charter' convoys that brought them by rail from their home towns to the camps and, in the case of the Warsaw ghetto, paying taxes for the wall.[21] Any effective resistance therefore had to smash the machines themselves and also deprive the Germans of the sources of booty. The first was impossible given the mechanization of transportation/reception, and the second would presumably only be possible when all Jews had been either incarcerated or killed, unless another Holocaust against other non-Aryan races was set in motion. (Though, in fact, the war against the Jews was the second Holocaust. 'The first victims of the German camps,' as Primo Levi reminds us, 'by the hundreds of thousands, were, in fact, the cadres of anti-Nazi political parties.')[22] Mechanization, convict labour and booty capitalism were the pillars that maintained the system of extermination.

A final point that emerges from *Shoah* is the extent to which the Nazis commandeered the everyday routines of those who did not go to the camps. In repeated cases workers who were responsible for doing their normal jobs (e.g. preparing timetables for trains, or working the railway signals) and villagers who were doing their everyday chores were interviewed to get a sense of what they remembered, what they thought they were doing and what the trains or the camps meant. And here, I think, we have the bloody sense that everyday, the normal continues, but that its end product has become abnormal, and that the functionaries, the market women, the railway workers, know that everything has changed but that everything seems to be the same. Blank stares, numb incomprehension, heads bowed, stealing a glance here, offering a cup of water there, back to work, to the store, to the fireplace, to the timetables. There is no such thing as commonsensical reality, because in the cattle-trucks the everyday, the personal, the private, the public have become criminalized, and the onlookers fear their own reality.

But from the camps, an angry prayer:

For the smoke that rises from crematoriums obeys physical laws like any other: the particles come together and disperse according to the wind that propels them. The only pilgrimage, estimable reader, would be to look with sadness at a stormy sky now and then.

And praised. Auschwitz. Be. Maidanek. The Lord. Treblinka. And praised. Buchenwald. Be. Mauthausen. The Lord. Belzec. And praised. Sobibor. Be. Chelmno. The Lord. Ponary. And praised. Theresienstadt. Be. Warsaw. The Lord. Vilna. And praised. Skarzysko. Be. Bergen-Belsen. The Lord. Janow. And Praised. Dora. Be. Neuengamme. The Lord. Pustkow. And praised . . .

Yes, at times one's heart could break in sorrow. But often too, preferably in the evening, I can't help thinking that Ernie Levy, dead six million times, is still alive somewhere, I don't know where . . .

The voice that cries out of the gas chambers is necessarily incoherent, death having put an end to talking and writing and myth-making. As Theodor Adorno wrote of Schoenberg, it is fragmentary music that may be the ultimate in transmuting the horror of the camps into a new articulation.

The late Schoenberg composed not works, but paradigms of a possible music. The idea of music itself grows all the more transparent as the works insist less and less on their appearance. They begin to acquire the character of the fragment, the shadow of which followed Schoenberg's art throughout his life. His last pieces give a fragmentary impression, not merely in their brevity but in their shrivelled diction. The dignity of the great works devolves on splinters. Oratorio and Biblical opera are outweighed by the tale of the Survivor from Warsaw, which lasts only a few minutes; in this piece, Schoenberg, acting on his own, suspends the aesthetic sphere through the recollection of experiences which are inaccessible to art. Anxiety, Schoenberg's expressive core, identifies itself with the terror of men in the agonies of death, under total domination. The sounds of Erwartung, the shocks of the Music for the Film, of 'impending danger, anxiety, catastrophe', finally meet what they had always prophesied. That which the feebleness and impotence of the individual soul seemed to express testifies to what has been inflicted on mankind in those who represent the whole as its victims. Horror has never rung as true in music, and by articulating it music regains its redeeming power through negation. The Jewish song with which the Survivor from Warsaw concludes is music as the protest of mankind against myth.[24]

But there are other responses in the post-culture. One of these is amnesic, another is politically utilitarian, another is a conscious cultural regrouping, and a final one (given that not everyone who went to the camps died) is a rethinking and retelling of what survival means: in Primo Levi's terms, contemplating the 'moments of reprieve'.[25] From the economically and politically assimilated Jews of Western Europe and North America to their satellite henchmen who control Israel, the politically utilitarian is paramount. Selective memory (the 'facts') may compete with the practical politics of getting by. The Holocaust as symbol may be conveniently used by politicians or the media to popularize a folk memory in order to project an ideological position which has little to do with understanding the Holocaust. (The television series *The Holocaust* was a dramatic example of just such reduction to banality, and should be contrasted with Claude Lanzmann's *Shoah*, which was an archival reconstruction.) Political utilitarianism is bound up with the vested interests of leaders of the rabbinate who absorb elements of the Holocaust into a moral blackmail on behalf of Israel. Rabid conservatism make the Horror an occasion for a one-dimensional paean of praise to the present ruling system. In opting for total North American cultural assimilation and an unspiritual Judaism, the political utilitarians gain their political power vicariously through the state of Israel, and their moral righteousness from the deaths of six million others. Their mouthpiece is *Commentary* and their political messiah is Ronald Reagan.[26] In many respects their position is not unlike that of those who suffer from total amnesia – gentile and Jew – except that their slight remembrance brings with it a price tag: to remember the Holocaust involves transferring to Russia the guilt for the past and the present. The 'Jews of Silence' replace the East European dead. For the second time in their recent history (the first was in the Germany of the First and Second Reich) the Jews have been co-opted by a dominant ideology; so much so that those other Auschwitzes of 1945, Hiroshima and Nagasaki, are barely mentioned in this form of remembrance. The sheer mechanization of terror and annihilation is swept aside in the interests of a knee-jerk capitalist solidarity.

The amnesic solution relates centrally to those who survived the Holocaust and those who were present when it took place. And in a more specific sense it relates to the majority of people who continued to live in East and Central Europe after 1945. Poland is a crucial case because half of all the Jews who died between 1939 and 1945 came from Poland, and the mechanism by which the Jews of the Holocaust were forgotten and then remembered is well documented. A Polish–Jewish scholar has put the problem succinctly:

> As an experience, the destruction of Polish Jewry was kept at a *distance*. It was something happening to an Other and something instigated by a foreign power. It was something that could be and was *bracketed* out from within the totality of Polish–Jewish relations, both for better and for worse. Furthermore, when Jews were being herded into the ghettos and then systematically murdered, theirs was an experience which could not be and was not shared, and yet it did not look altogether different from what Poles were subjected to in the course of Nazi occupation. Later, the memory of Jewish suffering was to be put again on a par with the memory of Polish victims, testimony to the evils of Nazism. And as it became more and more 'Polonized', the Holocaust lost its potential to undermine the existing structure of beliefs about the Jew. The message it had imprinted on Poland's memory was a universal one; it was also one which could be fitted into the overall 'victimological' vision of the national past. Jews *and* Poles as victims made no room, intellectually and emotionally, for considerations of the Poles' moral responsibility. They also left very little room indeed for an inquiry into the roots of anti-Jewish phobias. With the question 'Why the Jews?' never truly on the agenda, memory of the Holocaust, just as Auschwitz itself, was freed from its conscience-troubling aspects. And the very horror of the 'Final

Solution', when identified solely with the Nazis, only strengthened the Poles' conviction that 'we have nothing to account for.'

At this point, a brief comparative note might be of help. During recent years, a number of authors in the West have remarked on the remarkable phenomenon of a growing fascination with the Nazi period on the one hand and an increase in efforts to deny the very existence of gas chambers on the other. In countries such as West Germany and France in particular, there appears to have developed a counter-force to all the soul-searching prompted by the 'haunting Jew', a way of saying 'enough!' to guilt feelings and remorse. To some interpreters, the turnabout in positions vis-à-vis Israel or the cries of indignation at the Zionist 'final solution' in Lebanon, for example, are but one sign of people growing tired of having to account to the Jew.

The arrival of this new discourse designed to free Western conscience from the ghosts of the Holocaust and glorify Hitler is just beginning to be understood. But what is of direct relevance to us here is that nothing of the kind can be observed in Poland. It seems quite inconceivable indeed that anyone there would utter words in praise of the Nazi vision of the world or even attempt to deny the reality of the Auschwitz crematoria. By the same token, though, it is only very recently and very gradually that the Jews have been made to inhabit Auschwitz again, so to speak. Brief references, more often than not in the form of 'letters to the editor', emphasizing that it was Jews as Jews who were killed at various sites in Poland, constitute only the most direct indication of a more general trend introduced by the whole 'Jewish memory project'. To re-constitute the Jew in Poland's memory does begin to mean leaving Auschwitz without Jews behind.

It is then just at the time that some people in the West are trying to rid their world of the Jew's haunting presence, that the Poles appear set on offering him a permanent locale in their memory. Does it make any sense? Yes, it does, if we keep in mind that just as the 'silent Jew' had no means to disturb the collective conscience, the newly present Jew is not likely to do that either. Indeed, it might well be that his very status as someone who is now welcome is what best guarantees his 'good behaviour'. In other words, far from spelling trouble for the collective sense of self, the whole re-discovery of Poland's Jewish heritage may in fact provide the best means possible finally to *neutralize* the past.[27]

This very process, however, leads to a possible regrouping, to a rethinking of the concept of what 'Jew' means in Poland – or indeed, anywhere in Central Europe today. It is worth quoting again from the Marek Edelman interview:

What do you think it means to be a Jew nowadays?
Where? Here in Poland? . . . It means to be on the side of the weak, not of the government. The government here always beat the Jews, just like Solidarity is beaten today. Bujak is beaten by the government. I think that irrespective of who is being beaten you have to side with them. You should give them a place to stay, let them take refuge in your basement. You should not be afraid of them, and in general you should oppose those who are doing the beating. . . .

What do you think that people who call themselves Jews ought to identify with? Where should these people look to find their place in the world?
If they think of themselves as Jews in Europe, then they'll always be against the state. A Jew always has a sense of community with the very weakest.

In that case, is there any difference between a Jew who is on the side of the weak and those who are weak but not Jewish?
No. none. Bujak, Kuron, Michnik, Jaworski, Lis, Frasyniuk – they are the Jews of this system.[28]

What this argument presupposes, in contradiction to the conformist Zionism of North America, is that the very act of dissent is a 'Jewish' position and that to understand dissent in Central Europe we have to understand the continuing presence of Jews even after the Holocaust. The past may thus be not 'neutralized', as Irwin Zarecka argues, but made immediate and present. Something of the same position is adopted by liberal Jewish intellectuals, though with a different point of comparison. The Holocaust demonstrated that, given specific socio-cultural conditions and the necessary sophistication of technology, it was possible

to eradicate a whole people from the earth for reasons that had nothing to do with political realities. In a similar way, the idea of nuclear war lacks the most elementary political rationality, for it would necessarily destroy everything it meant to save: it would take genocide, invented in its most systematic form by the Nazis, to its global and suicidal conclusion.[29]

The Jewish experience of powerlessness becomes universal.

The Universal Auschwitz, now *that* is an eternal monument still waiting to be erected by some Super-Hitler who will not even mind that no one will remain to be horrified by his monument. So the warning of 'never again'? The warning to the rest of us to prevent such a Super-Hitler, *that* may remain as the only decently usable product of the Holocaust.[30]

But to do this requires seeing in the past, in the Holocaust, not only the Terror, but also the survival; to remember not only how a people died but how they lived, to work on the strategies of reprieve from the death sentences. It is in this respect that Primo Levi's autobiographies and fictions stand as the consummate literature of the Holocaust, the works which provide the cameos from which the wider issues of remembrance and action can be seen. It is Levi (who died in mysterious circumstances, with a suspicion of murder by neo-Fascists, in 1987) who provides the clue to rethinking the narrative, rescuing it from apocalyptic allegory or collective self-indulgence and placing it (just) within the realm of the daily practical.

Levi's writing began with his two early memoirs, *Survival in Auschwitz* (1947) (also published as *If This is a Man*), and *The Reawakening* (1965) (also published as *The Truce*), and continued with *The Monkey's Wrench* (1984), *If not Now, When?* (1985), *The Periodic Table* (1986) and *Moments of Reprieve* (1986). His vantage point for writing is unique. Levi was an Italian Jew, trained as a chemist, a member of the anti-Fascist partisan group; he was arrested in December 1943 and deported to Auschwitz in February 1944. He was one of twenty survivors of the convoy of 650 who were transported. He was released by the Red Army in January 1945, but, because of bureaucratic confusion, spent eight months travelling through East and Central Europe. His writing was spread over forty years, during most of which time he worked as an industrial chemist. The literary critical reception of Levi's work has been overwhelmingly superlative in tone[31] and most critics have caught the essence of Levi's achievement: his economy of phrase, his sense of the understatement, his commitment to the rational, his ability to project back into the past without allowing the political ideologies of the present to intervene. In addition, there is his sense of significant detail and his apparent detachment, though it is a detachment which is born, in Irving Howe's words, of total remembrance

> that leads Levi into despair and then at least partly beyond it, so that he does not flinch from anything, neither shame nor degradation, that actually happened at Auschwitz, yet refuses in his writings to indulge in those outbursts of self-pity, sometimes sliding into self-aggrandizement, which understandably mar a fair number of Holocaust memoirs and fictions.[32]

And yet there is another aspect of Levi's work which sets him apart from all writers who have tried to portray the Holocaust. His attempt at exploring the everyday aspects of camp experiences, of his release, of his travels through Eastern Europe, of his self-projection into the situations and lifestyles of other Jews, creates a polyphonic world of the camps that is quite unlike that of other Jewish writers. To do this he has not only to remember, read, and project himself backwards, but to read his own experiences against the popular fictions of what those situations *should* be like. In a series of answers to readers' questions which appear as an 'Afterword' to *The Reawakening*, he deals with the issue of why there were no large-scale revolts. His answer, in part, reads:

> The concept of escape as a moral obligation is constantly reinforced by romantic literature (remember the Count of Montecristo?), by popular literature, and by the cinema, in which the hero, unjustly (or even justly) imprisoned always tries to escape, even in the least likely circumstances, the attempt being invariably crowned with success.
>
> Perhaps it is good that the prisoner's condition, non-liberty, is felt to be something improper, abnormal – like an illness, in short – that has to be cured by escape or rebellion. Unfortunately, however, this picture hardly resembles a true one of the concentration camps.[33]

Levi's memoirs/fictions are therefore attempts to come to terms with the everyday nature of prison and escape *against* the misreading by others, especially his friends and allies. His deftness of touch consists, as with Dostoevsky, in writing into the script all the aspects of 'the demolition of man' that can be imagined without allowing one or other of the devils to have the dominating voice. Progressively – from *The Reawakening* on – there are two narratives competing with each other in Levi's work. One is the narrative of the camps – documented primarily in *Survival in Auschwitz* and *Moments of Reprieve* – and the other is the narrative outside the camps, the narrative based on establishing moments of resistance, of reclaiming the everyday world from the Nazi appropriation of it. Given the dominating power of the political–economic mechanism of terror, Levi's writing tries not only to reclaim humanity – though he does that – but to raise all the disturbing questions of what kind of humanity is to be reclaimed in what kind of society. Through his characters he urges us to make sense of all that continues to puzzle and disturb.

The significance or insignificance of religion is an important question. In his interview in *Across Frontiers*, Marek Edelman argues that religion played no major part in Jewish attitudes in Poland:

> In the ghetto, Religion got up and left. All those stories you hear about the Jews praying when the uprising began are just so many pleasant literary fantasies. People were killed for nothing. You might be walking along the street, or if your hair was black or even grey they'd kill you. How can you believe in God in a situation like that? A person who's done nothing wrong. He may have wanted to clean that German's boots or something like that. He stoops down. The German shoots him. So what do you think? If Christ passes the death sentence on 20 million Poles will the Poles all stay believers?[34]

These strong and extreme words are uncomfortable to Western ears, but the question of what importance there is in religious belief after God has apparently failed is a crucial one after the Holocaust. Levi deals with the issue cunningly, bypassing Edelman's theatrical and Hobbsean sense of polarities and seizing instead on the appropriation of belief in the minutae of everyday behaviour. It may not matter whether the ghetto prayed *en masse*; what matters more is what a prayer or belief means in the senselessness of an irrational situation. In *Moments of Reprieve*, Levi provides a series of pen-portraits of people trying to gain breathing space, and two of these (told as stories provided for him by others) give a glimpse of the problem inherent both in the continuation of any religious sensibility and in the moment of distancing from it.

In 'Lillith' a caballistic story is told of how God, because of his loneliness, took as his wife the *Shekhina*, the glory of his own presence in creation. She became the mother of all people, but when the temple in Jerusalem was destroyed and the Jews scattered and made captives, the *Shekhina* was angry with God, left him and went to live with the Jews in exile. But God, unable to be alone, took to himself a mistress. This was Lillith, the woman of the first creation, before Eve, who was created equal with man, but who rebelled against subservience to Adam and became the she-devil, the mother of all devils.

> It seems, in short, that things unfolded as in a quarrel when one insult is answered by a more serious insult, so the quarrel never ends; on the contrary it grows like an avalanche. Because you must know that this obscene tryst has not ended, and won't end soon. In one way it's the cause of the evil that occurs on earth; in another way, it is its effect. As long as God continues to sin with Lillith, there will be blood and trouble on Earth. But one day a powerful being will come – the one we are all waiting for. He will make Lillith die and put an end to God's lechery, and to our exile. Yes, even to yours and mine . . .[35]

In another story, 'The Cantor and the Barracks Chief', Levi tells the story of a Cantor who, on Passover Day, asked the chief of the barracks at Auschwitz to excuse him from eating his soup, but to save it for him until the next day. The barracks chief (an ex-member of the German Communist Party) is unable to understand such a bizarre request and is given explanations, 'sacred and profane'. And when the barracks chief tries to develop the logic of the Cantor's arguments ('What are you trying to tell me with this story of yours? That you are fasting for me too? And for everybody, even for – Them?') the Cantor replies that, 'unlike Jonah, he was not a prophet but a provincial Cantor'.[36] Muttering that the Cantor was *meshuge* (crazy), the barracks chief obliges and stores the soup for the next day. Levi concludes:

> Actually Ezra wasn't really *meshuge*. He was heir to an ancient, sorrowful, and strange tradition, whose core consists in holding evil in opprobrium and in 'hedging about the law' so that evil may not flood through the gaps in the hedge and submerge the law itself. In the course of the millennia, around this core has become encrusted a gigantic proliferation of comments, deductions, almost maniacally subtle distinctions, and further precepts and prohibitions. And in the course of the millennia many have behaved like Ezra throughout migrations and slaugh-

ters without number. That is why the history of the Jewish people is so ancient, sorrowful, and strange.[37]

In these two stories we have Levi's framework for the Jewish religious *angst*. The story of God and Lillith provides the structure for beginning to understand the wager of belief and unbelief, the story of the Cantor the problem of practice. The God who allowed this to happen to us is in bed with the she-devil (whom he created). Meanwhile the Ideal of his creation (the Lady Philosophy of Boethius) is living with us, giving us what support she can. It is she who, presumably, is goading the Cantor into preserving the minimal ritual of Passover, against all the logic of the rationalists, and who forces a stranger 'to repeat this impious tale, woven of poetry, ignorance, daring acumen and the unassuageable sadness that grows on the ruins of lost civilizations'.[38] Levi's religious commitment was never strong: his background was that of an Italian cosmopolitan. Being *branded* a Jew is a surprise. It is therefore even more important to bring the sense of religious turmoil into the realization of Jewishness.[39] Like Walter Benjamin (with the knowledge that the Caballists had been here before, and also that the practices of the present never seemed more remote than now) Levi tries to pull together the conflicting presences. But his work is a parody not of Goethe's *Faust* or the *Elective Affinities*, but of Dante. The images that come out clearly in Levi's withdrawal from total commitment to the God of Israel are those of the *Inferno* and the *Paradiso*. The *Shekhina* / Lady Philosophy / Beatrice is not always with us either. As he negotiates himself through the levels of hell (and how marvellous Levi is in describing, locating the pipes, the marshes, the abbatoirs!), the detached conspirator, the survivor, knows that he is not alone, but wonders who his allies are. The rediscovery of Jewishness, of the variety of Jewish people with their own idiosyncracies, is the hallmark of Levi's work. It is not just that Levi makes other people's survival his own – he doesn't even do that: he moves in, then stands back – it is that he knews that for other survivals to be part of his we have to recognize how problematic survival is. If not now, when? The war that invented the master spies on behalf of the Big Powers also produced the worried spy acting on behalf of a puzzled people. Levi's mischievous spying leaves us asking who we are. Walter Benjamin, in his 'Theses on the Philosophy of History', written with full awareness of the impending Holocaust, wrote that

the true image of the past flits by. The past can be seized only as an image which flashes up at the instant when it can be

recognized and is never seen again . . . for every image of the
past that is not recognized by the present as one of its own
concerns threatens to disappear irretrievably . . . Only that
historian will have the gift of fanning the spark of hope in the
past who is firmly convinced that *even the dead* will not be safe
from the enemy [the ruling class] if he wins. And, this enemy
has not ceased to be victorious.[40]

Levi's act of remembrance, of reclaiming the dead from the enemy,
is to tell the stories of the living and their survival, with all of its
continued echoes of a still-pending death sentence. The dead are no
different from us, and murmuring Kaddish prayers, in George Steiner's
sense, will not help them or us. Constructing bigger and better
ghettoes such as Israel will not help either, nor will the abdication of
all collective decisions to yet another Pharoah or another King
Herod.[41] The message of the camps is of our total fragility and the
importance of recognizing our strangeness in face of the terrifying
machinery of certainty. It is the ambiguity of life that is our hope of
survival. Our commitment, in Marek Edelman's words, is to be on
the side of the weak, our determination to reclaim the everyday, the
commonplace, the personal from those who would subject it to the
mechanism of inhuman power. The struggle is against all those
Holocausts that may yet be in store for us, under whatever name or
for whatever cause. And if the Enemy is not to win again and finally,
we have to know why we are *here* and not in some undiscovered
country that has never been ours.

For ultimately the message of the Holocaust is that the everyday
that was taken as normal by us was not taken as normal by *them*.
Our normalcy was taken as a threat, and shocked them. Every one
of them from Hitler down to the Polish peasant contemplating the
thirteen-year-old going to his bar-mitzvah, was shocked by *difference*
which became a challenge to his lifestyle, his everyday world. That
difference had to go. De Tocqueville prophesied it in the USA as the
'tyranny of the majority' in *Democracy in America*, Pascal as the
worry of Jewish rectitude in the *Pensées* in France, Oliver Cromwell
as he slit the Catholic noses in Ireland, Winston Churchill as he told
the Welsh mining rats to 'get back to their holes' after the 1926
General Strike, and, of course, Martin Luther as he provided reasons
for expelling the Jews from Prussia. The problem was that difference
was too much to bear if self-identifying power was to maintain itself.
Not only was it important to wipe out the 'Jew' (with his absurd
normalcy): it was also important to wipe out his creations, his

writings. Unfortunately for the exterminator, the Jewish writings were at the centre of his own sense of himself. He could not wipe out Jewish creation without wiping out himself. He, too, would make love, have children, live through differences. Even more now, he would only be able to do it by remembering, in his Biblical texts, those who had been here before. After reading the accounts of the Holocaust – whatever life was before – it is impossible to take children to school, play with them and look at beautiful women or marry them without realizing that life is more precious now than ever. The everyday has become very sacred.

NOTES

1   Thus, although there are accounts of slavery in the development of Western capitalism, of the forced labour camps in the development of Russia and even Australia, of the concentration camps in Germany and, indeed, of the Asiatic mode of production and its implications for social control and political ideology, there is no theoretical handle by which we can begin to grasp all of this in the development of contemporary societies. The concept of the Wretched of the Earth as developed by Fanon goes some way towards beginning a phenomenological approach, as does the work of Horkheimer, Adorno, Benjamin and Foucault, but it is a slender beginning.

2   Edward Percival Thompson, *The Making of the English Working Class* (London: Gollancz, 1963), p. 13.

3   This is, of course, not true in the same way of the Nazi concentration camps where the object was to eliminate the Jews, communists and homosexuals. Any remains of the pre-camp culture were thus accidental in that Germany was defeated before the inmates had all been exterminated. The internment of aliens and the kikuyu camps were too short-lived and also related to contiguous cultural hinterlands to attempt such clear deracinement as did the gulags, deportation to Australia and slavery in America.

4   Walter Benjamin, *Illuminations* (London: Cape, 1970), p. 148.

5   A suggestive comparison between writing out of prison and the preoccupation of modern fiction is made by Frank Kermode in *The Sense of an Ending* (Oxford: Oxford University Press, 1967).

6   George Steiner, *In Bluebeard's Castle: some Notes towards the Re-definition of Culture* (London: Faber, 1971), p. 63.

7   Frantz Fanon, *The Wretched of the Earth* (London: Weidenfeld and Nicolson, 1965), p. 23.

8   Steiner, *In Bluebeard's Castle*, p. 54.

9   Robert Hughes, *The Fatal Shore: the Epic of Australia's Founding* (New York: Knopf, 1986), p. 423. The very last Aboriginal Tasmanian was Trucanini, a former prostitute who died in 1876, followed by a funeral procession.

Huge crowds lined the pavements to watch her small, almost square coffin roll by; they followed it to the cemetery, and saw it lowered into a grave. It was empty. Fearing some unseemly public disturbance, the government had buried her corpse in a vault of the Protestant Chapel in the Hobart Penitentiary the night before. So Trucanini lay not 'behind the mountains,' but in gaol. In 1878 they dug her up again and sloughed the flesh off her bones, then boiled them and nailed them in an apple crate, which lay in storage for some years. The crate was about to be thrown out when someone from the Tasmanian Museum and Art Gallery read the faded label. The bones were strung together, and the skeleton of Trucanini went into a glass case in the museum, where it remained until feelings of public delicacy and humanitarian sentiment caused it to be removed, in 1947, to the basement. In 1976, the centenary of her death, the authorities – not knowing what else to do with this otherwise ineradicable dweller in their closet – had it cremated, and the ashes were scattered on the waters of the D'Entrecasteaux Channel. (Hughes, *The Fatal Shore*, p. 424)

10 As an example, in Brazil, the reader should refer to John Hemming, *Amazon Frontier: the Defeat of the Brazilian Indians* (London: Macmillan, 1987). In 1500 the Brazilian Indian population was 2.5 million. By 1827 there were 100,000.

11 See P. V. Glob, *The Bog People* (London: Faber, 1969), and also chapter 8 above, on Death Row.

12 Martin Gilbert, *The Holocaust* (London: Fontana, 1986).

13 Quoted from Martin Luther, *On Jews and their Lies* (1543), in Gilbert, *The Holocaust*, p. 19.

14 Max Horkheimer and Theodor Adorno, *Dialectic of Enlightenment* (London: Allen Lane, 1973), pp. 170–1.

15 Any chapter on the Holocaust should defend this statement. But the culture of the shtetl has been written long and thoroughly, and the sense of impending doom is present in all Jewish writing from the Babylonian captivity to the early twentieth century. Moralism was the fruit of a secular hope, Zionism the flickering flame of chiliastic despair.

16 Marek Edelman, 'You Have to be on the Side of the Weak: a Conversation', *Across Frontiers*, 3, 3 (Spring 1987), pp. 32–3.

17 Claude Lantzmann, *Shoah: an Oral History of the Holocaust. The Complete Text of the Film* (New York: Pantheon, 1985), pp. 147–8.

18 Ibid., p. 150.

19 Ibid., pp. 152–3.

20 Ibid., p. 153.

21 The only convoys that provided 'free' passages to death were those that came from Greece, because the travel agent did not know how to convert drachmas into marks (Lantzmann, *Shoah*, pp. 138–44).

22 Primo Levi, *If not Now, When?* (New York: Penguin, 1985), p. 205.

23 André Schwarz-Bart, *The Last of the Just* (New York: Bantam Books, 1961), p. 422.

24 Theodor Adorno, *Prisms* (London: Neville Spearman, 1967) p. 172.

25 Primo Levi, along with Isaac Bashevis Singer, is arguably the greatest of the post-culture retellers of the camp experiences. See in particular *Moments of*

Reprieve (London: Michael Joseph, 1981), *If not Now, When?* and *The Reawakening* (New York: Simon and Schuster, 1965).

26   'On one occasion, the President told a White House audience of Jews on Holocaust Day that, unlike right wing extremists who claimed the Holocaust was an invention, he *knew* it had happened because he had seen movies of it' (Michael Wallace, 'Ronald Reagan and the Politics of History', *Tikkun*, 2, 1 (1987), p. 18).

27   Iwona Irwin-Zarecka, *On a Memory Note: the Jew in Contemporary Poland* (PhD thesis, University of California at San Diego, 1987), pp. 176–7. Published in book form as *Neutralizing Memory: the Jew in Contemporary Poland* (New Brunswick, NJ: Transaction Books, 1989).

28   Edelman, 'You Have to be on the Side of the Weak', pp. 32–3.

29   David Biale, 'Rethinking the Holocaust', *Tikkun*, 2, 1 (1987), p. 73.

30   Arthur Waskow, 'Rethinking the Holocaust', *Tikkun*, 2, 1 (1987), p. 86.

31   See Irving Howe, 'Primo Levi: an Appreciation', in Levi, *If not Now, When?* pp. 3–16.

32   Ibid., p. 9.

33   Levi, *The Reawakening*, p. 202.

34   Edleman, 'You Have to be on the Side of the Weak', p. 5.

35   Levi, *If not Now, When?*, p. 44.

36   Ibid., p. 80.

37   Ibid., p. 82.

38   Ibid., p. 45.

39   Orthodox Jews have taken the secularization of Judaism as being the problem which created the Holocaust. But the Holocaust did not only involve the Jews – secular or not – but also communists, socialists and homosexuals. The Holocaust was an attack on difference, an attack on the marginality of those who were irrational against the seeming rationality of racial brotherhood. To resist another Holocaust, it is important to make a stand against *that* brotherhood.

40   Benjamin, *Illuminations*, p. 257.

41   And, of course, on the American right, there are those (of whose company the former President Ronald Reagan is apparently one), who seek for Armageddon, who believe that the Apocalypse is around the corner. There are those who, using Israel as their pretext, would like to blow us all out of the present into the never-never land. We, who want to live, must resist the Thanatos of the Christian-based nihilism. See Martin Gardner, 'Giving God a Hand', *New York Review of Books*, 13 August 1987, pp. 17–24, for a succinct account of the Christian fundamentalist 'Apocalypse Now'.

Part III

CONCLUSION

10

Inscribing the Everyday

No, no, no, no! Come, let's away to prison;
We too alone will sing like birds i' the cage:
When thou dost ask me blessing, I'll kneel down,
And ask of thee forgiveness: so we'll live,
And pray, and sing, and tell old tales, and laugh
At gilded butterflies, and hear poor rogues
Talk of court news; and we'll talk with them too,
Who loses and who wins; who's in, who's out;
And take upon's the mystery of things,
As if we were God's spies: and we'll wear out,
In a wall'd prison, packs and sects of great ones
That ebb and flow by the moon.

William Shakespeare, *King Lear*, V, iii, 8–19

I

Prison experience is brutal enough and the tapping on the walls conveys its own acoustic message; and yet the metaphorical appropriation of prison, though bizarre in some of its manifestations (how *dare* Norman Mailer talk about being a 'prisoner' of sex?)[1] is also real enough, in that the metaphorical prison has become integral to our perceptions of our everyday lives, as Shakespeare's 400-year-old words suggest. And yet, what interconnections can we make between the recorded accounts of prisoners and our own attempts at writing out of our commonplace experiences? In other words, does prison literature convey more to us than a separate existence of which we can never be a part, or must it always be appropriated as mere metaphor?

The perils of metaphorical appropriation are evident enough, and it might be useful to examine the more linear versions of these before working out a language of plausible congruence. Some versions of metaphorical use were hinted at in the early chapters – for example, that of Pascal, whose sense of the double prison (God and the world), and that of the political sociologists who coined the term 'totalitarian' to deal with whole societies as 'total' institutions. The problems of applying metaphors as methods of interpreting everyday life might be seen best by contrast. Two examples, by non-prisoners, suggest the complexity of the problem. The first of these, by Stanley Cohen and Laurie Taylor, is a direct metaphorical spin-off of an earlier study conducted by the authors on prison psychology. But whereas *Psychological Survival* was a careful documentation of case-histories of prisoners' survival strategies, *Escape Attempts: the Theory and Practice of Resistance to Everyday Life* was an attempt, using Erving Goffman and Georg Simmel as the templates, to read into everyday experience the lessons learned from studying deviant behaviour.

Cohen and Taylor's concern in writing *Escape Attempts* may not have been too far from mine in writing this book.

> We wanted to do more than show that deviance and crime were meaningful, we also wanted to characterize the consciousness of the deviant, to show that there was, perhaps, some homogeneous view of the world which linked together the individual groups that we studied. Specifically, we hoped to establish that the deviant held a picture of the world as a repressive place. His actions were a way of fighting against that repression. He was a social critic, a rebel, even a revolutionary.[2]

But the recognition that the deviant was not necessarily a revolutionary in that simplistic sense, and that behaviour and intentions were complex, led Cohen and Taylor to examine 'normalcy' and even boredom as features of everyday life:

> We put on one side books about rape, murder and revolution and started reading holiday brochures, gardening magazines, do-it-yourself manuals. We examined in detail the simple ways in which those around us got through their days.[3]

This transition from seeing the criminal as potential revolutionary to wanting to explore 'the mundane reality of getting by'[4] was manufactured at the price of imposing prison as the metaphor of everyday life. Cohen and Taylor's book owes everything to their research on 'deviants', 'criminals' and 'prisoners' and very little to the sense that the everyday routines might provide their own text. Every chapter is constructed around a topic or theme suggested by prison experience, even though the subject matter is derived from accounts of the activities of non-prisoners.[5] The metaphorical straitjacket squeezes the stories, preventing them from telling their own tale, or at least allowing the storyteller to establish his or her own correspondences.

What the book does, however, is to establish a link between the experience of the prisoner and the experiences of all of us at the level of our own reading of the texts that are superimposed on us. By preserving, if only tangentially, the utopian sensibility that things might be *better*, it allows for the possibility of a new reading of our literatures and theirs. But because the book is not sensitive to text itself as a problem, it is ultimately framed by text: by the textuality of its own metaphor.

Cohen and Taylor do not try to impose mega-texts on all of us. If anything, their book is modest. The French author Jean Baudrillard has created a wide apocalyptic vision of contemporary society where nothing exists apart from the multiple images of the real.[6] At least Cohen and Taylor invite us, through their metaphorical frame, to listen to the people talking, writing, singing, dancing, playing games, and the authors' effort at connecting the prison experiences and those of all of us is surely important if prison writing is not to be left in the margin of our discourses. An alternative route, and its accompanying pitfalls, is suggested by considering two books which are clustered around photographs by the same photographer, John Paskievich, a Canadian who was born of Ukrainian parents in Austria. The first is a collection entitled *Waiting for the Ice-Cream Man: a Prison Journal. Manitoba 1978*. Edited by Larry Krotz, it centres on various prisons in Manitoba, Canada. It includes fragments of prison autobiographies, poems, newspaper reports, articles on prison abolition, extracts from laws and parliamentary committee reports, statistics, a bibliography and Paskievich's photographs taken inside the prisons. The second book is called *A Voiceless Song: Photographs of the Slavic Lands*. It includes a foreword by Martha Langford, an introduction by Josef Škvorecký and sixty-seven photographs by Paskievich taken in the USSR, Poland, Bulgaria, Czechoslovakia and Yugoslavia. In the prison book the photography acts as a punctuation to the text, while in the Slavic book the texts are embellishments of the photographs.

And yet both books are 'framed': the prison book by the walls of prisons and the Slav book by an Orwellian totalism. Škvorecký in his introduction puts the Slav photographs directly into *1984* and all of these incredible photographs immediately become not statements in and of themselves but part of a master-metaphor, every bit as controlling as the thick walls, barbed wire and electronic surveillance of Stoney Mountain Institution. In some ways they are even bleaker, for at the end of his essay Škvorecký writes; 'Perhaps the only hope I can still retain is that all those people and their offspring, so marvellously captured in John Paskievich's photographs, will survive. But that is not a very encouraging hope, because the beautiful black and white images can tell me nothing about the quality of that survival – and I have my doubts.'[7] The Slav people have been put in prison by Škvorecký, and nothing that we or they can do will affect things much. It is, of course, quite remarkable that this should be written only a few years before the major political and social changes of the late 1980s in precisely these countries. It is, of course, true that the Slav countries have repeatedly experienced political terror and dictatorship, but the imposition of a totalizing metaphor does nothing to liberate either the people or Paskievich's images.

In *Waiting for the Ice-Cream Man* the textual and photographic images contend with each other so that, although prison is a brutalizing experience, no one version of that experience predominates. The lines of discourse from the legislation that frames the prison itself to the poems that prison generates are all there. From the matter-of-fact 'Rules Regarding Cell Maintenance' (Rule 4.1.4: 'Inmates must sleep with their heads towards the front of the cell' or 4.1.5 'An inmate may not paint or repaint his own cell') to a haiku ('summer breeze blowing/gently across the prairie/I turn on my fan'), the constellation of texts that implode in the cell are all there. There is even Oscar Wilde's laconic but bitter account of his induction into prison life:

> For I have come, not from obscurity into the momentary notoriety of crime, but from a sort of eternity of fame to a sort of eternity of infamy, and sometimes seem to myself to have shown, if indeed it required showing, that between the famous and the infamous there is but one step, if so much as one . . .
>
> On November 13th, I was brought down here [i.e. to Reading Gaol] from London. From two o'clock till half past two on that day I had to stand on the railway platform in convict dress and handcuffed, for the world to look at. I had been taken out of the hospital without a moment's notice being given to me. Of all positive objects I was the most grotesque. When people saw me they laughed. Each train as it came up swelled their amusement. That was of course before they knew who I was.

As soon as they had been informed, they laughed still more. For half an hour I stood there in the grey November rain surrounded by a jeering mob. For a year after that was done to me I wept every day at the same hour and for the same space of time.[8]

Larry Krotz's collection invites discourse on the prison system as an expensive waste of lives, money and natural resources, while Josef Škvorecký's monologue on behalf of Paskievich's photographs imposes foreclosure on any possible discourse. And yet something is happening as we look at the two books, which adds to what Cohen and Taylor try to put together in *Escape Attempts*. The first thing to note is that the comparisons are not explicit: Paskievich did not set out to create two books about total institutions (his other collections of photographs are based on North End Winnipeg and Urban Indians, and it is clear that his photography tries to express the individuality of his subjects by locating them in a space which sets off their own uniqueness). The comparisons emerge out of the juxtapositions of the subject matter and the written texts, while focusing on Paskievich's photography. It is the images that sing against the texts, though it is the texts with which we ultimately have to come to terms, because they train us to look. But if, as Walter Benjamin argued, 'the caption becomes the most important part of the photograph,'[9] so, too, the photograph becomes alternatively the caption to a text. The interplay of image and text is what gives these two books their prominence in prison writing and its relationship to our everyday world. The camera makes all of us into 'God's spies' and into criminals:

Not for nothing have Atget's photographs been likened to those of the scene of a crime. But is not every square inch of our cities the scene of a crime? Every passer-by a culprit? Is it not the task of the photographer-descendant of the augurs and the haruspices – to reveal guilt and to point out the guilty in his pictures?[10]

What Benjamin suggests here is the interconnection of the photographer/spy and the guilty author, setting the scene for mutual authorship of crime, detection and punishment. Paskievich fulfils this role admirably, letting the objects of his art act out their guilt and at the same time displaying the framework of their incarceration. Through his eyes we become the detectives, not only of crime but of our own complicity both in its execution and in the administration of punishment. How the text 'captions' the photographs does, however, affect the way that the images can have any meaning in our everyday lives. If we are 'told' how to read them, as Škvorecký does in the Slav collection, then it is possible that we may not be able to read them at all.

II

The relevance of prison writing to everyday concerns must, however, be pursued along another path: that of the prisoner taking the experience of writing in gaol and transforming it into a language that might be applied to non-prison situations. This may be a different project to those outlined above in that the writer is not necessarily concerned with metaphorical appropriations, but rather with the development of his own writing experience into a non-prison context. Ignoring writers who were imprisoned because of their writing, or those who were imprisoned for political or religious reasons, very few writers have addressed themselves to the life of the others who are not in prison. One of the reasons for this is that so many prison writers never write more than one autobiographical book; another is that, for the many of them who came from minority groups, the relationship between community and prison was so close that it would be difficult to think of any writing about everyday life that was not about prison. Another is that the fantasies of release were so banal that 'outside' could only read like what it was before going in:

> Now that I'm out of prison I think about the other guys I met in Collins Bay who sunk themselves in remote crevices of time dwelling on Glen Miller's music. Or the ones who bought guitars and practiced ten hours a day, but never learned more than four or five chords. And the guys who build their dreams of a happy, prison-free future on a girl they've modelled after someone they knew in grade three. Or the funny ones who only live for the moment when they get out and they can buy a '49 Ford, just like the one they had back in '58. All chromed. If only they can get that car, then like everything will be all right.[11]

One author, however, systematically explored the connection between his prison experience and its relevance for understanding the outside world. This writer is Jean Genet. In four plays, *The Balcony*,

The Maids, The Blacks and *The Screens* Genet probed resistance and rebellion in a brothel, the murder of an aristocratic woman by her maids, a slave uprising and revolution in Algeria. In *Prisoner of Love*, a posthumously published memoir, Genet reflects on his fifteen-year relationship with Palestinian guerrillas. Taken together, these works display the increasing politicization of Genet's literary output. They also mark his transition from novelist to dramatist (his first and only other play, *Deathwatch*, about Death Row, was set entirely in prison, and owed much to the philosophy developed in his novel, *The Miracle of the Rose*) and his ultimate transformation into political essayist, pamphleteer and revolutionary diarist. The images that persist in his dramatic and political work are nevertheless bound up with his prison experiences: so persistent are they that they transform, perhaps for ever, how we will look at ourselves, not because they impose metaphor, as Cohen and Taylor do, but because they invite correspondences, as Benjamin suggested. In Genet's political writings the questions of social and sexual identity as well as textuality remain paramount in deciding what *any* politics is about. For Genet it is the experience of criminality that provides the occasion for engaging with the 'real' world.

Prisoner of Love is as good a place to begin because its disorganized structure allows Genet to engage in correspondence-making much as Theodor Adorno did in *Minima Moralia*, Walter Benjamin in his 'Paris Project', Gertrude Stein in *The Journal of Alice B. Toklas*, Alexis de Tocqueville in *Democracy in America* or Virginia Woolf in *A Room of One's Own*. It is Genet trying to put his entire prison script together in terms of a people 'outside' yet very much 'inside' his own prison writing. *Prisoner of Love* is part autobiography, part travelogue, part political manifesto, part auto-critique. The theme of all the plays and in *Prisoner of Love* is the reclamation of a lost childhood ('the melodious child dead in me long before the axe chops off my head'):

> The dream, but not yet the declared aim, of the fedayeen was clear: to do away with the twenty-two Arab nations and leave everyone wreathed in smiles, childlike at first but soon foolish. But they were running out of ammunition and their main target, America, was endlessly resourceful.[12]

The child can only be reborn by recognizing the violence of the system that has denied him his childhood. As Sartre noted in *Saint Genet*,

Having died in boyhood, Genet contains within him the dizziness of the irremediable, he wants to die again. He abandons himself to the instant, to the cathartic crises that reproduce the first enchantment and carry it to the sublime: crime, capital punishment, poetry, orgasm, homosexuality. In each case we shall find the paradox of the before and after, a rise and fall, a life staked on a single card, the play of the eternal and the fleeting.[13]

Thus the tension in all of Genet's work is that between what we conventionally take to be the innocent, playful nature of the child's imagination and life and the violent suppression of that life that is the active ingredient of the biography of most prisoners.[14] But whereas most prison writers do not get beyond trying to recall a destroyed childhood, in one sense using it as an excuse for a wasted life, Genet's writing probes that connection in the situations of other people as well as himself where the traumas of childhood become linked to a mythopoeic rebellion.[15]

Being abandoned and left to be brought up as an orphan was a birth that was different from but not any worse than most. Childhood among the peasants whose cows I tended was much the same as any other childhood. My youth as a thief and prostitute was like that of all who steal or prostitute themselves, either in fact or in dream. My visible life was nothing but carefully masked pretences. Prisons I found rather motherly – more so than the dangerous streets of Amsterdam, Paris, Berlin and Barcelona. In gaol I ran no risk of getting killed or dying of hunger: and the corridors were at once the most erotic and the most respectful places I've ever known.

The few months I spent in the United States with the Black Panthers are another example of how my life and my books have been misinterpreted. The Panthers saw me as a rebel – unless there was a parallel between us that none of us suspected. For their movement was a shifting dream about the doings of Whites, a poetical revolt, an 'act', rather than a real attempt at radical change . . .

By agreeing to go first with the Panthers and then with the Palestinians, playing my role as dreamer inside a dream, wasn't I just one more factor inside both movements? Wasn't I a European saying to a dream, 'You are a dream – don't wake the sleeper!' . . .

But from these thoughts there emerged another: all that we

know of men, whether famous or not, may only have been invented to hide the abysses of which life is made up. In that case the Palestinians were right to set up the Potemkin camps, the camps of the young lions – though their wretched guns served to reveal rather than conceal them.[16]

In this version the mythology of the rebels is a dream, though a necessary dream, in order to reclaim the poetry of childhood, but a dream which is predicated on the necessity of a violent rewriting of the white text, much as a child will doodle in the margin of a textbook or eliminate phrases in order to make fun of a teacher, a concept or a set of ideas. But the rebel's rewriting is deadly serious. As he writes on the Black Panthers:

> The black words on the white American page are sometimes crossed out or erased. The best disappear, but it's they that make the poem, or rather the poem of the poem. If the Whites are the page, the Blacks are the writing that conveys a meaning – not of the page, or the page alone. The abundance of Whites is what the writing is set down on, and it forms the margin too. But the poem is written by the absent Blacks – the dead, if you like – the nameless absent Blacks who wrote the poem, of which the meaning escapes me but not the reality.
>
> Let the absence of invisibility of the Blacks we call dead be well understood. They are still active. Radioactive.[17]

This sense of the child/rebel rereading history and literature is almost, but not completely, unique in the study of child's play and development. Contrary to Piaget's view that children needed to abandon the unformed, inchoate imagination of their early years in favour of an adaptive developmental sequence towards 'adulthood', Walter Benjamin argued in favour of the child's early reappraisal of the artefacts that he or she found around.

> Children are particularly fond of haunting any site where things are being visibly worked upon. They are irresistibly drawn by the detritus generated by building, gardening, housework, tailoring, or carpentry. In waste products they recognize the face that the world of things turns directly and solely to them. In using these things they do not so much imitate the works of adults as bring together, in the artefact produced in play, materials of widely differing kinds in a new, intuitive relation-

ship. Children thus produce their own small world of things within the greater one.[18]

Developmental theories and practices of pedagogy worked against any revolutionary solution, and one of the features of all revolutions was their attempt to *continue* the work of bourgeois pedagogy rather than to take revolution as a new beginning in its sense of pedagogy. As Susan Buck-Morss has written of Benjamin's approach:

> Benjamin took the story of the Messiah coming as a child literally, but collectivized it. In children, the capacity for revolutionary transformation was present from the start. Hence all children were 'representatives of Paradise', and each generation was 'endowed with a *weak* Messianic power.' Stripped of its metaphysical pretensions, history was the begetting of children, and as such, it was always a return to the beginnings. Here revolutions appeared, not as the culmination of world history, but as a fresh start.[19]

Genet's work can thus be seen as an attempt at seeing how that fresh start might be possible by taking as his theme those whose life-projects were based on rediscovering a lost childhood – but also discovering it through a violent restructuring of the conditions which made childhood traumatic. There are few illusions in this exercise. Benjamin at the end of his life said that 'Only that historian will have the gift of fanning the spark of hope in the past who is firmly convinced that *even the dead* will not be safe from the enemy if he wins. And this enemy has not ceased to be victorious.'[20] He also argued that only people who lived out their childhood really grew up.[21] Genet's pedagogy of the prisons and the revolutionary *maquis* also hinged on this sense of pessimism (if the Palestinians managed to win, they really wanted to become 'comfortable' and therefore avoid 'rigour and intelligence': 'One of the things I couldn't go along with . . . was their optimism').[22] The revolution will be swallowed up in the idea of 'progress'. Thus the concept that the pedagogy involves a new beginning, based on the playfulness of childhood, is vitiated by the text that writes itself over the whole endeavour. The 'playful' violence of teenagers with wretched ammunition over their shoulders is pre-empted by the need to have a 'civilized' opposition, which learns the tricks of the oppressor in order to continue its military strategy. 'Having been slaves, shall we be terrible masters when the time comes?' 'A rebellion or a revolution may not be so much a matter of conquering or winning back land as a deep breath on the part of people who have suffered from . . . stereotyping.'[23]

The children's crusade, in Ajloun, Derra, Akaba, Soledad or in Tiananmen Square is littered with the bodies of those of whom the adults were afraid. And therefore two questions linger in Genet's account of his perigrinations. First: 'Is this childish play simply a dream? A Dream within a dream by people who are Fakes?' And the second, in the form of a prayer (written by someone who seems to be speaking the same language), if the first question is answered in the negative:

> I am afraid not of what they will do to us, but of what they can make us into. For people who are outlaws for a long time may feed on their own traumas and emotions which, in turn, strangle their reason and ability to see reality . . . I pray that we do not return like ghosts who hate the world, cannot understand it, and are unable to live in it. I pray that we do not change from prisoners into prison guards.[24]

III

Of course, the message here is central if any utopian sense is to emerge out of prison experience. If prison is to be used as more than a metaphor to enclose everyday life, its message has to speak out of the inscriptions on the prison walls. The appropriation of prison by those of us who are outside tells more about us than about prison. But there are other ways of approaching the issues that Genet wants to raise, and three of these are worth exploring in conclusion. The first relates to the mechanical constitution of violence, the second to prisons as home territory and the third to gender and the construction of prison knowledge.

Although Genet is not flippant about violence ('An ancient people restored to youth by rebellion and to rebellion by youth can seem very sinister'),[25] he appears to accept it as a state of affairs to which there can be no alternative and to give much greater priority to the ambiguities of political struggle. Ultimately also for Genet the *writings* of other prisoners seem to be of little consequence, although their experiences are. Violence is the occasion for his own mythopoeism. At least four chapters in this book have discussed the issue of violence and prison and the mechanization of writing, and yet, just because violence is both an abstract, technological space and, as well, a set of very personal encounters, the resolution of that discussion may need to be spelled out. The issue of incarceratory violence is not simply that a mechanized writing constructs the instruments of death and that there is a structural opposition to it, but that people die in the cross-fire. For some (perhaps most) societies, over time, there has been a structural propensity to violence, where violence within the system is a built-in ritual of preserving the status quo. The deportations to prison camps in the American and Australian colonies by the English in the eighteenth and nineteenth centuries, slavery, the use of Siberia and the gulags by various Russian governments from the eighteenth to the twentieth centuries, the executions by the Iranian government in the name of Islam, the continued deportations and mass-executions by the government of China, the destruction of entire civilian populations through saturation or nuclear bombing in the Second World War, and the establishment of death camps by Nazi Germany in the 1930s and 1940s — all have provided the deep structural patterns of violence within modern society which provide the measurements (negative and positive) by which all other features of incarceration, as well as our ability to deal with difference, are judged. These are the texts which continue to influence the *eidos* or form of institutionalized violence. Just as the route from slavery to the modern penitentiary in the United States lay through peonage and lynchings, so the relationship between white and black in Australia is deeply influenced by the foundations of that society as a penal colony, and the treatment of prisoners in modern Britain or Canada by the convict system.[26]

This relationship is explored by Kafka in his short story *In the Penal Colony*, where the mechanization of torture is quite explicitly related to writing (the prisoner will have his sentence written by a needle on to his body until ultimately he is dead) and where, even though the prisoner goes free and the executing officer is finally destroyed by the machine, the threat that the old system will return provides the concluding section of the story.[27] If all ritual is, in Derrida's sense, a writing, the rituals of mass-killings, mass-incarceration, and mass-deportations become the ultimate dominant texts. The attempts to create an alternative narrative, whether through the rethinking of history, the enormous canvas of the novel, or the redrafting of legislation, are reduced to pinpricks in the corpus of the superdeterminate text. Personal belief systems, demonstrations, hunger strikes, scratchings on the wall live in the crevices between the flagstones over which the machines of violence continue to rumble.

Within this context, prison writing appears in a different guise, though one which has already been suggested by Genet's work. The power of prison writing lies not in an attempt to establish a unity of purpose or a commonality of experience among all prisoners, but in its faltering steps towards tracing out a new beginning within which the world might be rethought. What the French philosopher Jean-François Lyotard has written about the post-modern artist or philosopher applies even more powerfully to the prison writer:

> A post-modern artist or writer is in the position of a philosopher: the text he writes, the work he produces are not in principle governed by preestablished rules, and they cannot be judged according to a determining judgement, by applying familiar categories to the text or to the work. Those rules and categories are what the work of art itself is looking for. The artist and the writer, then, are working without rules in order to formulate the rules of what *will have been done*.[28]

Every scrap of prison writing or singing is not only a rethinking of what was done, or of the future consequences of past actions, but a recognition that the text itself (frequently published long after its inception and in a context where it is necessarily translated) is a projectile into our futures out of other histories. But Lyotard's formula need not be completely devoid of empirical foundations or history, nor should we think that there is anything particularly 'post-modern' about prison writing. If so, prison writing has been 'post-modern' for the past two thousand years or so. What is, perhaps, 'post-modern' is a set of contending texts which now allow us a greater opportunity to assess the rules of what will have been done. Maurice Blanchot has drawn attention to the strategic significance of the literature of disaster in understanding the contemporary human condition.[29] Although his theme is the two world wars, concentration camps, Hiroshima/Nagasaki and the Holocaust, the argument must be extended back to slavery, the deportations to the American and Australian colonies and to the Siberian salt mines, and forwards to Vietnam and the other Asiatic wars, and the textual examples to include songs, folk tales and other, non-literary, texts such as graffiti and tattoos. And the texts, as he observes, must not be allowed to be used as 'documentary evidence' for other ideas, but must speak directly for themselves (poor, blind mouths: as if that could ever be really done, for *we* are the translators, the texts ultimately speak to us and thus we have the responsibility of situating them and ourselves).

This means a rethinking of our own means of making connections across quite disparate fields, and of entering into a discourse with those who have been the victims of earlier imposed connections. This is not the same as Cohen and Taylor's attempt at establishing a neat fit between prisoners' experiences and those of the rest of us. Although the impetus for making any correspondences might have been similar, the end result will be markedly different. People go to prison for different reasons. They may manufacture 'crime' alone out of their personal life history; they may act in groups out of what is sometimes termed a subculture; they may engage in activities (from writing or politics to drinking alcohol or taking drugs) which, formerly considered legal, are now declared illegal; whole communities (ethnic, sexual or gender-based, religious, class, or political) may suddenly or over time acquire pariah status; acts of war (international or civil) may incarcerate civilians and soldiers – for any of these reasons the houses within which people live might be declared prisons, or territories of their own or other countries may become prisons through an act of banishment. In this century the amount of literature that has emerged out of these autobiographical experiences far exceeds that of *all* previous prison literature, and therefore any attempts to weld the literature into one continuous narrative are doomed to failure.

And yet, there are interconnecting narrative themes which provide clues to making a new reading of the literature, which must both be conscious of a very long history of prison writing and also confront both the explosion and the particularity of prison writing in this century. In the 1990s prisons provide a constant element across all societies, more constant than chains of hamburger stores, films, television, radio or money markets; probably, in a world of dwindling ecological resources, as constant as zoos.[30] The universality of prisons lies in a perception by government in every society that those who, for whatever reason, are seen not to fit into the dominating norms of that society must be expelled from it, or brainwashed, or incarcerated or, in extreme cases, ultimately exterminated. Thus from the petty thief to the noblest author, from the gangster's moll to the collective exiles, the arm of the law, as arbitrary as the governments that extend it, pulls them into its grinding maw.

This blanket universalism – in which the Ayatollah's thuggery in the name of Islam and the execution of Ruth Ellis for murder come to much the same thing – is naïve enough to hold together for a moment, but not for long enough to be self-sustaining, for it would lead to the ultimate nihilism of which Lyotard's apolitical, ahistorical philosophy is the apogee. We *do* have to start with the awareness that 'the nineteenth and twentieth centuries have given us as much terror as we can take',[31] but we have to recognize that this debate requires a sense of the social and intellectual history of terror, and of a basis from which to read both the texts that seemed to be complicit in the terror and the texts that surround us from those who experienced it.

What this means, if we are not to wallow in nostalgia (as the French Romantics seemed to do) or be swept away by a post-modernist philosophy of panic which seizes texts as immediate and historically unrooted, is a need for a vision of the relationship of text to (different) social actions, of how text is creatively used both in the context of its own genesis and in its subsequent appropriations. One of the clues to how this might be done is developed in E. P. Thompson's *Whigs and Hunters*, a study of the introduction in England of the Black Act in 1723, which established a criminally based property law in England that was to last for the next century. The Act was vicious in the extreme, imposing the death penalty for poaching and other crimes against landlords. Many people suffered and died under this law, and on the surface the law clearly showed that government, the legal system and the power of the property-owning classes were in collusion. And yet, counter to received wisdom from other sources, a tradition was formed which established the basis both for resistance and for an alternative reading of the role of the law.

> Such law has not only been imposed *upon* men from above: it has also been a medium within which other social conflicts have been fought out. Productive relations themselves are, in part, only meaningful in terms of their definitions at law: the serf, free labourer; the cottager with common rights, the inhabitant without; the unfree proletarian, the picket conscious of his rights; the landless labourer who may still sue his employer for assault. And if the actuality of the law's operation in class-divided societies has, again and again, fallen short of its own rhetoric of equity, yet the notion of the rule of law is itself an unqualified good.[32]

For Thompson, then, the notion (and perhaps the text) of the law, from wherever it may come, becomes the site of social struggle. He makes a distinction between particular laws and the forms within which they were drafted.

No defence, in terms of natural justice, can be offered for anything in the history of the Black Act. But even this study does not prove that all such law is bad. Even this law bound the rulers to act only in the ways which its forms permitted; they had difficulty with these forms; they could not always override the sense of natural justice of the jurors; and we may imagine how Walpole would have acted, against Jacobites or against disturbers of Richmond Park, if he had been subject to no forms of law at all.[33]

Ultimately, the ideal of law as an equitable principle, after being fought over by governments and freemen, landlords and peasants, jurors and lawyers, becomes enshrined in the folklore of constitutional practice. The enormous script of common and legislative law becomes the terrain within which rights and freedoms are negotiated, because it embodies both the form within which any discourse can take place and also the experiences of earlier negotiations. As a model of theorizing the past it is attractive, centring as it does on history, textuality and social practice, and provides a convenient method of linking politics, history and social control. This book is concerned with prison writing, a writing which stands over and against the legally discursive texts, the end product of the legal process. Prison writing is largely subjective; Thompson's in spite of his disclaimers, is an attempt to find a universality within which the particular inscriptions of the prisoners might be situated. How helpful are these two approaches to each other?

In his earlier work, Thompson, fighting against structuralist and deterministic categories of historical writing, provided an interactionist interpretation of social history which would rescue the abandoned authors of history from the archival refuse-dump. In *Whigs and Hunters*, the task is related, but ultimately reformulated by asking how, with the texts they inherited, these authors changed the definition of the controlling text. The (foreclosed) universalism of *The Making of the English Working Class* is seen in *Whigs and Hunters* as the catalyst for legal universalism. Although the ground has shifted, it has shifted to a history which has become more developmental, structural. What Thompson has done is to bring his social history as close to the present as he dare.

Thompson does not address the writing itself, except in so far as it is related to a collective goal, nor does he dare make comparisons with other societies, nor does he consider prisons as places which are the end product of law (whether it be considered just or unjust). Yet with these qualifications, Thompson's work raises the issue of which writing is important in what context, of how deterministic are the structures of law and how malleable to social pressure, of whether there is one legal text or many, and whether, in spite of the essential inegalitarianism of legal codes, it is still possible to talk of justice and, if so, on what epistemological grounds. In other words, if we are to accept that prison writing has something to do with our everyday lives, in what ways should we locate it without abandoning the exercise to pure relativism.

By itself this idealism is not enough. Any lawyer would see it as the legitimation of his existing practice, any policemen doing his job would bask in its reflected glory, and any criminal would see himself as planting the liberty tree. Furthermore, transplanted to other countries, in spite of Thompson's disclaimer that 'there is a difference between arbitrary power and the rule of law' (Germany between 1933 and 1945? South Africa after 1948? the Southern United States during and after Confederation? Northern Ireland after 1988? North American Indians over the past century?) the argument seems perverse. Even though there is some validity in Thompson's subsequent arguments that recent distortions in the practice of law in Western Europe are attributable to the cold war, they do not seriously affect his central thesis that the rule of law is the core of civil society.

The question that is begged in all this is 'what civil society?' That is a question that brings us back to the literature from prisons. For law, in whatever form, is not the *Geist* that holds and moves the fragile parts of our societies onwards, but a segment of the hegemonic apparatus on which we all draw, to be reassembled by whoever will. Parts of what hegemony have their own store of historical experiences, other parts have others. If Thompson (separating his social historical self from his anti-nuclear one) is arguing that law is the secular hegemony, so be it. The messages from the inscriptions on the prison walls suggest other ways of reading that hegemony which provide a different sense of what we ought to be thinking about and one which might put the two E. P. Thompsons together.

Prison writing is about guilt, but the ultimate guilt of not knowing whether one's own actions were locked into a world over which one had no control or into one's self (which comes to the same thing). Prisoners (whether political, religious, civil or criminal) write to make sense to themselves and others of that predicament. Apart from some bombastic writing of self-aggrandizement and a little which is purely querulous, prison writing is self-reflexive. It is about trying to establish authorship (collective or individual) where that has been denied by the operation of the law. For most prison writing there is no evident author, and when there is, the text is often buried in instant remaindership. Prison writing, from Boethius to Sarrazine, confronts the writing machine that commands, appropriates, spews out.

The correspondences that might be traced in order to focus on how prison writing affects us must therefore not only hinge on the machines themselves and their terrible incisions, but on the ways that prison writers have tried to rewrite the incarcerating text. As Thompson has suggested elsewhere,[34] the fact that writers were anonymous does not mean that they were not serious ('Given the opportunity, such insurrectionary voices could be followed by insurrectionary actions').[35] What it does mean, however, is that attempts at rewriting the dominant texts have to be given greater scrutiny, and according to corresponding lines that make sense to us now.

IV

The connecting links to the outside include writers who (unlike Genet, who was something of a voyeur in his contacts) were directly connected to a community. H. Bruce Franklin's study of American black writers is a monument in this respect, and so is Judith A. Scheffler's anthology *Wall Tappings* which attempts to bring together in a thoughtful way international writing by women prisoners.[36] Similar collections or interpretations might be produced on gypsies, immigrants and other transients in many societies, native ethnic minorities in North and South America and Australia, blacks in South Africa, Jews everywhere, and the Irish in and out of Ireland. But none of this is available in any systematic way. What evidence exists suggests that the bulk of this writing displays a strong bond between prisoner and community and that, as the twentieth century draws to a close, the affirmative voice of this alternative literature is pronounced and clear. For what is important is the way in which community acts as a base for reviewing the social organization of our knowledge, not only as it relates to prisons, but as it relates to the wider questions of how we construct our everyday worlds. The differences in style that might be seen if we contrast black with, say, women's writing are not as great as the overwhelming power of the deconstructive act of all community-related writing which peals away the pretentiousness of the values which seem to hold our societies together. As Judith Scheffler writes in discussing an anthology of women's prison writing:

This declaration of women prisoners' intention to reclaim self-respect and undermine the system's power, even in a 'friendly' way, is a recent development that negates the traditional 'fallen woman' stereotype. The poems are unmistakably women's, yet the concept of collective publication has nothing exclusively to do with being female; it has intriguing parallels with the tradition of black American protest as well as the celebrated rebelliousness of male prison literature that seeks to change society.[37]

The writing that emerges out of a collective experience displays a symbiotic relationship between the individuals who are incarcerated and the community of which they see themselves as a part. It is an interpenetration of the self and the whole, the ultimate metaphor of the one and the many. None of it says 'I was incarcerated only because I was black/Jewish/female/gypsy' but rather that 'Given that I was black/Jewish/female/gypsy, I have a unique vantage point on the system you call justice, and hence on your entire system of values. My writing is an attempt to communicate with you but more essentially with those of my own community in order to create a new value system.' Scheffler quotes from Patricia McConnel, a woman prisoner who writes fiction:

> An extremely important element in my motivation to write these stories is to give the reader some sense of the reality of this form of societal madness – that these are real human beings being destroyed by a machine designed and run by madmen, for the most part. In spite of this dark theme, most of the stories are life-affirming in some way. I am impressed, all these years afterwards, at the resiliency of the spirits of the women I knew.
> My stories are about women struggling to preserve their wills, their self-respect, in a system intent on destroying them.[38]

This 'life-affirming' writing provides a sharpened version of what non-imprisoned women are concerned with, and the relationship to gypsy, black or Jewish writing is clear enough. But it would be foolish to pretend that these sparks of *gnosis* are enough to rewrite the entire narrative of our violent complacency, our imposition of a violent space to which we banish our outsiders. What is surprising is how little of violence comes through in their writing. If most of prison writing is parodic, it is hardly mimetic. The acoustic space that we have constructed for ourselves echoes with messages which resound against those that erected the building.

You took away all the oceans and all the room.
You gave me my shoe-size in earth with bars around it.
Where did it get you? Nowhere.
You left my lips, and they shape words, even in silence.[39]

Outside prison, the challenge involves the complete rethinking of institutionalized violence as part of the *normal* way of conducting social affairs. Since the end of the Second World War, even though crime rates have increased only marginally in most Western countries, the increase in prison construction and prison populations has been phenomenal. Between 1950 and 1985 the prison population of England and Wales increased from 20,000 to 48,000, that of the United States from 264,000 to 736,000.[40] Increases in the building of prisons (which have become electronically-controlled fortifications) and the employment of prison guards are even more pronounced than the increase in numbers of prisoners. In Canada, for example, between 1950 and 1985 the number of prisons tripled, and the number of officers employed in the system increased from one per prisoner to three per prisoner over the same period.[41] Thus more prisoners are being locked up in more technologically sophisticated prisons and guarded by more wardens. In a time of 'new' conservative economic policies, the state economy of incarceration continues unchecked. For the frayed ends of a system which cannot hold itself together are knotted together in the 'correction house', and a politics which emphasizes the survival of the economically fittest legitimizes itself by tightening the screws on blacks, gypsies, Puerto Ricans, native Indians, mestizos, drugged and demoralized women . . .

The mood in society as a whole is therefore far from promising. The appeals to law and order attest to that. Occasionally, however, there are surprising flashes of recognition, in the most unlikely places, that the legal and prison system is outrageously cruel. In *The Spectator*, for example, Auberon Waugh refers to the case of Rosie Johnston who was

> . . . imprisoned by the wretched judge for 'supplying' drugs when she had merely fetched some for a friend. So far as one could make out, this was because the gutter press had inaccurately labelled her 'privileged'. Reading Johnston's book of her prison experiences (*Inside Out*, Michael Joseph, 1989, £12.95) you meet many victims of even more capricious injustice: the gentle 18-year-old who received six years for grievous bodily harm because she had illegally bought alcohol for a delinquent,

14-year-old sister who proceeded to terrorise the neighbourhood; another woman serving nine months for stealing a bottle of vodka . . . Having read Johnston's book, I feel I have looked in the jaws of hell. Prison is a vile place, and I feel ashamed that I have even for a moment smiled that anyone . . . should be sent there.[42]

Waugh's elitist reading of the Johnston case may not take us very far; though for him, as for any person, the reading of prison literature together with the recognition that anyone may be caught in the mesh of the prison system is certainly the beginning of wisdom. A further and deeper connection is suggested by Dorothy Smith in her feminist sociology. Understanding of how the texts may realize their liberating potential depends on discovering

> . . . from within the expanded relations that contain, organize, and provide the dynamic interconnections linking our one-sided knowledge of our own existence into a larger knowledge of a historical process in which we are active and to which we are captive.[43]

Smith uses examples of women's writing as her point of departure. But the urgent need to transform the institutions of violence is more than a feminist preserve. Raymond Williams, speaking of Welsh culture, wrote

> To the extent that we are a people, we have been defeated, colonized, penetrated, incorporated. Never finally, of course. The living resilience, in many forms, has always been there. But its forms are distinct . . .
>
> Real independence is a time of new and active creation: people sure enough of themselves to discard their own baggage; knowing the past as past, as a shaping history, but with a confident sense of the present and the future, where the decisive meanings and values will be made. But at an earlier stage, wanting that but not yet able to get it, there is another spirit: a fixation on the past, part real, part mythicized, because the past, in either form, is one thing they can't take away from us, that might even interest them, get a nod of recognition. Each of these tendencies is now active in Wales. The complexity is that they are so difficult to separate, because they live, often, in the same bodies, the same minds.[44]

The sensibilities that inform the work of Dorothy Smith and Raymond Williams should be conjoined in our approach to prison writing. It is important not only to read the accounts by prisoners as documents of their experiences, but also to recognize that these experiences are refracted through very specific contradictions of memory, place and social structure. If we are to be more than reflectively impotent ('fixated on the past' in Williams's language), the writings must be placed in our own communities, with a connectedness that is able to deal with social structures not simply as alien impositions, but as human creations that must be remade, transformed. And to do that we have to rethink our entire sense of human relationships and why incarceration is situated at the centre of our proclivities to find violent solutions to everyday human problems. That is the challenge that is presented to us by the vast literature that has been created out of the prison cells of the world. It is the ultimate cry of the oppressed; but also the eyes in a sightless world.

NOTES

1   In a diatribe against feminists in his book of the same name: Norman Mailer, *The Prisoner of Sex* (New York: Warner Books, 1982).
2   Stanley Cohen and Laurie Taylor, *Escape Attempts: the Theory and Practice of Resistance to Everyday Life* (Harmondsworth: Penguin, 1978), p. 3.
3   Ibid., p. 5.
4   David Mercer, *A Suitable Case for Treatment* in *Three Television Plays* (London: Calder and Boyars, 1966).
5   The titles of the chapters deal with 'open prison', repetition, routine, the 'inner theatre of the mind', 'free areas, escape routes and identity sites', 'mistaken identity', 'over the wall', etc. The stories, however, are about jobs, going to work, fantasy, watching movies, going on holiday, a meal out, taking drugs, religion, alcohol, sex, etc.
6   See Jean Baudrillard, *America* (London: Verso, 1988), in which the concept of us now having more images than meanings that can be attached to them is taken to imply that our lives are dominated by a communications system which refers only to itself. Thus power, values, the social, disappear under the signs of their own imitation. The sense of continuous desire which capitalism engenders consumes its own tail. As Robert Hughes has argued in his review of Baudrillard's *America*, 'The Patron Saint of Neo-Pop', (*New York Review of Books*, 36, 9 (1989), pp. 29–32), this is a perfect legitimation for the activities of all people who work in the media and for art dealers, but it hardly offers a basis for understanding what goes on in everyday encounters.
7   Josef Škvorecký, 'A Revolution is Usually the Worst Solution', in Toronto

Arts Group for Human Rights, ex., *The Writer and Human Rights* (Toronto: Lester and Orpen Dennys, 1983), p. 21.
8   Oscar Wilde, *The Complete Works* (London: Collins, 1973), p. 183.
9   Walter Benjamin, *One Way Street* (London: New Left Books, 1979), p. 256.
10 Ibid.
11 Don Bailey in Larry Krotz, ed., *Waiting for the Ice-cream Man: a Prison Journal* (Winnipeg, Manitoba: Converse, 1978), p. 58.
12 Jean Genet, *Prisoner of Love* (London: Picador, 1989), p. 88.
13 Jean-Paul Sartre, *Saint Genet* (London: W. H. Allen, 1964), p. 4.
14 In a large measure most prison autobiographies deal at length with a fractured childhood, in many cases going so far as to pinpoint the precise moment when children's play and imagination died. One of the most dramatic appears in Caryl Chessman's *Cell 2455, Death Row*, in which he describes how he realized as a small boy that he had a natural talent for music: 'To him it was a natural enough phenomenon – he heard music and he "saw" colors. Only there was a greater intimacy, a more perfect oneness. In a way that he couldn't possibly explain, music was color.' His parents arrange for the young Whit (he adopted the name Caryl later, as a writer) to take music lessons. He proves to be a brilliant pupil. But

> one summer day he returned home tired and feverish. That day and for several preceding days he had been building a cave with two pals near a creek. He had been stung several times by mosquitoes but had paid the bites no heed. That night his condition worsened; his fever rose. A lethargy settled upon him. A doctor was hastily summoned and at first thought Whit was suffering from the flu. The diagnosis was later changed – and changed, too, was the whole course and pattern of Whit's life.
> Whit had been attacked by encephalitis. The disease apparently destroyed, literally ate away, that portion of his brain which gave him his tonal sense. He was left tone deaf. Except mechanically, he was never able to play again. He never tried. Gone were the beautiful colors, the lively, wonderful colors, the friendly colors; left behind was a murky residue, gray, inanimate, dead. (Chessman, *Cell 2455, Death Row*), pp. 23–5)

15 That Genet's writing is not simply the creation of an alternative myth to that of the dominant ones is, however, suggested by Jacques Derrida in *Glas* (Lincoln, Nebraska: University of Nebraska Press, 1986), his reinterpretation of Genet and Hegel, where he juxtaposes texts and commentaries on both authors in order to force *us* to make our own new readings of them. The comparison/contrast is suggestive primarily because it is Hegel's master/slave dichotomy that seems to be at the heart of Genet's writing, and because in his plays Genet, following Brecht, invites the spectator to be the decision-maker. In Derrida's intertextual reading the apparently totalizing Hegel is set side-by-side with the apparently detotalizing Genet. The exercise is clearly intended not to produce an answer but to compel us to meditate on the correspondences.
16 Genet, *Prisoner of Love*, pp. 148–50.
17 Ibid., p. 218.
18 Benjamin, *One Way Street*, pp. 52–3.

19   Susan Buck-Morss, 'Walter Benjamin – Revolutionary Writer, II', *New Left Review*, 129 (September–October 1981), p. 87.
20   Walter Benjamin, *Illuminations* (London: Cape, 1970), p. 257.
21   Walter Benjamin (with Asja Lacis), 'Program for a Proletarian Children's Theater', *Performance*, 1, 5 (March–April 1973), p. 32.
22   Genet, *Prisoner of Love*, p. 180.
23   Ibid., p. 181. In this sense Genet's plays would appear to be an attempt at going beyond the basic theme of Sartre's *No Exit*, where the three characters have to strip away each others' masks of bad faith and self-deception before they can get on with a relationship among themselves – a relationship which is, apparently, structurally improbable. In Genet's plays the political message is paramount but the resolution ambiguous. All posit a power-struggle between rulers and ruled, but in all the ruled are at loggerheads with each other, a difference which is based on their envy of the social lifestyle and values of the rulers. Within this dichotomy, the ruled either betray each other and become heroes in their own eyes, or else organize together in order violently to achieve power. The masks that they wear are therefore strategic, the most strategic being the ones worn by the rulers, whose violent, selfish actions are camouflaged by their show of morality and 'culture'. The rules, however, act out their frustrations in order to achieve a measure of self-assertion denied them by their servile status. Play-acting is thus a form of liberation, whereas for Sartre play-acting is evidence of imprisonment in a false ego. After Sartre published *Saint Genet*, which portrayed Genet as a man suffering a metamorphosis from one form of masquerade to another, but decidedly not political, Genet's own work took on a more decidedly political stance. For an interpretation of Genet's plays, see Jeannette Savona, *Jean Genet* (New York: Grove Press, 1983).
24   Adam Michnik, *Letters from Prison and other Essays* (Berkeley, Cal.: University of California Press, 1985), p. 99.
25   Genet, *Prisoner of Love*, p. 115.
26   There is a considerable literature on this subject, much of which is outside the scope of this book. But in his study of the Australian penal colonies, Robert Hughes concludes with an assessment of the impact of the system on Australian society. After dismissing the idea that Australian social conduct can be traced back to the convict era as a 'sterile line of inquiry', he does, however, deal with the impact on Australian culture:

>   Would Australians have done anything different if their country had not been settled as the jail of infinite space? Certainly they would. They would have remembered more of their own history. The obsessive cultural enterprise of Australians a hundred years ago was to forget it entirely, to sublimate it, to drive it down into unconsulted recesses. This affected all Australian culture, from political rhetoric to the preception of space. Space, in America, had always been optimistic; the more of it you faced, the freer you were – 'Go West, young man!' In Australian terms to go west was to die, and space itself was the gaol . . . At the heart of each proclamation of renewal was a longing for amnesia. And Australians embarked on this quest for oblivion with go-getting energy. They wanted to forget that their forefathers had ever been, or even rubbed shoulders with, government men; and,

before long, they succeeded. (Hughes, *The Fatal Shore: the Epic of Australia's Founding* (New York: Knopf, 1987), pp. 596–7)

27   See Franz Kafka, *The Complete Stories and Parables* (New York: Quality Paperback Book Club, 1983), pp. 140–67.

28   Jean-François Lyotard, *The Post-modern Condition: a Report on Knowledge* (Minneapolis: University of Minnesota Press, 1984), p. 81. Compare this with E. P. Thompson's conclusion to his study of the English working class in the Industrial Revolution:

> These years appear at times to display, not a revolutionary challenge, but a resistance movement, in which both the Romantics and the Radical craftsmen opposed the annunciation of Acquisitive Man. In the failure of the two traditions to come to a point of junction, something was lost. How much we cannot be sure, for we are among the losers. (Edward Percival Thompson, *The Making of the English Working Class* (London, Gollancz, 1963), p. 832)

30   For a superb critique of the implication of zoos for looking at the fate of the planet, see John Berger, 'Why Look at Animals?', in Berger, *About Looking* (New York: Pantheon, 1980).

31   Lyotard, *The Post-modern Condition*, p. 81.

32   Edward Percival Thompson, *Whigs and Hunters* (Harmondsworth: Penguin, 1977), p. 267.

33   Ibid.

34   See E. P. Thompson, 'The Crime of Anonymity', in Douglas Hay et al., eds, *Albion's Fatal Tree: Crime and Society in Eighteenth-century England* (Harmondsworth: Penguin, 1975), on anonymous letters.

35   Ibid., p. 306.

36   Judith A. Scheffler, ed., *Wall Tappings: an Anthology of Writings by Women Prisoners* (Boston: Northeastern University Press, 1986).

37   Ibid., p. 260.

38   Ibid., p. 261.

39   Osip Mandelstam, *Selected Poems* (Harmondsworth: Penguin, 1977), p. 108.

40   Andrew Rutherford, *Prisons and the Process of Justice* (Oxford: Oxford University Press, 1986), pp. 43–63.

41   Brian MacLean, 'What is to be Done about the Correctional Enterprise in Canada?', *Journal of Prisoners on Prisons* (Toronto), 1, 2 (Winter 1988/9), pp. 59–74.

42   Auberon Waugh, 'The Day I nearly Kissed an Unknown Young Woman on the Tube', *The Spectator*, 14 October 1989, p. 8.

43   Dorothy E. Smith, *The Everyday World as Problematic* (Toronto: University of Toronto Press, 1987), p. 223.

44   Raymond Williams, *Resources of Hope* (London: Verso, 1989), p. 103.

Appendix

Biographical Outlines of Prison Writers Mentioned Most Frequently in the Text

BAKHTIN, Mikhail Mikhailovich (1895–1975). Russian philosopher and cultural theorist. In internal exile for most of his working life, Bakhtin's major work was only published after his formal retirement in 1961, though some may have been published earlier under pseudonyms. His studies of Dostoevsky, Rabelais and Freud and part of his study of Goethe appeared in English in the 1970s and 1980s, as well as works on language and the sociology of verbal and playful communication. In the early 1940s his study of Goethe was sent to a Russian publisher whose archives were destroyed by German bombs. Running short of cigarette paper, Bakhtin used paper from his own copy, starting from the last page. What remained was the first chapter. Hence the dedication at the beginning of this book.

BIENEK, Horst (1930–). Born in Gleiwitz, Upper Silesia (now part of Poland) and worked with Brecht at the Berliner Ensemble. On political grounds he was arrested and sentenced to twenty-five years in Siberia. Released after four years, he went to West Germany, where he now lives. In addition to *The Cell*, he has written novels, collections of poetry, critical essays and film scripts.

BOETHIUS, Anicius Manlius Severinus (c.480–c.524). Roman philosopher and theologian. Translator of works by Aristotle and neo-Platonists, and author of philosophical works, mainly on logic. Appointed Consul in 510. Served under Theodoric the Great. Accused of treason and executed. While in prison wrote *The Consolation of Philosophy*.

BREYTENBACH, Breyten (1939–). South African novelist, poet and painter; has lived in Paris (with interruptions) since 1961. Was arrested and imprisoned in South Africa in 1975 for trying to negotiate contacts with the black trade union movement, and served seven years in various prisons. *Mouroir* and *The True Confessions of an Albino Terrorist* are the direct products of this experience. *A Season in Paradise* is an account of an earlier visit to South Africa.

BUNYAN, John (1628–88). English writer and preacher. He refused to obey royal fiats condemning nonconformist preaching and was imprisoned twice, from 1660 to 1672, and again in 1675. During his first sentence he wrote *Grace Abounding to the Chief of Sinners* and during his second, *Pilgrim's Progress*. His simple, narrative yet didactic style had a powerful effect on the subsequent direction of English writing.

CELLINI, Benvenuto (1500–71). Florentine goldsmith, sculptor and author who wrote one of the most lively and informative autobiographies ever. First published two hundred years after his death, it provides a vivid (though egotistical) account of Renaissance society and artistic life, including a verse 'Capitolo in Praise of Prison' based on his imprisonment in the dungeon of S. Angelo, Rome.

CHESSMAN, Caryl (1921–60). American writer. Sentenced to death for rape and robbery in 1948, spent the next twelve years defending himself by a series of appeals and the writing of four books. Two of these, a novel *The Kid was a Killer* and his autobiography *Cell 2455, Death Row* are classics of prison writing. Finally executed at San Quentin in 1960.

CLEAVER, Eldridge (1935–). Black American writer, political activist and, latterly, evangelical Christian minister. Imprisoned at the age of eighteen for possession of marijuana, he became active in the Black Panther Party. His prison memoir, *Soul on Ice*, was published in 1968, followed by *Post-prison Writings and Speeches* in 1969. Pursued by the FBI on a murder charge, he moved to Algeria, returning in 1978. His account of his conversation to evangelical Christianity is told in *Soul on Fire*.

COLSON, Charles (1937–). Sentenced to Maxwell Prison, Alabama, for his part in the Watergate break-in authorized by President Richard Nixon, Colson, a minor functionary in the Federal bureaucracy, experienced a religious conversion, and published his accounts in *Born Again* (1976) and *Life Sentence* (1979). He subsequently organized an evangelical ministry for inmates and campaigned for prison reform.

DE SADE, Donatien Alphonse François, Comte, known as the Marquis de Sade (1740–1814). French novelist, dramatist and pamphleteer. Major theorist of violence as the mechanization of desire. Imprisoned before and after the French Revolution, about one quarter of his works were ordered destroyed during the Consulate and the Empire and most were banned in France until the mid-twentieth century. Spent his last days in the mental institution of Charenton where he helped to organize dramatic therapy. Strong influence on French, and some world, literature. Major works: *Justine* (1791), *Philosophy in the Boudoir* (1795), *Juliette* (1797), and *120 days in Sodom* (1931–5).

DJILAS, Milovan (1911–). Former Yugoslav revolutionary leader and colleague of Tito, he was imprisoned in 1933–5 under the Fascists and again from 1956–61, and in 1962–6 under Tito. His two most famous books, *The New Class* (1957) and *Conversations with Stalin* (1962) marked him as one of the most trenchant critics of communist bureaucracy and cynicism, while *Memoirs of a Revolutionary* and *Of Prisons and Ideas* (1986) reflected on his experiences in and out of prison.

DOSTOEVSKY, Fyodor Mikhailovich (1821–81). Russian novelist. Sentenced to death for reading subversive (socialist) literature, but ultimately exiled and imprisoned for four years in Siberia and a further four years in the army, Dostoevsky's early major work stemmed from these experiences. *The House of the Dead, Notes from the Underground, Crime and Punishment* and *The Gambler* were all directly informed by life in prison and the army, while his later work, notably *The Idiot, The Possessed* and *The Brothers Karamazov* explored the relationships between religious belief and social order, individual self-discovery and political movement. His contribution to world literature, philosophy and psychology is incalculable. Unfortunately his contribution to political thought and practice is almost zero.

FALUDY, György (George) (1913–). Hungarian poet. Became well known because of his translations of François Villon's poetry in the 1930s. 'Villon, in Faludy's translation, was quoted, discussed, learned by heart and recited in public. Faludy made Villon one of the most popular poets in Hungary, and he has remained a Hungarian hero to this day,' wrote George Mikes in 1981. Imprisoned by the Fascists and the Communists, Faludy, after touring the world, ultimately left Hungary for Canada, where he now lives. His autobiography, *My Happy Days in Hell* (1962), and his various collections of poetry, in particular *Learn This Poem of Mine by Heart* (1983) offer both the poetic and autobiographical versions of his experiences.

FIRST, Ruth (1926–82). South African journalist, social worker, political animateur, political researcher. Was incarcerated by the South African government in 1963 for being a member of the African National Congress and the South African Communist Party. Her book documenting this event was published in 1965 as *117 Days*. It was the subject of a film, *A World Apart*, in 1988. In 1982 Ruth First was killed by a letter bomb in Mozambique.

GENET, Jean (1910–86). French dramatist, novelist, autobiographer and tourist of apprehended revolutions. Gay, pimp and professional thief, the classic protagonist of the absurd as pushing ourselves to our limits. His early novels, essays and autobiography plumbed the depths of his prison experiences (*A Thief's Journal, Our Lady of the Flowers, The Miracle of the Rose* and *Querelle of Brest*) while his later drama and his travelogue in Palestine expressed the mystery of those others with whom he felt he had some affinity – blacks, women, slaves and other rebels.

GRAMSCI, Antonio (1891–1937). Italian Communist leader, brought up in abject poverty, student at Turin, influenced by the Italian Hegelian, Beneditto Croce, and the works of Marx and the challenge of Marxism as a practice. Involved in the factory councils of Turin (1919) and in the editorship of *L'Ordine Nuovo*, the left-wing socialist newspaper. Elected to parliament, but denied the chance to take his seat. Was in a sanatorium in Moscow in the mid-1920s suffering from TB. Arrested by Mussolini's police in 1926 and spent the last eleven years of his life in prison, the last six in a prison hospital. Wrote the *Prison Notebooks* while in prison, most parts of which were smuggled out by Julia Schucht. Rejected crude versions of historical materialism. Theoretically and practically opposed to Stalinism, and therefore became the voice of a cultural Marxism when the full effects of Stalin's brutalism became manifest in the West. Was released from the prison hospital one day before his death.

HAVEL, Václav (1936–). Czech dramatist, poet and essayist. Plays focus on the crisis of communication (see *The Memorandum*, 1967, and *The Increased Difficulty of Concentration*, 1968, both of which acted as fulcrae for the Prague Spring of 1968). Sometimes saw himself as the expositor of George Orwell's ideas on the lack of communication in totalitarian society. Was imprisoned or sentenced to house arrest frequently during the 1970s and 1980s. Two books deriving from these experiences were *The Power of The Powerless* (1985) and *Letters to Olga* (1988). Since 1969 his works have been published only in samizdat or abroad. Elected President of Czechoslovakia in late 1989.

HIMES, Chester (1909–84). Black American novelist. While imprisoned in Ohio State Penitentiary for armed robbery, started to write fiction and accounts of prison life. Early novels: *If He Hollers Let Him Go* (1945), *Cast the First Stone* (1952) and *The Third Generation* (1954). After 1953, lived in France and Spain and wrote his best known series of detective fiction, featuring the Harlem policemen, Grave Digger Jones and Coffin Ed Johnson: see *The Big Gold Dream* (1960), *Cotton Comes to Harlem* (1965) and *Run Man Run* (1966). Wrote two autobiographies: *A Quality of Hurt* (1972) and *My Life of Absurdity* (1976).

JACKSON, George (1941–71). Sentenced to prison when he was eighteen (for one year to life at the discretion of the prison authorities, for stealing $70 from a gas station), Jackson spent the next eleven years of his life in prison, eight-and-a-half of them in solitary confinement. When he was twenty-eight he was charged with the murder of a prison guard in Soledad prison. On 21 August 1971, two days before the opening of his trial, he was shot in San Quentin Prison by a prison guard in what was claimed to be an escape attempt. *Soledad Brother*, published one year before his death, with an introduction by Jean Genet, was based on letters to members of his family, friends and his lawyer. Jackson was perhaps the most eloquent writer to emerge from the Black Panther Party.

KOESTLER, Arthur (1905–83). Hungarian/British writer. Imprisoned by the Fascists during the Spanish Civil War, and in a French transit camp in 1940. (*Spanish Testament*, 1937, and *Scum of the Earth*, 1941, are accounts of these experiences.) His novel, *Darkness at Noon* (1940), based on his reflections on his membership in the Communist Party and the Stalin purges of the 1930s, is, with George Orwell's *1984*, a classic exposure of totalitarian thought control. His later work popularized ideas on the analysis of mechanization, creativity, individual psychology and the mythology of Jews as the chosen people. He and his wife died together in a suicide pact.

LEVI, Primo (1919–87). Italian chemist and writer. Arrested as member of the anti-Fascist resistance, was deported to Auschwitz in 1944. His reclamation of his Jewish heritage and his accounts of the survivors of the camps is the theme of most of his writing, notably *Survival in Auschwitz, The Reawakening, If not Now, When?* and *The Periodic Table*. He died in mysterious circumstances, with a suspicion of murder by neo-Fascists, in Turin.

LUXEMBURG, Rosa (1871–1919). Polish/German revolutionary writer. Major theorist of left communist opposition to Eduard Bernstein and Karl Kautsky in Germany and Lenin in Russia. Imprisoned in Russian Poland in 1906 and in Germany twice, in 1915 and in 1916–18. Her first major theoretical work, *The Accumulation of Capital*, was written in 1912, while her two critiques of the Russian Revolution, *The Russian Revolution* and *Leninism or Marxism*, were written in prison between 1916 and 1918. Wrote anti-war tracts from prison (known as the *Spartakusbriefe*, or Spartacus letters) and established the Communist Party of Germany (with Karl Liebknecht) in early 1919. On the night of 15–16 January 1919 she and Liebknecht were murdered by the Freikorps troops, orchestrated by the Social Democratic Government.

LYTTON, Lady Constance (1869–1923), third daughter of Robert, First Earl of Lytton and Viceroy of India. English suffragette who was imprisoned at different periods from 1909 to 1912, in the later cases posing as working-class woman 'Jane Warton' because she believed that she was given preferential treatment as an aristocrat. Suffered a heart attack after being released from Walton Gaol, Liverpool, and wrote, with her left hand, *Prisons and Prisoners*, her account of the suffragette movement and her experiences in prison.

MANDELSTAM, Nadezhda Yakovlevna, née Khazina (1899–1980). Russian author and wife of Osip Mandelstam. Accompanied her husband during his two exiles, memorizing his poetry and transcribing it to ensure its survival. At sixty-five she published two volumes of an autobiography (*Hope Against Hope*, 1971, and *Hope Abandoned*, 1973) which have established the aesthetic and moral standard for Russian biography.

MANDELSTAM, Osip (1891–1938). Russian poet and essayist. Born into a middle-class Jewish family and brought up in St Petersburg, which became the subject of much of his poetry. Various collections of poetry published in the 1920s (*Tristia*, 1922, *Poems*, 1928, *Armenia*, 1931) as well as prose. In 1934 he was exiled first to Cherdyn in the Urals then to Voronezh where he composed the poetry known now as *The Voronezh Notebooks*. Allowed to return to Moscow in 1937, he was rearrested in 1938 and sentenced to five years hard labour, moving from one camp to another. In one of these he died.

MARKIEVICZ, Countess Constance, née Gore-Booth (1868–1927). Irish revolutionary who helped found the Irish Republican Army and campaigned for women's rights. One of the organizers of the 1916 Easter Rising in Dublin, was arrested and sentenced to death, though this was commuted to life imprisonment. Spent the last ten years of her life in prison or on the run. The first woman ever elected to the British parliament, she never took her seat. First Minister of Labour in the Dáil Éireann. Her *Prison Letters* were written to her sister, Eva Gore-Booth.

MICHNIK, Adam (1947–). Polish historian and political writer. Was an adviser to KOR (the Workers' Defence Committee) and to Solidarity. Prolific writer, imprisoned several times for his political stance. Main writing in English: *Letters from Prison and other Essays* (1985). Also available: *On Trial in Gdansk: a transcript of the proceedings against Adam Michnik, Bogdan Lis, Wladyslaw Frasyniuk, May–June 1985* (1986). Editor-in-chief of the pro-Solidarity Polish daily *Gazeta*; in 1989 became a member of the Polish senate.

POUND, Ezra (1885–1972). American poet who spent most of his working life in Europe. Influential champion of modernist writers and artists. Large poetic output, much of which was based on free translations from Anglo-Saxon, Latin, Provençal, Early Italian, Mandarin and Greek, incorporated into the *Cantos*, commenced in 1917. During Second World War broadcast on behalf of Mussolini's Fascists from Italy, where he had lived since 1925. Arrested by US Army in 1945 and kept in the US Army Disciplinary Training Centre near Pisa until 1948. Here wrote the *Pisan Cantos*. Was transferred to Washington where he was confined to a mental institution because he was considered unfit to plead. Released in 1958, he returned to Italy to live out his remaining years.

RIVIERE, Pierre (1813–1840). French author, rediscovered by Michel Foucault and his colleagues after a 150-year-old burial in court archives. Having murdered his mother and brother and sister, he wrote an account of the whole affair in gaol, in which he justifies his act as one which would free his father from his mother's tyranny. His place in our sense of the writing of criminal history owes everything to Foucault's archaeological investigation. (see Foucault, ed., *I, Pierre Riviere, having slaughtered my mother, my sister and my brother . . .*).

ROSENBERG, Ethel, née Greenglass (1916–53), American housewife, and Julius (1918–53), electrical engineer. Charged in 1950 with spying for the Soviet Union and passing on atomic secrets. Their trial at the height of the cold war was part of the climate fostered by the McCarthy hearings. Sentenced to death in 1951, after several unsuccessful appeals, they were executed in Sing-Sing on 20 June 1953. Basic documents: *The Rosenberg Letters* (to each other from prison, 1953), and Walter and Miriam Schiner, *Invitation to an Inquest* (1983).

SACCO, Nicola (1891–1927) and VANZETTI, Bartolomeo (1888–1927). Italian/American labourers and anarchists. Charged and convicted in May–July 1921 of the murder of a paymaster and a guard and of the theft of over $15,000, at a shoe factory in Massachusetts, they were condemned to death. The case became a major political scandal. Both men denied knowledge of the crime, and it was believed that they were convicted because of their politics. After many stays of execution, a committee appointed by the Governor of Massachusetts and headed by President Lowell of Harvard University upheld the original verdict. Sacco and Vanzetti were executed in June 1927. The case provided the focus for many literary works, notably by Edna St Vincent Millay, Upton Sinclair, Maxwell Anderson and the Welsh poet Alun Lewis. Katherine Anne Porter published her recollections of the trial, *Never-Ending Wrong*, in 1977. See *The Letters of Sacco and Vanzetti* (1928).

SERGE, Victor (1890–1947). Sequentially an Anarchist, Bolshevik, Trotskyist, revisionist-Marxist, but above all, in his own terms, a 'personalist'. Belgian by birth, French by adoption, Russian by parentage and later by citizenship, put down as 'Spanish' by the Mexican authorities on his death certificate. Journalist, poet, pamphleteer, novelist, historian and agitator. Imprisoned in several countries, his classic study, *Men in Prison* (1968) was written in the Santé Prison in Paris. Other books in English translation: *Memoirs of a Revolutionary, 1901–1941* (1963), *Destiny of a Revolution* (1937), *Birth of our Power* (1967), *The Long Dusk* (1946) and *The Case of Comrade Tulayev* (1950).

SOLZHENITSYN, Aleksandr Isayevich (1918–). Russian novelist. Sentenced to eight years in prison camps for referring to Stalin as 'the boss', spent a further four teaching physics and mathematics (in which he had received his first degree) in Kazakhstan. On returning to Moscow, the literary magazine *Novy Mir* published *One Day in the life of Ivan Denisovich* (1962) plus a number of short stories. Although *Novy Mir* accepted both his novels, *The*

First Circle and *Cancer Ward*, they were not published at that time in Russia, but were instantly published abroad. In 1969 he was expelled from the Writers' Union, and in 1974 he left Russia. In the same year his historical saga *The Gulag Archipelago* was published in the West. Since 1976 he has lived in the USA, though continuing to declaim how Slavic Russia's unique moral destiny has been compromised by its flirtation with Western culture and its admixture with non-Slavic races.

VANZETTI, Bartolomeo *see* SACCO, Nicola.

VILLON, François (1431–?). French poet who, after a brilliant period at the Sorbonne (he received his MA before he was twenty-one), landed himself in trouble, killed a priest in a drunken brawl and was either in prison or on the run thereafter. His parodic and self-critical verse (especially in the *Petit Testament* (1465), parodying legal documents, and the *Grand Testament* (1461), castigating himself as a beggar and thief) are the major texts, but his *Ballad des pendus* ('The Ballad of the Hanged Men'), written while he was under sentence of death, was written not only as his own epitaph, but taken by other literary prisoners as their own. Villon's poetry has become, over time, the clarion cry of the incarcerated intellectual, and since the end of the eighteenth century has been translated by a large number of authors into every major language and many minor ones.

WILDE, Oscar Fingal O'Flahertie Wills (1854–1900). Irish-born dramatist, poet, essayist, and novelist. Perhaps the major satirist of English established society whose plays, short stories and essays have become the major benchmarks for what critical style might aspire to in the twentieth century. His plays, e.g. *Lady Windermere's Fan* (1892), *Salome* (1893), *The Importance of Being Earnest* (1895), displayed a versatility of style, language and content, while his novel, *The Picture of Dorian Gray* (1891), his parodic tales, e.g. *Lord Canterville's Ghost* and *The Happy Prince* (1888), and his social criticism, e.g. *The Soul of Man under Socialism* (1896) provided a spectrum of styles and observations that no one at the *fin-de-siècle* could match. His trial for homosexuality and his sentence to imprisonment with hard labour displayed the viciousness of an established social class which had been pilloried by his art. His self-examination and his critique of prison conditions were published in *The Ballad of Reading Gaol* (1898) and *De Profundis* (1905). Wilde died in Paris in 1900. For a biography see Richard Ellman, *Oscar Wilde* (1987).

References

In order not to over-burden the reader, this list contains only books, articles and other texts discussed or quoted in the body of this book and its notes. It also only refers to the editions I consulted, though if the version I have was a reprint, I refer to the first date of that printing.

Abbott, Jack Henry. *In the Belly of the Beast: Letters from Prison*. With an introduction by Norman Mailer. New York: Random House 1982.

Adorno, Theodor. *Prisms*. Translated by Samuel and Shierry Weber. London: Neville Spearman, 1967.

Algren, Nelson. *A Walk on the Wild Side*. New York: Farrar, Straus and Cudahy, 1956.

Arendt, Hannah. *On Revolution*. New York: Viking, 1963.

Bachelard, Gaston. *The Poetics of Space*. Translated by Maria Jolas. Boston: Beacon Press, 1969.

Baker, Houston A., Jr. *Blues, Ideology and Afro-American Literature: a Vernacular Theory*. Chicago: University of Chicago Press, 1984.

Bakhtin, Mikhail. *Rabelais and his World*. Translated by Helene Iswolsky. Cambridge, Masso: MIT Press, 1968.

—— *The Dialogic Imagination*. Edited by Michael Holquist, translated by Caryl Emerson and Michael Holquist. Austin: University of Texas Press, 1981.

—— *Problems of Dostoevsky's Poetics*. Edited and translated by Caryl Emerson with an introduction by Wayne C. Booth. Minneapolis: University of Minnesota Press, 1984.

Baraka, Imamu Amiri (alias Leroy Jones). *Blues People: the Negro Experience in White America and the Music that Developed from it*. New York: William Morrow, 1963.

Barthes, Roland. *Sade/Fourier/Loyala*. Translated by Richard Miller. New York: Hill and Wang, 1976.

—— *The Grain of the Voice: Interviews 1962–1980*. Translated by Linda Coverdale. New York: Hill and Wang, 1985.

—— *Literature and Evil*. London: Marion Boyars, 1985.

Bataille, Georges. *Visions of Excess: Selected Writings, 1927–1939*. Edited and with an introduction by Allan Stoekl. Translated by Alan Stoekl, with Carl R. Lovitt and Donald M. Leslie, Jr. Minneapolis: University of Minnesota Press, 1985.

Baudrillard, Jean. *America*. Translated by Chris Turner. London: Verso, 1988.

Bell, Gregory. *Birdsong*. London: Arrow Books, 1986.

Benjamin, Walter. *Illuminations*. With an introduction by Hannah Arendt. Translated by Harry Zohn. London: Cape, 1970.

—— *One Way Street*. With an introduction by Susan Sontag. Translated by Edmund Jephcott and Kingsley Shorter. London: New Left Books, 1979.

—— with Asja Lacis. 'Program for a Proletarian Children's Theater', translated by Susan Buck-Morss, *Performance* 1, 5 (March–April 1973): 28–32.

Berger, John, *About Looking*. New York: Pantheon, 1980.

Bernstein, Basil. *Class, Codes and Control*. London: Routledge, 1971.

Biallke, David. 'Rethinking the Holocaust.' *Tikkun*, 2, 1 (1987): 73.

Bienek, Horst. *The Cell*. With an introduction by Daniel Berrigan, SJ. Translated by Ursula Mahlendorf. Santa Barbara: Unicorn Press, 1972.

Black, Max. *Models and Metaphors*. Ithaca, NY: Cornell University Press, 1962.

Blanchot, Maurice. *The Writing of the Disaster*. Translated with an introduction by Ann Smock. Lincoln, Nebraska: University of Nebraska Press, 1986.

—— *Death Sentence* Translated by Lydia Davis. Barrytown, NY: Station Hill Press, 1978.

Blum, Alan. *Theorizing*. London: Heinemann, 1974.

Boethius, Anicius. *The Consolation of Philosophy*. Translated by V. E. Watts. Harmondsworth: Penguin, 1969.

Bourdieu, Pierre. *Distinction: a Social Critique of the Judgement of Taste*. Translated by Richard Nice. Cambridge, Mass.: Harvard University Press, 1984.

—— and Passeron, Jean-Claude. *Reproduction in Education, Society and Culture*. With a foreword by Tom Bottomore. Translated by Richard Nice. London: Sage, 1977.

Breytenbach, Breyten. *A Season in Paradise*. Translated by Rike Vaughan. New York: Persea Books, 1980.

—— *The True Confessions of an Albino Terrorist*. London: Faber, 1984.

—— *Mouroir: Mirrornotes of a Novel*. London: Faber, 1985.

Brombert, Victor. *The Romantic Prison: the French Tradition*. Princeton, NJ: Princeton University Press, 1978.

Brown, Clarence. *Mandelstam*. Cambridge: Cambridge University Press, 1973.

Brown, Michael F. 'History and History's Problem'. *Social Text*, 16 (Winter 1986–7): 136–61.

Bruce, Lenny. *The Essential Lenny Bruce*. Compiled and edited by John Cohen. New York: Ballantine Books, 1967.

Buck-Morss, Susan. 'Walter Benjamin – Revolutionary Writer, I', *New Left Review*, 128 (July–August 1981): 50–75; 'Walter Benjamin – Revolutionary Writer, II', *New Left Review* 129 (September–October 1981): 77–95.

Bunyan, John. *Grace Abounding to the Chief of Sinners*. Grand Rapids, Mich.: Baker Book House, 1978.

—— *Pilgrim's Progress*. London: Dent, 1954.

Camus, Albert. *The Rebel*. Translated by Anthony Power with a foreword by Herbert Read. London: Hamish Hamilton, 1953.

Caron, Roger. *Go Boy!* Toronto: McGraw–Hill Ryerson, 1978.

—— *Bingo!* Toronto: McGraw–Hill Ryerson, 1985.

Carpenter, Humphrey. *A Serious Character: the Life of Ezra Pound*. London: Faber, 1988.

Cellini, Benvenuto. *The Life of Benvenuto Cellini*. Translated by John Addington Symonds, with an introduction and appreciation by Arthur Calder-Marshall. London: Heron Books, 1968.

Chessman, Caryl. *Cell 2455, Death Row*. Montreal: Permabook, 1956.
—— *The Kid was a Killer*. Greenwich, Conn.: Fawcett Publications, 1960.
Clay, James A. *A Voice from the Prison: or, Truths for the Multitude and Pearls for the Truthful*. Boston, 1856 (privately printed).
Cleaver, Eldridge. *Soul on Ice*. New York: McGraw–Hill, 1968.
—— *Post-prison Writings and Speeches*. London: Cape, 1969.
—— *Soul on Fire*. Waco, Texas: World Books, 1978.
Cohen, Stanley and Taylor, Laurie. *Escape Attempts: the Theory and Practice of Resistance to Everyday Life* Harmondsworth: Penguin, 1978.
Coleridge, Samuel Taylor. *Selected Poetry and Prose*. Edited by Donald A. Stauffer. New York: Random House, 1951.
Colson, Charles. *Born Again*. New York: Bantam, 1976.
—— *Life Sentence*. New York: Bantam, 1979.
Cook, David. 'The Dark Side of the Enlightenment', *Canadian Journal of Political and Social Theory*, V, 3 (Fall 1981): 3–14.
Dante Alighieri, *Inferno*. Translated and annotated by Dorothy L. Sayers. Harmondsworth: Penguin, 1949.
—— *The Divine Comedy: Paradise*. Translated by Dorothy L. Sayers and Barbara Reynolds. Harmondsworth: Penguin, 1962.
Davidowicz, Lucy. *The War Against the Jews 1933–45*. Harmondsworth: Penguin, 1977.
Davies, Ioan. 'Lenny Bruce: Hyperrealism and the Death of Tragic Jewish Humor', *Social Text*, 22 (Spring 1989): 92–114.
Davis, Angela, ed. *If They Come in the Morning: Voices of Resistance*. With a foreword by Julian Bond. New York: New American Library, 1971.
—— *With my Mind on Freedom: an Autobiography*. New York: Random House, 1974.
d'Eaubonne, Françoise. *Les Ecrivans en Cage*. Paris: André Balland, 1970.
de Lauretis, Teresa. *Technologies of Gender: Essays on Theory, Film, and Fiction*. Bloomington and Indianapolis: Indiana University Press, 1987.
de Sade, Donatien Alphonse François (Marquis de Sade). *120 Days in Sodom*. Compiled and translated by Austryn Wainhouse and Richard Seaver, with introductions by Simone de Beauvoir and Pierre Klossowski. New York: Grove Press, 1966.
—— *Justine: Philosophy in the Bedroom and other Writings*. Compiled and translated by Richard Seaver and Austryn Wainhouse, with introductions by Jean Paulhan and Maurice Blanchot. New York: Grove Press, 1966.
Deleuze, Giles and Guattari, Felix. *Kafka: Toward a Minor Literature*. Translated by Dana Polan with a foreword by Reda Bensmaia. Minneapolis: University of Minnesota Press, 1986.
—— *Anti-Oedipus: Capitalism and Schizophrenia*. Translated by Robert Hurley, Mark Seem and Helen R. Lane. New York: Viking, 1977.
Derrida, Jacques. *Of Grammatology*. Translated with an introduction by Gayatri Chakravorty Spivak. Baltimore: Johns Hopkins University Press, 1976.
—— *Writing and Difference*. Translated with an introduction and additional notes by Alan Bass. Chicago: University of Chicago Press, 1978.
—— *Glas*. Translated by John P. Leavey, Jr and Richard Rand. Lincoln, Nebraska: University of Nebraska Press, 1986.
Diderot, Denis. *The Nun*. Translated with an introduction by Leonard Tancock. Harmondsworth: Penguin, 1974.

Djilas, Milovan. *Of Prisons and Ideas.* Translated by Michael Boro Petrovich. New York. Harcourt Brace Jovanovich, 1986.

Dostoevsky, Fyodor. *The Brothers Karamazov.* Translated by Constance Garnett with an introduction by Edward Garnett. London: Dent, 1927.

—— *Crime and Punishment.* Translated with an introduction by David Magarshack. Harmondsworth: Penguin, 1951.

—— *Notes from the Underground; The Double.* Translated with an introduction by Jessie Coulson. Harmondsworth: Penguin, 1972.

—— *The House of the Dead.* Translated by David McDuff. Harmondsworth: Penguin, 1985.

Douglas, Mary. *Natural Symbols.* Harmondsworth: Penguin, 1973.

Eco, Umberto. *The Name of the Rose.* Translated by William Weaver. New York: Harcourt, Brace, Jovanovich, 1983.

Edelman, Marek. 'You Have to be on the Side of the Weak: a Conversation', *Across Frontiers*, III, 3 (Spring 1987): 3–7, 30–33.

El Sa'adwi, Nawal. *Memoirs from the Women's Prison.* Translated by Marilyn Booth. London: Women's Press, 1986.

'Eipenor,' 'A Drunkard's Progress', *Harper's*, October 1986: 42–8.

—— *Learn This Poem of Mine By Heart.* Edited by John Robert Columbo, translated by the editor and seven others, with an appreciation by George Mikes. Toronto: Hounslow Press, 1983.

Faludy, George. *My Happy Days In Hell.* Translated by Kathleen Szasz. Don Mills, Ontario: Totem Press, 1985.

Fanon, Frantz. *The Wretched of the Earth.* London: Weidenfeld and Nicolson, 1965.

Farrell, Peter. 'This Stors is written by me *Peter Demitro*, (the master) of modern mystery (by hook or by crook) or by me' and 'An Interview with Peter Farrell by Peter Murphy and Janet Urquhart', *Prison Journal*, 7 (1988): 6–7, 8–14. Burnaby: Simon Fraser University, Department of Continuing Education.

Fekete, John, ed. *Life after Postmodernism: Essays on Value and Culture.* Montreal: New World Perspectives, 1987.

Fiori, Guiseppe. *Antonio Gramsci: Life of a Revolutionary.* Translated by Tom Nairn. London: New Left Books, 1970.

First, Ruth. *117 Days.* Harmondsworth: Penguin, 1982.

Flynn, Elizabeth Gurley. *The Alderston Story: My Life as a Political Prisoner.* New York: International Publishers, 1963.

Foster, Hal, ed. *Postmodern Culture.* London: Pluto Press, 1985.

Foucault, Michel. 'On Attica: an Interview', interviewed, edited and translated by John K. Simon, *Telos*, 19 (Spring 1974): 154–161.

—— *Discipline and Punish.* Translated by Alan Sheridan. New York: Vintage Books, 1979.

—— *Power/Knowledge: Selected Interviews and Other Writings.* Edited by Colin Gordon, translated by Colin Gordon, Leo Marshall, John Mepham and Kate Soper. New York: Pantheon, 1980.

—— ed. *I, Pierre Riviere, having Slaughtered my Mother, my Sister, and my Brother . . .: A Case of Parricide in the 19th Century.* New York: Pantheon, 1975.

Franklin, H. Bruce. *Prison Literature in America: the Victim as Criminal and Artist.* Westport, Conn.: Lawrence Hill, 1982.

—— *American Prisoners and Ex-Prisoners: Their Writings. An Annotated*

Bibliography of Published Works, 1798–1981. Westport, Conn.: Lawrence Hill, 1982.

Fraser, George Macdonald. *The Hollywood History of the World.* London: Michael Joseph, 1988.

Frye, Northrop. *The Great Code.* New York: Harcourt Brace Jovanovich, 1982.

Gardner, Martin. 'Giving God a Hand', *New York Review of Books,* 13 August 1987: 17–24.

Gaucher, Robert. 'The Prisoner as Convict: an Interpretive Study from a Canadian Penitentiary', MA thesis, Carleton University, Ottawa, 1974.

—— 'Teaching Criminology: Crime Fiction and Crime News. Offsetting the influence of the Mass Media', in H. Bianchi and R. Swaaminger, eds, *Abolitionism: Towards a Non-repressive Approach to Crime.* London: Wiley, 1986.

Gelfland, Elissa. *Imagination in Confinement.* Ithaca, NY: Cornell University Press, 1983.

Genet, Jean. *The Miracle of the Rose.* Translated by Bernard Frechman. New York: Grove Press, 1966.

—— *Prisoner of Love.* Translated by Barbara Bray with an introduction by Edmund White. London: Picador, 1989.

Genovese, Eugene. *The Political Economy of Slavery.* New York: Random House, 1967.

Gilbert, Martin. *The Holocaust,* London: Fontana, 1986.

Glob, P. V. *The Bog People.* Translated by Robert Bruce-Mitford. London: Faber, 1969.

Goldmann, Lucien. *The Hidden God.* London: Routledge, 1964.

Goody, Jack. *The Logic of Writing and the Organization of Society.* Cambridge: Cambridge University Press, 1986.

—— *The Interface between the Written and the Oral.* Cambridge: Cambridge University Press, 1987.

Gramsci, Antonio. *Selections from the Prison Notebooks.* Translated with an introduction by Quentin Hoare and Patrick Nowell-Smith. London: Lawrence & Wishart, 1971.

Graves, Robert. *The White Goddess.* London: Faber, 1952.

Hall, Stuart, Critcher, Chas, Jefferson, Tony, Clarke, John and Roberts, Brian. *Policing the Crisis.* London: Macmillan, 1978.

Hall, Stuart et al.: Centre for Contemporary Cultural Studies. *On Ideology.* London: Hutchinson, 1980.

Harding, Vincent. 'Beyond Chaos: Black History and the Search for the New Land', *Amistad,* 1 (1970): 267–92.

Hardwick, Elizabeth. *A View of my Own.* New York: Farrar, Straus & Co., 1963.

Havel, Václav. *The Power of the Powerless.* Translated by Paul Wilson et al. Boston: E. J. Sharp, 1985.

—— 'Stories and Totalitarianism', *Index on Censorship,* 17, 2 (1988): 14–21.

Hay, Douglas et al., eds. *Albion's Fatal Tree: Crime and Society in Eighteenth-Century England.* Harmondsworth: Penguin, 1975.

Heaney, Seamus. *The Haw Lantern.* London: Faber, 1987.

—— *The Government of the Tongue.* London: Faber, 1988.

Hebdige, Dick. *Subculture: the Meaning of Style.* London: Routledge, 1979.

—— *Cut 'n' Mix.* London: Routledge, 1987.

—— *Hiding in the Light*. London: Routledge, 1989.

—— 'After the Masses', *Marxism Today*, January 1989: 48–53.

Hector, Mario. *Death Row*. London: Zed, 1984.

Helwig, David. *A Book about Billie*. Toronto: Oberon Press, 1972.

—— *The Rain Falls like Rain*. Toronto: Oberon Press, 1982.

Hemming, John. *Amazon Frontier: the Defeat of the Brazilian Indians*. London: Macmillan, 1987.

Hill, Christopher. *A Turbulent, Seditious, and Factious People: John Bunyan and his Church, 1628–1688*. Oxford: Clarendon Press, 1988.

Himes, Chester. *Cotton Comes to Harlem*. New York: Putnam, 1965.

—— *Cast the First Stone*. New York: Signet Books, 1972.

—— *The Big Gold Dream*. London: Allison & Busby, 1988.

Hobsbawm, Eric J. *see* Newton, Francis.

—— *Bandits*. Harmondsworth: Penguin, 1972.

—— and Terence Ranger, eds. *The Invention of Tradition*. Cambridge: Cambridge University Press, 1985.

Hofstadter, Douglas R. *Godel, Escher, Bach*. New York: Basic Books, 1980.

—— *Metamagical Themas: Questing for the Essence of Mind and Pattern*. New York: Basic Books, 1985.

Horkheimer, Max and Adorno, Theodor. *Dialectic of Enlightenment*. London: Allen Lane, 1973.

Howe, Irving. *World of our Fathers*. New York: New American Library, 1976.

—— and Kenneth Libo, eds. *How we Lived*. New York: New American Library, 1979.

Hughes, Robert. *The Fatal Shore: the Epic of Australia's Founding*. New York: Knopf, 1986.

—— 'The Patron Saint of Neo-Pop', *New York Review of Books*, 36, 9 (1989): 29–32.

Hutcheon, Linda. *A Theory of Parody*. London: Methuen, 1985.

Ignatieff, Michael. *A Just Measure of Pain: the Penitentiary in the Industrial Revolution*. London: Macmillan, 1978.

Irwin-Zarecka, Iwona. *Neutralizing Memory: the Jew in Contemporary Poland*. New Brunswick, NJ: Transaction Books, 1989.

Jackson, George. *Soledad Brother*. With an introduction by Jean Genet. New York: Bantam Books, 1972.

Jameson, Frederic. *The Political Unconscious*. Princeton, NJ: Princeton University Press, 1981.

Jones, Nate. 'Trans-Canada Highway Revisited: Holiday '72'. With an introduction by Suzanne Bellrichard, *Canadian Journal of Political and Social Theory*, 10, 3 (Fall 1986): 1–23.

Kafka, Franz. *The Complete Stories and Parables*. With a foreword by Joyce Carol Oates. New York: Quality Paperback Book Club, 1983.

Katz, Gertrude, ed. *The Time Gatherers: Writings from Prison*. With comments by Gertrude Katz, introduction by Hugh MacLennan. Montreal: Harvest House, 1970.

Keane, John. *Democracy and Civil Society*. London: Verso, 1988.

Kermode, Frank. *The Sense of An Ending*. Oxford: Oxford University Press, 1967.

Kipling, Rudyard. *A Choice of Kipling's Verse*. Selected with an essay on Kipling by T. S. Eliot. London: Faber, 1963.

Koestler, Arthur. *Darkness at Noon*. Harmondsworth: Penguin, 1968.
—— *Scum of the Earth*. London: Hutchinson, 1968.
Konrad, György. *Anti-Politics*. Translated by Richard E. Allen. New York: Harcourt Brace Jovanovich, 1984.
Krotz, Larry, ed. *Waiting for the Ice-Cream Man . . . a Prison Journal*. With photographs by John Paskievich. Winnipeg, Manitoba: Converse, 1978.
Laclau, Ernesto and Mouffe, Chantal. *Hegemony and Socialist Strategy*. London: Verso, 1986.
Lantzmann, Claude. *Shoah: an Oral History of the Holocaust. The Complete Text of the Film*. With a preface by Simone de Beauvoir. New York: Pantheon, 1985.
Leach, Edmund. *Lévi-Strauss*. London: Fontana, 1970.
Levi, Primo. *Survival in Auschwitz*. New York: Simon & Schuster, 1961.
—— *The Reawakening*. New York: Simon & Schuster, 1965.
—— *Moments of Reprieve*. London: Michael Joseph, 1981.
—— *The Periodic Table*. London: Michael Joseph, 1984.
—— *If not Now, When?* With an introduction by Irving Howe. New York: Penguin, 1985.
Lifton, Robert Jay. *Thought Reform and the Psychology of Totalism: a Study of Brainwashing in China*. New York: Basic Books, 1960.
—— *The Future of Immortality and other Essays for a Nuclear Age*. New York: Basic Books, 1987.
Lloyd, A. L. *Folk Song in England*. London: Panther, 1969.
Luxemburg, Rosa. *The Letters of Rosa Luxemburg*. Edited by Stephen E. Bronner. Boulder, Col.: Westview Press, 1978.
Lyman, Stanford M. and Scott, Marvin B. *A Sociology of the Absurd*. New York: Appleton-Century-Crofts, 1970.
Lyotard, Jean-François. *The Post-Modern Condition: a Report on Knowledge*. Translated by Geoff Bennington and Brian Massumi with a foreword by Fredric Jameson. Minneapolis: University of Minnesota Press, 1984.
Lytton, Lady Constance. *Prison and Prisoners*. London: Women's Press, 1988.
MacIntyre, Alasdair. *After Virtue*. Notre Dame, Indiana: University of Notre Dame Press, 1984.
MacLean, Brian. 'What is to be Done about the Correctional Enterprise in Canada?', *Journal of Prisoners on Prisons* (Toronto), 1, 2 (Winter 1988/9): 59–74.
Mailer, Norman. *The Executioner's Song*. New York: Warner Books, 1979.
—— *The Prisoner of Sex*. New York: Warner Books, 1982.
Malcolm X (with the assistance of Alex Haley). *The Autobiography of Malcolm X*. New York: Grove Press, 1965.
Mandel, Eli. *On Oscar Wilde and Jean Genet*. In The Literature of Prison and Exile Series. Montreal: CBC Enterprises, 1968.
Mandelstam, Nadezhda. *Hope against Hope*. Translated by Max Hayward with an introduction by Clarence Brown. New York: Atheneum, 1970.
—— *Hope Abandoned*. Translated by Max Hayward. New York: Atheneum, 1972.
Mandelstam, Osip. *Selected Poems*. Translated by Clarence Brown and W. S. Merwin. Harmondsworth: Penguin, 1977.
Markievicz, Countess Constance de. *Prison Letters*. London: Women's Press, 1984.

Mercer, David. *A Suitable Case For Treatment* in *Three Television Plays*. London: Calder and Boyars, 1966.

Merleau-Ponty, Maurice. *Humanism and Terror: an Essay on the Communist Problem*. Translated with notes by John O'Neill. Boston: Beacon Press, 1969.

Michnik, Adam. *Letters From Prison and other Essays*. Translated by Maya Latynski with a foreword by Czeslaw Milosz and an introduction by Jonathan Schell. Berkeley, Cal.: University of California Press, 1985.

Murdoch, Iris. *The Fire and the Sun: Why Plato Banished the Artists*. Oxford: Oxford University Press, 1977.

Nettl, Peter. *Rosa Luxemburg* (2 volumes). London: Oxford University Press, 1966.

Neugroschol, Joachin, ed. *The Shtetl*. New York: G. P. Putnam's Sons, 1979.

Newton, Francis (alias Eric J. Hobsbawm). *The Jazz Scene*. Harmondsworth: Penguin, 1959.

O'Neill, John. *Sociology as a Skin Trade*. New York: Harper & Row, 1972.

Orwell, George. *Nineteen-Eighty-Four*. Harmondsworth: Penguin, 1949.

—— *Collected Essays, Journalism and Letters* (4 volumes). Edited by Sonia Orwell and Ian Angus. Harmondsworth: Penguin, 1970.

Pascal, Blaise. *Pensées*. Translated with an introduction by A. J. Krailsheimer). Harmondsworth: Penguin, 1966.

Paskievich, John. *A Voiceless Song: Photographs of the Slavic Lands*. With an introduction by Josef Škvorecký. Toronto: Lester and Orpen Dennys, 1983.

Pfeil, Fred. 'Policiers Noirs', *The Nation*, 15 November 1986: 523–5.

Porter, Roy. *A Social History of Madness*. New York: Weidenfeld & Nicolson, 1987.

Pound, Ezra. *The Cantos of Ezra Pound*. New York: New Directions, 1970.

Praz, Mario. *The Romantic Agony*. Oxford: Oxford University Press, 1933.

Priestley, Philip. *Victorian Prison Lives: English Prison Biography, 1830–1914*. London: Methuen, 1985.

Rabelais, François. *Gargantua and Pantagruel*. Translated with an introduction by J. M. Cohen. Harmondsworth: Penguin, 1955.

Reid, Stephen. *Jack-rabbit Parole*. Toronto: Seal Books, 1988.

Ricoeur, Paul. *The Rule of Metaphor*. Toronto: University of Toronto Press, 1978.

Rilke, Rainer Maria. *Duino Elegies*. Translated with an introduction and commentary by J. B. Leishman and Stephen Spender. London: Hogarth, 1952.

—— *Poems from the Book of Hours*. Translated by Babette Deutsch. London: Vision, 1957.

Rosenberg, Ethel and Julius. *The Death House Letters of Ethel and Julius Rosenberg*. New York: Jero, 1953.

—— *We are your Sons: the Legacy of Ethel and Julius Rosenberg*. Letters edited by Robert and Michael Meeropol. Boston: Houghton Mifflin, 1975.

Ross, Andrew. 'Intellectuals and Ordinary People: Reading the Rosenberg Letters', *Cultural Critique*, 9 (Spring 1988): 55–86.

—— ed. *Universal Abandon*. Minneapolis: University of Minnesota Press, 1989.

Rushdie, Salman. *The Satanic Verses*. London: Penguin/Viking, 1988.

Rutherford, Andrew. *Prisons and the Process of Justice*. Oxford: Oxford University Press, 1986.

Sacco, Nico and Vanzetti, Bartolomeo. *The Letters of Sacco and Vanzetti*. Edited by Marion D. Frankfurter and Gardner Jackson. New York: E. P. Dutton, 1960.

Sacks, Sheldon, ed. *On Metaphor*. Chicago: University of Chicago Press, 1979.

Said, Edward W. *Orientalism*. New York: Random House, 1978.

Sartre, Jean-Paul. *No Exit and three other Plays*. Translated by Stuart Gilbert. New York: Vintage, 1955.

—— *Saint Genet*. Translated by Bernard Frechtman. London: W. H. Allen, 1964.

Savona, Jeannette L. *Jean Genet*. New York: Grove Press, 1983.

Scheffler, Judith A., ed. *Wall Tappings: an Anthology of Writings by Women Prisoners*. Boston: Northeastern University Press, 1986.

Schroeder, Andreas. *Shaking it Rough*. Halifax, Nova Scotia: Formac Publishing, 1983.

Schwartz-Bart, André. *The Last of the Just*. Translated by Stephen Becker. New York: Bantam Books, 1961.

Scott, George D., with Bill Trent. *Inmate: the Casebook Revelations of a Canadian Penitentiary Psychiatrist*. Montreal: Optimum Publishing International, 1982.

Serge, Victor. *Destiny of a Revolution*. Translated by Max Schachtman. London: Hutchinson, 1937.

—— *Memoirs of a Revolutionary 1901–1941*. Translated with an introduction by Peter Sedgwick. Oxford: Oxford University Press, 1963.

—— *Men in Prison*. Translated with an introduction by Richard Greenman. London: Writers & Readers Publishing Cooperative, 1977.

Shorris, Earl. 'To Be a Hero in our Time it is Necessary to Write a Book', *The Nation*, 10 May 1986: 641–8.

Smith, Dorothy E. *The Everyday World as Problematic*. Toronto: University of Toronto Press, 1987.

Sorel, A. *Reflections on Violence*. Translated with an introduction by Edward A. Shils. Glencoe, Ill.: Free Press, 1950.

Soyinka, Wole. *The Man Died*. New York: Farrar, Straus & Giroux, 1988.

Spriano, Paolo. *Antonio Gramsci and the Party: the Prison Years*. Translated by John Fraser. London: Lawrence & Wishart, 1979.

Steinburunner, Chris and Penzler, Otto. *Encyclopedia of Mystery and Detection*. New York: St Martin's, 1976.

Steiner, George. *In Bluebeard's Castle: some Notes towards the Re-definition of Culture*. London: Faber, 1971.

—— *After Babel*. London: Oxford University Press, 1975.

—— ed. *The Penguin Book of Modern Verse in Translation*. Harmondsworth: Penguin, 1966.

Stevenson, Robert Louis. *The Strange Case of Dr Jekyll and Mr Hyde*. New York: Charles Scribner's Sons, 1912.

Symons, A. J. *Bloody Murder*. Harmondsworth: Penguin, 1985.

Theiner, George, ed. *They Shoot Writers, Don't They?* London: Faber, 1984.

Thompson, Edward Percival. *The Making of the English Working Class*. London: Gollancz, 1963.

—— *Whigs and Hunters*. Harmondsworth: Penguin, 1977.

Toronto Arts Group for Human Rights, ed. *The Writer and Human Rights*. Toronto: Lester and Orpen Dennys, 1983.

Villon, François. *Selected Poems*. Translated by Peter Dale. Harmondsworth: Penguin, 1978.

Wa Thiong'o, Ngugi. *Detained: a Writer's Prison Diary*. London: Heinemann, 1981.

Wallace, Michael. 'Ronald Reagan and the Politics of History', *Tikkun*, 2, 1 (1987): 18.

Waskow, Arthur. 'Rethinking the Holocaust'. *Tikkun*, 2, 1, 1987: 86.

Waugh, Auberon. 'The Day I nearly kissed an Unknown Young Woman on the Tube', *The Spectator*, 14 October 1989: 8.

Weis, Rene. *Criminal Justice: the True Story of Edith Thompson*. London: Hamish Hamilton, 1988.

Weiss, Peter. *The Persecution and Assassination of Marat as Performed by the Inmates of the Asylum of Charenton under the Direction of the Marquis de Sade*. English version by Geoffrey Skelton, verse adaptation by Adrian Mitchell. Introduction by Peter Brook. London: Calder & Boyars, 1965.

White, Allon, 'The Struggle over Bakhtin: Fraternal Reply to Robert Young', *Cultural Critique*, 8 (Winter 1987–8): 217–41.

White, Matthew and Ali, Jaffer. *The Official Prisoner Companion*. New York: Warner Books, 1988.

Wilde, Oscar. *The Complete Works*. London: Collins, 1973.

Williams, Raymond. *Resources of Hope*. London: Verso, 1989.

Yeats, W. B. *The Poems: A New Edition*. Edited by Richard J. Finneran. New York: Macmillan, 1983.

Zwelonke, D. M. *Robben Island*. London: Heinemann, 1973.

Index

DATE DUE
